In This Day and Age?!

A Community at the Crossroads of Religion and Homosexuality

My Diary of Being Outed and Excommunicated

Compiled, Edited, and Written by Isaac Namdar, M.D.

This book is dedicated to the love of my life,

Andrew Mitchell-Namdar,

whose courage and generosity of heart

have inspired and guided me

ever since the first day I met him.

Table of Contents

<u>Preface</u>

The true events in this book relate to the story of my outing, and the reaction among a tight-knit religious community. Although the storyline deals with the issue of homosexuality, I believe that the greater lesson to be learned can be extrapolated to any situation where individual freedoms may be voluntarily or habitually be suppressed with secrets, fear of banishments and excommunications.

My entire story started, progressed, and ended with internet-based content. Actually, at many points the whole thing felt so surreal, almost like a virtual reality video game. Hence, I thought it was appropriate to document the story and tell it through the original internet excerpts. I used actual emails, Facebook messages, and the soon-to-be-familiar-to-you Discussion Board entries almost verbatim to give the reader a first-person perspective rather than a digested narrative. I chose to insert my narrative to make the story more fluent, and to give the reader an inside view of emotional turbulence through the whole ordeal. Although I am aware of a current trend to tell a story mimicking the style of internet media, my story actually did happen as told here. No gimmicks!

The major advantage point of my story is that it is not told from the perspective of just one person. Obviously, as the protagonist, I would be highly biased and portray myself as the victim. Any protagonist in any conflict would be guilty of providing a compassionate argument for his side of the story, and either fail to provide a valid counterargument or provide one that is what *he* might think is the core of his counterpart's beliefs. Rather, I was able to capture the actual voices of a most interesting variety of people. While some saw in me a case of civil rights in need of protection, others went all the way to compare me to Osama Bin Laden, and compared homosexuality to bestiality. Through it all, the protagonist (me) was the only one who was fully transparent and open about his identity and ideology. Most others sent me private emails, or posted anonymous comments on the Discussion Board. I found it astounding that even those denouncing me in the name of religion, who obviously thought their ideas were divinely inspired and justified, still chose to make their comments anonymously, and were not courageous enough to own up to their ideals. Even more amazing is that the only medium of free speech was provided, free of charge, by the most recent excommunicated member of the community.

This book should be viewed as a chronicle of an extraordinary amount of personal events and circumstances that happened to me during a very short period of time. I compiled an immense amount of communications in the form of entries in the Discussion Board as well as emails to provide a diary of my life for those two weeks. Although much of the content was not written by me, it is the compilation of all the text, along with my narrative, that together serve as a diary of my life for that period of time. Thus, the content here should be considered as my personal diary, all told in the original language and tone of the people interacting with me, that I share with you.

The purpose of telling my story is not to seek retaliation on my community or its leaders, who took certain positions against me. Some may argue that the content I am publishing in this book was intended for private use only, and that the 'secrets' of the community were never meant to be discussed with the wider population. I would counter-argue that if those narrow-minded views and actions could not be justified and validated within the larger population with democratic values and safeguards, they should certainly not be justified within the confines of a smaller community with very limited resources of guaranteeing justice. Much the same way that I am 100% accountable for my decisions and action, those who represent an opposing view should be accountable for their actions, in public and in private. The one major difference is that my homosexual lifestyle had no direct or intended impact on the community, as I kept my distance from them. But the actions of those outing me and advocating my banishment had a direct impact on me. I am not 'outing' the community in response to the way I was 'outed' and humiliated. My only intent in telling my story is to showcase that any type of discrimination, banishment, exclusion, excommunication, or sanctioning of any individual or minority group solely based on their identity is not acceptable in this day and age, as the book title implies.

Therefore, I have taken extreme care to disguise the names of people and places, and hide the identity of the original community under discussion. Most names have been anglicized or biblicized to protect the anonymity of everyone involved. Minor changes to the text of communications have also been applied to once again protect all parties in the story. If the reader sees themselves or anyone else they know in any of the people described in this book, they should consider the resemblance purely coincidental. I can guess that if the reader is decently knowledgeable about Middle East geography, or is otherwise familiar with the history of my community, they would be able to trace the story here to the community under discussion. For these people, you probably have already heard of what happened and don't need this book as a new revelation. For the vast majority of you who otherwise don't fall within that category, I do not want your one and only knowledge of my community to be the events of this book.

In the next section of this book I will give you a brief history of my community, the Kartaqis. I will also give you some information about our community's norms and mode of operation. My intention is not to expose to the larger public the inner thinking of a community that has tried over the centuries to maintain its privacy, and this book was not written to tell the history of the Kartaqis. My intention is to give the reader just enough information to be able to make sense of the story, while trying to extrapolate the circumstances to any other group of people or community.

I hope that you will appreciate the magnitude of the social interactions that engulfed me and my ethnic community in the span of two weeks. What started as a shaming of a gay person by outing him, progressed so rapidly into a positive learning experience for everybody involved. Polar opposite opinions were expressed, and an unprecedented community-wide discussion served as a communal therapy session. I was able to bring a discussion about gay weddings in particular, and gay rights in general, to a community that would otherwise adhere to a strict religious view, never dare to deviate from a biblical code of behavior, and otherwise claim: "we have no gays." I am certain that any student of Sociology will describe this book as fascinating.

A few stylistic notes as you read this book:

- There is a large cast of characters you will encounter in this book, as well as hundreds of comments from anonymous people. I will introduce each character and his/her relations to me as they appear chronologically. I have also added a list of these characters at the end of the book in case later reference is needed.

- There are a large number of emails included in My Diary section. Please make the effort to read the headings so you can establish the connection to the many concurrent conversations I was conducting with the various characters.

- In a few emails, and in some of the Discussion Board entries, people quoted a previous comment to establish a link or to validate a point. I indented all the quoted texts to differentiate them from original text, and to make it easier for the reader to skip if you remember the original text well.

- As many comments in the Discussion Board pertain to Jewish laws and values, at times Hebrew words are used to convey widely known concepts amongst the forum participants. I have translated these terms to plain English as each term was introduced, and a glossary page is provided at the end of the book as many terms are repeated throughout the book.

__Background__

__The Kartaqi Community:__

My name is Isaac. I was born in 1968 to a Jewish family in Zameen (imaginary name), the capital city of a Muslim country in the Middle East. My mother's family is one of the original and prominent Jewish families in Zameen. My ancestry from my father's side is from the town of Kartaq (another imaginary name). It is a very tight-knit community with intense bonds between its members.

The Jews of Kartaq had suffered many tragedies in the past few centuries. There were pogroms, forced conversions, and some very strict limitations on their ability to live life freely and practice their religions, even in closed quarters. All these hardships led to a very cohesive community. The small size of the community, and their relative geographical distance from other Jews in our country, led to multiple first-cousin marriages, and other marriages that were specifically condoned and arranged by community elders.

In the Sephardic communities (Jews of Middle East), we do not have a formal division into Orthodox, Conservative, and Reform movements. By default, we are considered to be Orthodox, or 'original', since none of the new movements ever reached us. Yet we are far from the picture of Orthodox that comes to the minds of most readers of this book. Over centuries, we have loosened certain restrictions, and adopted milder versions of practicing our religion. We never gave it a framework or specific definition. It was a matter of comfort rather than a set ideology. The correct terminology for this brand of Judaism is called *Masorti* (tradition-driven), which implies we practice our religion based on a communal sense of connection to G-d and each other, rather than individual revelation or spiritual awakening. By the way, you will encounter in several places in this book that the name of our Creator is spelled G-d, as a sign of respect for not using his name in vain.

Before I was born, there was a mass immigration of Kartaqi Jews to Zameen due to more optimal religious and economic climate there. Yet the community was so cohesive that they largely refrained from socializing with other Jews already in Zameen. They maintained their own separate synagogues, and did not intermarry with other Jews. While some viewed this practice as necessary to maintain and preserve the community's identity, others saw this as snobbery. This self-imposed insulation persisted back then, and still persists to this date in the United States. My father was one of the 'radicals' of his time when he fell in love with a Zameeni Jewess and married my mother.

A few years after I was born, as the entire Middle East grew more radical, the Jews in my country immigrated to safer countries. Some went to Israel, some came to the United States, and some went to various countries in Europe.

My own nuclear family first moved to Israel in 1980. We already had a large group of immediate family present there, and assimilating with them sounded like the logical next step. However, most Kartaqi Jews settled in one of the major metropolitans in the United States. Again, their cohesive nature led to better economic opportunities as they all nurtured and supported each other. Most members of the community initially settled in one of the neighborhoods of the big city they immigrated to. With the passage of time, and better prosperity, most Kartaqis moved to the rich suburb of Green Hills (imaginary name). The community was able to rapidly acclimate itself to the new surroundings. They set up their own synagogue and education system in their new home, this time able to be completely open and proud of their Jewish identity.

In 1984, my parents and I packed our bags again and moved to the United States. By then, my two older sisters were married, and stayed behind in Israel. Unlike most Kartaqi high school graduates of the time who chose not to continue higher education and entered the family businesses (mostly in only a few business fields), I had the brains and the will to continue to become a doctor. At the time, my family was struggling financially, and many other Kartaqis disdained my father for "letting" me go to college and medical school instead of entering the marketplace and help him with household expenses. We struggled, and we managed.

However, my relative isolation in college and medical school from the rest of the Kartaqis allowed me to integrate more freely into the American society, especially those in the academic fields. Most of my interactions with the Kartaqi community were limited to visiting extended family during major holidays, going to the Kartaqi synagogue while back in town, and the rare hanging out with few Kartaqi friends I had made. Since I was a "half-breed" Kartaqi, it was not odd to them that I had other sources of social and economic resources than they did.

At the present time, the great majority of Kartaqis in the United States live in Green Hills. The population approaches 5000 people. Since basically everyone in the community marries each other, we are all related to each other at most through one degree of separation. First and second- cousin marriages are very common, and the entire community feels like one big family. We all call each others 'cousins', often because we *are*, and mostly because that's how it feels. An average Kartaqi wedding has 600-1000 guests, and is often hosted in the same 4-5 venues near Green Hills that can accommodate that many people. There are usually a couple of Kartaqi weddings, Bar Mitzvahs, or Briths (circumcisions) per week. Just keeping your social calendar in sync with these events could be a full time job!

Being exposed to American values, some in the community have embraced a more strict Orthodox practice of our religion, yet others have assimilated into the greater American culture and the freedoms it affords us. This has been a source of contention between the various groups within the community. An alarming recent trend is the polarization of the opposing camps, and the distrust and friction it has brought to our ranks.

The umbrella organization for the entire community is called the Central Board, abbreviated as CB in many discussions in this book. It is a body of elected officials, regulating the tone and day to day affairs of the community. Some may disagree, but generally those elected to the CB come from the more prominent families in our community, both from financial and social status perspectives. They are given the difficult task of pulling together all the different factions of our community, and often they default to a strict Orthodox code since they believe that it is the most correct practice of Judaism, and the lowest common denominator among us. Unfortunately, this attitude aligns them with one end of the spectrum of thought, and they may be seen as dividers rather than uniters. Additionally, they have needed to frequently intervene and set guidelines for many community activities that may seem out of line to an outside observer, such as regulating what are appropriate gifts for weddings, how late should the youth parties go at night, what is considered appropriate foods at a funeral, what should be the maximum guest list for bar mitzvahs, etc. Many who disagree with this level of regulation of our daily lives have become embittered with the authority of the Central Board.

There is also a Kartaqi Youth Committee, called the KYC, which is the young adult version of the Central Board. They often arrange programs pertaining to social interactions, and publish the quarterly magazine called Scrolls. Kartaqis of all ages look forward to Scrolls to update them on current social issues, recent wedding announcements, and other community events. Technically, The KYC is under the financial and leadership control of the Central Board, significantly curtailing their ability to be innovative or otherwise deviate from the standard.

The spiritual leader of the Kartaqi community in the United States is Rabbi Levy (imaginary name). Rabbi Levy traces his origins to a different Muslim country in the Middle East. His virtues as an energetic and charismatic Rabbi took him through a multi-national career before he was recruited to the Kartaqi synagogue in Green Hills. Not being a Kartaqi himself, he showed outstanding ability to adapt to our customs and assume his role as the religious authority. Since by the time of his arrival to our community I went to the Kartaqi synagogue on major Jewish holidays only, I never had the chance to get to him personally. As such, I am not able to provide any personal reference on his character.

Membership in the Kartaqi synagogue is by birthright only; there are no annual dues. Instead, the expenses of the community are covered by voluntary donations. These donations are usually pledged in public, where various parts of the prayer are auctioned off to the highest bidder. Members with lesser financial success may nonetheless feel pressured to make larger donations to keep up the appearances with the richer crowd.

The major social event of the Kartaqi community is the Saturday (Shabbat) morning services. It is an opportunity for community members not just to pray together, but also to exchange news and other information on a weekly basis. Most people leave the services completely updated on all matters of personal and community significance.

The Kartaqis, in general, tend to live their lives by consensus. Usually derived from religious values, and often influenced by guidelines spelled out by the Central Board, a communal style of life has prevailed for centuries. They voluntarily live in the same neighborhoods, vacation together at the same spots, shop from the same stores, and typically work in the same few industries. Many in the margins often complain that this mode of life leaves no room for individuality, while those at the center claim that individuality would spell out the end of the community.

My Life and Sexual Orientation:

My relative social and geographical distance from other Kartaqis made it easier for me to deal with my homosexuality. Although I knew since college that I am attracted to the same sex, I felt it was my duty to my family and my community to suppress those feeling and marry a woman one day and raise a family amongst my people. The more I tried to play it straight, the more it became evident to me that the struggle is futile. At some point in medical school I started making some moves to explore my sexuality. By the time I was in residency, I had made more progress, and had my first sexual experience with someone of the same sex. As time went on, I became more comfortable with it myself, yet had a tough time trying to reconcile this with my family and friends.

In the Middle East, including in Kartaq, there is simply no such thing as openly gay people. Homosexuality is actually a crime. Quite a few gay men are executed every year with the sole crime of homosexuality. That same mentality is still prevalent among the elder Kartaqis and the religious people now living in the United Sates. The alternatives for homosexuals are either lie to yourself and everyone else and marry someone of the opposite sex (which is what most do), or never get married and have people always get into your business. For me, none of the above options would do, and I needed to find a better way.

Skip forward to 2003, when I met Andrew Mitchell. Up until then, for the past 35 years of my life, my sexuality had prevented me from opening my heart to anyone, of either gender. Yet it became evident to me in just two weeks after I met Andrew that I was meant to spend the rest of my life with this wonderful man. I had met my soulmate, and there was no way I was letting him go. I am so lucky that the feeling was mutual. Andrew had come out of the closet at age 22, and led a completely transparent life since then. His courage and honesty was most inspiring to me, serving as a role model for how to be comfortable with oneself.

Over the next few years, our bond grew stronger. I was eventually able to discuss my relationship and sexuality with my close American friends and with my sisters. By then, my mother had passed away, and my father was entirely from a different generation to be able to handle a gay son, especially coming from an older Kartaqi point of reference. A couple of years later, my father moved back to Israel so he can be near my sisters and their children. I later shared the information with a few cousins in Israel. But since I lived my life in isolation to the Kartaqi community, I did not voluntarily disclose my sexuality to anyone there. Many had suspected, and some had enough clues to put pieces of the puzzle together. Yet those people allowed me my personal space to live my life as I see fit, as long as I was not blatantly exposing them to anything that was contrary to their practices and beliefs. I imagined there were other Kartaqi gays, but I was not interested in finding them out, nor did I want to become part of any such network.

On July 1st, 2009, Andrew and I got married. We had an intimate civil ceremony in our country home, in one of a few states where gay marriage is legal. On

October 18, 2009, we had a wedding party for our friends and family (mostly his family). The event was fabulous, if I must say so myself! We also used a wedding website to share stories, photos, and other information about our engagement, wedding, and honeymoon with our guests. The domain name was www.Micthell-Namdar.com, which made it very easy for people to refer to it.

Unfortunately, my wedding was sandwiched on both ends with deaths in my immediate family. In June 2009, my older sister passed away after battling breast cancer for 17 years. As miserable as I felt personally, seeing my father attend his daughter's funeral was absolutely devastating. In December 2009, my second sister's husband died rather suddenly from recurrent brain cancer. And because of my brother-in-law's sudden illness, my sister Jenny and her kids were not able to attend my wedding even though they planned on it for months.

The ensuing events detailed in this book cover the course of two weeks in January 2010, when an inadvertent discovery of our wedding website caused a major uproar within the Kartaqi community. This was the first case of same-sex marriage of any member of the Kartaqi community, and was quite a shock to all everyone in the community. As stated in the Preface section, in this book I will try to be as true to the actual events as possible, while disguising the real names of people and places in order to provide protection by anonymity for those involved.

My Diary

Tuesday, January 5, 2010

Today marked the 30th day anniversary of the death of my second brother-in-law, David. Unlike my older sister, who suffered from a long battle with breast cancer, and whose death in June 2009 was sadly expected, David had a rapid decline in his health that resulted in his sudden demise. He was initially diagnosed with brain cancer 8 years ago. He underwent initial treatment with surgery and radiation back then, which left him with significant impairment of his left arm and leg. He then had a recurrence a year later, and he needed additional surgery and radiation for treatment. He was very compliant with his follow up doctor visits every few months, and was considered to have been cured.

My sister Jenny and her two daughters had planned for months to come to my wedding party in October. She was overjoyed to see her baby brother finally find the right person and settle down, although a blond American Episcopalian man was not quite what she had dreamed up for me. Nonetheless, she proved to be very supportive, and totally looked forward to the wedding party

When I called her the day before her flight to the United States, her voice was trembling. She told me that David was sick. Naturally, I thought she meant that David might have come down with a cold. She clarified for me that David was having additional weakness in his already impaired limbs. She wasn't sure if this was due to medication imbalance, or something of more significance. She told me that she was really torn what to do given the circumstances. As much as I wanted her to attend my wedding, I knew her obligation to her husband was much more important. I kept my silence. She called me again later and told me that she arranged for David's brother to accompany him to the doctors the following day, and that she was on the way to the airport.

Andrew volunteered to pick up my sister and nieces from the airport. During the car ride home, they called back to Israel to announce they had arrived safely, and to ask for David's condition. They were told that David had fallen significantly sicker since my sister and the girls took off, and they are taking him to the emergency room for prompt evaluation. As soon as they came upstairs, they had to call the airline company to look for the next flight home. In the airport, my sister was inconsolable. Not only she was not able to attend her brother's wedding, but she was heading into a situation that most likely was not going to have a good outcome for her and her entire family.

After the initial round of tests, Jenny told me that David had a massive recurrence of his brain tumor. He was going to need another brain surgery, and the doctors were shocked how a completely disease-free CT scan of his brain from just two months ago now had such a large tumor in it. The surgery was emergently scheduled for Thursday October 15, 2009, just three days before my wedding party. I immediately offered to cancel the wedding party and to fly to Israel to be with her and the entire family in support during the surgery and recovery phase. She told me, in so many words, that chances are I will not be able to reschedule the wedding party for quite some time if I cancel, and that she would actually prefer I came to Israel in a few weeks for the inevitable outcome. I fully understood what she was talking about. Reluctantly, I went ahead with the wedding plans, as Andrew and I were glued to the telephone from Israel for updates.

Despite the surgery, David's condition continued to deteriorate. With each daily phone call I asked my sister to tell me when to drop everything and take the next flight to be with her and the kids. Finally, seven weeks later, she told me that the time had come. That afternoon I took the next flight. David died on Friday night, December 4th, 2009. He was buried on Sunday morning, with a most impressive crowd honoring his life as a decorated war hero in the Israeli Army and as a model husband and father. I stayed in Israel for the entire week of *shiva* (seven days of mourning), and then came from Israel back home a broken man. This was the second trip I had made to Israel as an emergency to bury a loved one.

Fast forward to today, which was the 30th day of David's passing and burial. As is custom in many Jewish communities, we had a memorial service in the synagogue to honor David's memory. David's two sisters live in the United States, and arranged for the services in the Kartaqi synagogue in Green Hills. Especially since his *shiva* service was entirely conducted in Israel, this served as an opportunity for the Kartaqi community in the United States to pay their respects. His sisters asked me to attend the memorial service as the other next of kin. At the end of the services, it is customary for the mourners to stand in the hallway as visitors line up to pass us by and express their sympathies. I got the chance to see many Kartaqis who I had not seen for quite a long time. A select few also inquired, as they always do when talking to young single eligible men in our community, when was I going to find the right girl and settle down. The standard line usually includes that since we all already know of all the eligible young Kartaqi women of my age, and it wasn't as though a new one was going to show up out of nowhere, it was time to just basically learn to like one them sufficiently to marry her and establish a family. And that if I lived in Green Hills and not so far away in the City, and that if my mother was still alive, I would have settled down already. I was there in the synagogue to pay my respects to my brother-in-law, but by now I couldn't wait to get out of there.

Thursday, January 7, 2010

Thursday was just like any other day. Go to work, see patients, check email in between, and see what happened on Facebook on lunch break. That Thursday would end up being the last normal day I would know in months. During lunch break, I got the following email:

Email

From: Wedding Website

To: Isaac

Date: 1/7/2010 12:33:29 P.M.

Subject: I am also Namdar

Hello Andrew & Isaac!

You have received this comment from the contact page on your wedding website:

Name: Jacob Namdar

E-mail: *****@aol.com

Comment: I was interested to know your background

Have a great day

I didn't know who Jacob Namdar was. He shares the same last name with me, but there are approximately five families of Namdars among the Kartaqis. We probably shared an ancestor a few generations ago. Additionally, there are some Muslim Namdars who are not related to us. So this Jacob could be anyone. I didn't know how to respond to him discovering our wedding website. For the time being, I was going to ignore him and hopefully he would just disappear.

Andrew had gotten the same message from the wedding website. He sent me this inquiry.

Email

From: Andrew

To: Isaac

Date: 1/7/2010 12:38:59 P.M.

Subject: Fwd: I am also Namdar

Who is this?? Should I respond?

> ----- Original Message -----
> From: Jacob Namdar <support@*********.com>
> To: Andrew Mitchell-Namdar
> Sent: Thu Jan 07 12:33:23 2010
> Subject: Wedding: I am also Namdar
>
>
> Hello Andrew & Isaac!
>
> You have received this comment from the contact page on your wedding website:
>
> Name: Jacob Namdar
>
> E-mail: *****@aol.com
>
> Comment: I was interested to know your background
>
> Have a great day.

Email

From: Isaac

To: Andrew

Date: 1/7/2010 2:32:59 P.M.

Subject: Fw: I am also Namdar

I don't know him. Ignore for now.

I saw patients the rest of the afternoon. When I got home, I went back on the computer.

Email

From: notification+mh3-hudi@Facebook email.com

To: Isaac

Date: 1/7/2010 9:08:36 P.M. Eastern Standard Time

Subject: Natusha added you as a friend on Facebook...

Hi Isaac,

Natusha added you as a friend on Facebook. We need to confirm that you know Natusha in order for you to be friends on Facebook.

I looked up Natusha on Facebook before responding. She was a Kartaqi, but I did not recognize her personally. I ignored the friendship invite. Two more friends invitations from Facebook came later that night from other Kartaqis I did not personally know. I found the sudden interest odd, but did not make any connection to what really was going on.

Friday, January 8, 2010

Andrew left town for business today. I had a quiet dinner at home that night and was able to organize some paperwork and other matters that needed attention.

I received one more friends request on Facebook from a Kartaqi woman I did not know personally. I declined.

Saturday, January 9, 2010

Since Andrew was out of town, I decided to do some errands downtown. Before I left, I got the message below:

Email

From: notification+mh3-hudi@Facebook email.com

To: Isaac

Date: 1/9/2010 9:23:24 A.M.

Subject: Arielle added you as a friend on Facebook...

Hi Isaac,

Arielle added you as a friend on Facebook. We need to confirm that you know Arielle in order for you to be friends on Facebook.

I checked out Arielle on Facebook, and she too is a Kartaqi whom I did not know personally. I thought it was odd, so I declined her invite too. I thought the sudden interest from the Kartaqis I didn't otherwise know to become friends with me on Facebook was very unusual. In hindsight it is easy to make the connections and decipher what the source of the sudden interest was, but at the time I was too naïve to understand what was going on behind my back.

After finishing some of the errands, I went to a coffee shop to order lunch. I placed my order, and sat by the window to enjoy the view as I ate. I randomly checked my emails on my smartphone as I waited.

Email

From: Nathan (my 22 year old nephew in Israel, my sister Jenny's son)

To: Isaac

Date: 1/9/2010 12:06:36 P.M. Eastern Standard Time

Subject: Hey

hey listen .. call me . dont go to synagogue ... everyone knows. and talking about it. call mom !

O-M-G!!!! That one sentence from my nephew forever changed everything else in my life. It was the doomsday scenario I was not ready for. It was like someone dumped a truckload of ice water on my head. It was as though my heart just plummeted to the floor. It was as though there was no oxygen in the air. It was as though there was a ton of bricks on my chest and I was suffocating. You name the cliché metaphor, I felt it!

I was just numb. What does this mean? What happened? Who knows? How did they find out? What are they saying? I'm ruined!

In the past few months, ever since I went to Israel for my brother-in-law's funeral, select members of the family had slowly discovered the news about my wedding. The ones who came forward to congratulate me were all supportive. Could this new discovery be an extension of the same? Did someone cross the line of decency and decide to divulge the information to strangers? Was there a violation of trust? Some kind of betrayal? Or some kind of backstabbing?

I figured I owed myself the next 15 minutes of peace to finish my lunch before calling Israel to talk to my sister. Not that lunch was enjoyable at that point, but I just needed to breathe before digging in. I needed to organize my thought before reacting.

Last bite, and it was time to call. I called my sister Jenny, and just listened. She had received a phone call from a relative in the United States, telling her that someone got into our wedding website, saw all the pictures, and sent an email to all his friends telling them about our gay wedding. In retrospect, again, that email from Jacob Namdar two days ago was the source of the massive discovery. People also got into the Facebook accounts of Andrew and myself, and saw the video of our wedding ceremony. Apparently everyone, EVERYONE, all 5000 Kartaqis, found out about it in a matter of hours. She wanted to make sure I had not gone to synagogue that Saturday, so not to run into any awkward situations or confrontations. Especially since our synagogue is a major source of gossip exchange, a topic like this would be way too juicy for them not to discuss on the spot. I told her I hadn't planned on going to synagogue, and had stopped going regularly for a while. Jenny then asked me to quickly decide how much of this we should share with our father.

My father belongs to the same generation of older people from the Middle East, to whom an openly gay lifestyle is not comprehensible. Up until that point, my father had enough clues (intentional and not) to figure out my sexuality, and knew of my special connection with Andrew. Yet he made it clear to me that he preferred not to talk about it directly. This gave us the opportunity to quietly respect each other's wishes, yet maintain our father-son relationship unaffected. I was saddened that I could not share my happiness and love with my father, yet did not need to upset him with something that was beyond his comprehension. Obviously, this meant that I did not tell him about the wedding.

Under the new circumstances, Jenny and I decided that I should tell our father about the wedding personally and immediately, before some idiot calls him to 'congratulate' him and catch him by surprise. That was another tough call I had to make right then and there in the coffee shop. I called my dad, and very slowly approached the subject with him. Of course he knew Andrew and I were together, but I guess he had hoped that it was a phase, and that I would eventually stop 'playing games' and settle down with a woman. I told him that it was not a phase, and that in fact we had gotten married. His immediate concern was to find out why we needed to make it official, and why couldn't we just continue to be together without making it official. I enumerated some of the 1500 reasons that marriage makes a difference legally and socially, and now that we are allowed to do it in certain states, we cannot live as strangers any more. I am sure he was crushed. He said that he could not congratulate me, but still wishes me all the best.

After I hung up the phone, I returned back to the present. All my senses were numb. This was the biggest invasion of my privacy I could have possibly imagined. And to make it worse, it was done by people whom I had slowly and seamlessly tried to cut out of my life. And now they are coming back to haunt me and discuss me to no end behind my back. The worst part of it was the powerlessness. There was not a single thing I could do to change things, or take back what happened.

At that moment it was obvious to me that I will be banished, or even officially excommunicated by the leadership of the Kartaqi community. My frame of reference was the story of a previous Kartaqi who married a Gentile. Although the woman went through a strict Orthodox conversion before the wedding, the couple was excommunicated. His family was strongly encouraged to stop accepting him within their homes, or else face alienation themselves. A so-called Green Letter, named after the color paper it was printed on, was mailed to every Kartaqi household after that incident. All community members were strictly instructed to shun the couple at all social events. The instructions went as far as demanding Kartaqis to leave any community wedding or events if that couple was spotted at any gathering. Surely, the same fate was awaiting me and my innocent family. I just couldn't bear to mind that my poor relatives would be punished or otherwise put in an awkward situation on account of me.

Concentrating again on my own story, it was time for damage assessment, or even damage control. I remembered that our wedding site had a visitor counter on it. I immediately logged on and saw that there were almost 1000 new visitors to the site since the last time I checked on it a few weeks ago! I immediately got the mental image of thousands of Kartaqis, sitting in groups and in families, looking at my wedding pictures with ridicule and disgust, and making fun of my homosexual life. "Cocksucker!" "Faggot!" "Fudgepacker!" "Abomination!" "Sinner! "Disgrace!" "Is he *that* gay that he couldn't just marry a woman anyways?" "Is he *so* gay that he couldn't get it up for a woman even if he tried to?" "So much for the esteemed doctor, that fucking deviant!" These are only a handful of jokes and ridicule I surely was the subject of within many Kartaqi homes for the past two days.

Denial, predictably, was my first reaction. This couldn't be happening. Desperately, I wanted to minimize the damage. My immediate reaction was to deactivate the wedding website, and go back to Facebook and see what should be eliminated or otherwise restricted. I used the small screen of my smartphone to get into the account settings of my wedding website and deactivate it. I couldn't do any Facebook changes since the mobile app is really not set up to control privacy settings. In the meantime, I got two more Facebook friends request from young people in the community, and I decided to hold off on taking any action.

I thought that given the situation, retail therapy would be good to just escape the bitter new reality. I browsed a few stores, restless and queasy the whole time. All the images of people looking at my wedding photos, giggling, and cracking faggot jokes behind my back was just too overbearing.

I then suddenly realized that in addition to my own ruining, the news could be so damaging to my sister and her kids after they just recently lost their father. I had to apologize. I got back on the smartphone to write an email.

Email

From: Isaac

To: Nathan

Date: 1/9/2010 2:22:31

Subject: Re: hey

Thanks for the warning. I had not gone to synagogue, it was too cold.

I spoke to your mom. I am sorry if my personal life choices are going to cause you and your family any unnecessary grief. Especially right now, when your own life is in turmoil. Please accept my apologies. Please refer all the yentas to talk to me directly instead of hassling you and your mom.

Right after that I got another phone call from my sister. She insisted that I should never think I am a burden or source of embarrassment to them. She loves me from the bottom of her heart, and she would never have me any other way. I apologized again to her directly, knowing that she will have to face quite a few critical people or other yentas trying to be opportunists with this situation, as is the custom among the Kartaqis.

Email

From: Alon (my first cousin, living in Israel)

To: Isaac

Date: 1/9/2010 3:05:11 P.M.

Subject: Synagogue

hi doc

if you don't know, everyone talked about you in synagogue today.

be ready for kartaqi attack.

Email

From: Isaac

To: Alon

Date: 1/9/2010 3:15:06 P.M.

Subject: Re: synagogue

Thanks. I got the call already from my sister. I usually go there for holidays anyway, was not planning on going today. How did the word get out? Who was the major nosey?

Email

From: Alon

To: Isaac

Date: Sat, Jan 9, 2010 at 03:20 PM

Subject: Re: synagogue

Facebook

after they changed the settings andrew's page got open and everyone saw what he got there.

now kartaqis will stop asking you when are you going to get marry.

  :-)

Email

From: Nathan

To: Isaac

Date: Jan 9, 2010, at 4:04 PM

Subject: Re: hey

Do you want me to tell my other uncle and my cousins here before they hear it from someone else?

Email

From: Isaac

To: Nathan

Date: 1/9/2010 4:35:43 P.M.

Subject: Re: hey

I am just in awe. The amount of love and support I have received from you over the years is absolutely amazing.

I'll leave it up to you to figure out who should be told how much and when.

Look, after all, I am not that involved with the Kartaqis like I used to, and I have pretty much stopped hanging out with them. I rarely show up, just basically for the High Holidays. So this will not change too much for me.

But you and your mother are involved in the community daily over there. So make your decisions based on what is going to make life the easiest for you. And don't take me or my feeling into considerations. Again, I apologize if I and my lifestyle have caused you any unnecessary inconvenience or embarrassment, especially in these difficult times.

Email

From: Jenny (my sister)

To: Isaac

Date: 1/9/2010 5:12:38 P.M.

Subject: None

I read the email you sent to Nathan. Just want you to know that we love you and we are proud of you just as you are. We're not embarrassed or anything, and I didn't like it that you thought we were. Don't even think that it bothers me a bit, and I would not exchange you with anyone else even for a moment.

I am happy that you are happy and I am so proud of you so don't ever say again that you are sorry.

You have only given us happiness and I don't owe any explanations to anyone.

Email

From: Isaac

To: Jenny

Date: 1/9/2010 5:29:05 P.M

Subject: Re:

I spoke with dad and told him. It was hard for him to take it, but it went OK altogether. He asked who else in the family knows, and I was honest about it. He asked that at this time he does not want anyone else in the family to talk to him about it directly, and he prefers if they think he doesn't know and to let him have some privacy. I think it is games, but if that is the way he wants it, then I can respect it too.

I really really really really appreciate your support all this time. It means the world to me. At any time that the news was going to get out, there was going to be some noise about it. I am just so sorry it happened at this time that you and Nathan are so absorbed in your own troubles after David passed away so suddenly. You really did not need any extra stress in your life right now.

Email

From: Nathan

To: Isaac

Date: 1/9/2010 6:11:44 P.M.

Subject: Re: hey

Uncle, I am going to ask you never to say we are embarrassed of you. Embarrassed? Of what? That you live your real life with happiness, something that none of those Kartaqis have there?

Live your life in peace. I imagine it is a bit hard now for you, but you have enough experience in life to know that all is going to be well, and the main thing is we should all be healthy.

You also know that there will be some noise to begin with, but it will die down and everyone will move to the next topic.

Email

From: Isaac

To: Nathan

Date: 1/9/2010 6:24:29 P.M

Subject: Re: hey

Thanks. I already talked to my dad. He wants everyone to act as though he does not know and not to talk to him about it. I think it is silly, but if that is what he wants, so be it.

My real concern is if there would be too much of a hassle on you all. And if anyone wants to call me or write an email, I am available.

I later got home from errands. It was mostly a waste of time, just to keep my mind distracted a bit. Just a mental game for me to deny the reality of what had just happened to me.

I logged onto Facebook to change the privacy settings for our pictures and other personal information. I deleted the wedding video from Andrew's account, and limited access to any additional data mostly to our American friends. I even deleted a few vacation videos I had previously posted on YouTube. While I was busy with digging in deeper into the details, I got the message below.

Facebook Message

From: Zach (a total stranger with a Kartaqi last name)

To: Isaac

Date: January 9 at 6:32pm

Congrats on your wedding!

So far, I had spent the better part of the day getting more and more emotionally withdrawn. I was in touch with my sister and my nephew a few times, but otherwise sank myself into the safety of self-isolation. I had quickly come to terms that I will never have any more contact with my Kartaqi heritage, or my family from that side. Not in a million years did I expect that a day that started so dismally would at some point include any congratulatory or supportive message, much less from a stranger I never met. There is a Kartaqi saying: once bitten by a snake, always scared of a shoelace. Although I wanted to bask in this message of support, I was hesitant to open up.

Facebook Message

From: Isaac

To: Ted

Date: January 9 at 6:43pm

Thanks. Remind me where I know you from?

Facebook Message

From: Ted

To: Isaac

Date: January 9 at 6:51pm

Umm... we dont know each other. I am a non-community kartaqi, my mom told me this morning about your wedding (i guess gossip runs fast lol) and as another gay kartaqi I thought it was very cool.

:)

Although it is only natural that in a community of 5000 Kartaqis there should be other gay people, I never knew of any personally, nor did I ever imagine any kind of sharing or networking. This was the first instance that it occurred to me others within the community might be homosexuals too, and that they might have dealt with it in their own individual and possibly open ways.

Facebook Message

From: Isaac

To: Ted

Date: January 9 at 6:57pm

Wow, that makes at least the two of us. Does your family and the rest of the community know about you? I guess today was my day in the minds and mouths of everyone....LOL.

Facebook Message

From: Zach

To: Isaac

Date: January 9 at 7:07pm

My family knows about me and are very cool about it but since I'm not in the kartaqi community (nor I wanna be lol) they ask me not to wave a rainbow flag when I come visit them in green hill. I live in the city for the last 13yrs. How is your family accepting the good news and your husband? I assume you live in the city..?

Although we never met I was sooo happy this morning when I heard the news, hopefully your action will pave a new attitude and somewhat of an acceptance among kartaqis.

Facebook Message

From: Isaac

To: Zach

Date: January 9 at 7:49pm

I told my sisters and nieces/nephews a few years ago. They are totally cool with it. My father really does not want to talk about it, although he knows too (my mom passed away some time ago). Before the wedding I also told some cousins in Israel and invited them too. Some came for the party all the way from Israel.

Yes, we live in the city, so we're neighbors too.

So, by now you know so much about me. Tell me about you? Are you dating? What do you do for life? Can I 'friend' you on Facebook? BTW, when your mom told you, did she feel relieved that you were not the first one to be outed? Did she have any other comments?

Facebook Message

From: Zach

To: Isaac

Date: January 9 at 8:32pm

My mom told me your news as a 'by the way' and then she moved on to the next subject (the weather I think…lol) afterwards when I spoke to my sister she told me your name and I looked you up on FB, btw you're the only Isaac Namdar on FB so it was easy to track you down

My parents live in Israel but my bro and sisters all live in Green Hills and married to kartaqis… (im sure you know all my family) you can 'friend me although lets keep our new discovery about each other in low key as my family asked me not to spread my life too much among kartaqis (although I assume most people who know me must know im gay) you can tell your family though, im sure they'll be happy there's more than one of us… I am sure there are MANY of us but they are major closeted. Last time I was in

Green Hills (my bro's wedding) my gaydar was working and was pretty sure I spotted a few...

I'm single now, was in a 6 yrs relationship that ended this summer.

Are you involved in the Kartaqi community at all?

Facebook Message

From: Isaac

To: Zach

Date: January 9 at 8:51pm

I understand, once you friend someone on FB, everyone knows. Smart idea. Instead, you can call me anytime you want, 789 555-1212. Or just on FB messages, that's cool.

And I am really not that involved in the Kartaqi community. There are about 7-8 people I used to hang out a bit more like 10 years ago. Now some are married, and we parted ways. I now basically go to the synagogue on Rosh Hashannah and once on Passover. I have been going to the local synagogue for Yom Kippur and Purim etc for the past few years, with my hubby. My immediate family are all in Israel, have cousins and second cousins here. Some cousins and acquaintants from Israel have called or sent messages in the past few days saying mazal tov and that they are supportive. That is a good sign, although I do not expect miracles of any sort.

Sorry to hear your relationship ended. Time to find you a new cutie. My hubby and I have a beach house summer share we have been going to for the past few years. You are welcome to crash with us and see what happens with all the single and available men there

Facebook Message

From: Zach

That night, I got a phone call from Rachel, my second cousin's wife, the same person who had called my sister in Israel to alert her to the situation. Having grown up in the Kartaqi community in Israel, she had been a good friend of my sister before she married out second cousin. She figured my sister should be the one to tell me about the mass outing. She told me that there was an email that went around two days ago, and it could be traced to Jacob Namdar at the bottom of the forwards list. Jacob had sent an email with the link to our wedding website to a handful of his friends, and they in turn forwarded it to everybody else. It then got forwarded virally to almost everyone in the Kartaqi community. Rachel was so surprised and shocked that she did not know what was the right thing to do. She said that she now regrets not calling me directly right away to tell me what is happening, so I could have had a chance to limit all the exposure. Rachel indicated to me that she was very supportive, and that the new revelation would not change anything in her relations with me. She was raised in Israel, and she attributed her open-mindedness to growing away from most Kartaqis in an otherwise egalitarian society. She then changed the focus to a lighter note, telling me that the pictures were gooooooooorgeous! What a ceremony! What a party! And who is the photographer? We all need to hire him instead of the same bozo everybody hires for all the Kartaqi weddings.

As I digested all this new information, the one factor that was beyond all comprehension is that even my family members and friends could not call me to let me know what was happening. Like deer stuck in the headlights, they just watched my demise in the eyes of the community. Worse even, knowing that our Saturday morning services at the synagogue are the central weekly social gathering, where much news and gossip is exchanged, not one of them bothered to call me that morning to tell me to be prepared just in case I was planning on going to our synagogue that day. I kept imagining what could have happened if in fact I had gone to the Kartaqi synagogue in Green Hills that morning, and was confronted mobs of homophobes harassing me into leaving in shame. Yet nobody, absolutely nobody, bothered to call me and warm me against walking into the lion's den by going to synagogue on that very day.

Later that evening I got a few more Facebook friendship request, I declined them all. I finally understood what all the sudden interest from people on Facebook asking to be my friends was all about. I couldn't tell if they wanted to gain better access to my personal information, or they indeed wanted to express their support. I decided that given all that had transpired, it was not worth the risk at the moment. I ignored all those requests.

Sunday, January 10, 2010

I was restless all night. There was a heavy feeling in my chest. It was a sense of total despair. I kept replaying the images of an entire community gathering at services and cracking faggot jokes at my expense. The unforgiving nature of the masses could be horrifying. I also kept imagining that just in case I *had* gone to services yesterday, after the great discovery, the confrontation and not being prepared for it would have been completely disastrous.

There was also a huge sense of loss. It was obvious to me that I will never see all my relatives from my father's side, and even perhaps from my mother's side, as the news will surely travel from the Kartaqi to the Zameeni community. I will never be able to go and visit them for the holidays. I will never be able to attend services at my synagogue. Overnight, I lost all my identity, and become a different person. Everybody from my country of origin will surely ostracize and alienate me. Even if people like Rachel and other open-minded people express their support, I will never be invited to their homes or be able to attend another community wedding. I am a liability to them, and they can't be seen associating with me.

Trying to put the pieces of the puzzle together, I figured that Jacob Namdar, whose message I had ignored on Thursday, was really the first one who got into the website and told everyone else. Even though he has the same last name, I don't know him. I tried to find out who he was.

Email

From: Isaac

To: Alon

Date: 1/10/2010 11:22:17 A.M.

Subject: Re: synagogue

I think a Jacob Namdar is the one who sent the email to everyone. Do you know him?

Email

From: Alon

To: Isaac

Date: 1/10/2010 1:18:17 P.M.

Subject: Re: synagogue

who is he?

do i know him?

real asshole sending e-mails to everyone.

but what did you think will happen that you have your names and pictures together all over google?

Email

From: Alon

To: Isaac

Date: 1/10/2010 3:52:41 P.M.

Subject: Re: synagogue

i asked my cousin Ron ,this is what he said:

Jacob is some kartaqi guy who is very involved with community things, and the syng.

Anyway he will be ok ,he's a good guy and smart ,he can handle it

I was puzzled at that last sentence by Alon. Why was he more concerned about him than me? Why was he concerned that Jacob will be OK? OK from what?

That afternoon I went to the gym. I always get a much better workout when I am upset or angry. All the banging of the metal is a good stress relief mechanism for me. Plus, I do some of my best thinking when I am working out. As I was lifting weights, I got the inspiration that I cannot retreat. I can't let this be the lasting image of me. I was violated, and I need to let it be known that I was wronged. I can't just disappear in shame.

My initial instinct had been to immediately destroy everything that had led to my demise in the eyes of others. I had taken down the wedding website, changed Facebook settings for Andrew and myself, and even deleted some videos of our vacations from YouTube. Somehow, in my instinctive denial phase, that made perfect sense.

Now that I had more time to think things out, I knew that it was not the right thing to do. I have lived my life to the fullest, and rejoiced in my love for Andrew. Personally, I am proud of whom I am, and if people have problem with it, then that's *their* problem. I did not want the actions of others to force me into hiding, into a state of paranoia. I had made so much progress coming to terms with my sexuality; I couldn't let *them* determine how open and transparent I should be.

It was going to be a delicate balance of showing others I am confident and proud, yet not provide them material that could be used to ridicule me further. I decided that instead of taking down the wedding website as though it never existed, maybe I should put up a one-page response letting everyone know that the way my life was invaded was not acceptable.

I re-opened the website, and posted the following as the homepage. I chose "I've Got a Feeling that Somebody's Watching Me" by Rockwell as the background music. Altogether, I needed to convey that I was hurt, yet not lash out, and maybe even show some sense of humor and a bit of humanity. I also knew that most people will use religion to point out that homosexuality is wrong. I, too, needed to use religion to point out what they did to me was wrong as well.

HELLO!!!!

1.   Welcome to our web-casa!

2.   We wish that everyone would have the happiness and romance that we have experienced for the past few years. And we would love to share our stories and pictures with you. Contact us at Namdar@aol.com, and we would love to have you over for coffee or tea. We'll even watch the videos together. We are open to sharing everything, just not behind our backs.

---

3.   A certain member of our community, who shares the same last name, took the story of love between two people and made it into a mockery in the eyes of the community.

As said in Pirkey Avot (Ethics of Fathers) 3,15: "Rabbi Elazar of Modiim said: If a man puts his fellow to shame publicly, he has no share in the world to come."

Rabbi Yonason Goldson elaborates: "Parallel to one's relationship with G-d is his relationship with his fellow Jews and, ultimately, his relationship with himself. In the eyes of the sages, embarrassing or humiliating another person publicly constitutes so severe a transgression that they equated it to murder. One who disdains another person with no concern for the emotional pain he causes has effectively denied the G-dliness within the other and, by extension, the G-dliness within oneself."

Still, we have it in our hearts to forgive. If that person who started the first leak (and we all know who he is) wants to make amends, he can contact us anytime he wants.

4.   If you think that the way this issue has been handled by the community is totally inappropriate, we would be glad to direct you to a couple of charitable causes who were the recipients of our registry so that you can get over your guilt by making a donation. Better yet, there are still a few gifts left on our store registries, and we just LOVE presents! (and to think the first time you came to this website you didn't leave a little mazal tov note, or bothered to check the registry and send us a little something... Nothing! Oy!)

PS. After all that has happened we have nothing but love and respect for you and everyone in the community. We hope the feeling is mutual.

In the meantime two more cousins and second cousins called to say that at some level they had known for some time, and that it doesn't change a thing in their dealings with me. They were also generally very upset the way the community reacted. I told them that I had changed the website to reflect a one page response; they should check it out.

Monday, January 11, 2010

Well, that was a very eventful weekend! My world came crashing over my head, and any trace of respect among my people was lost. Ironically, the only contacts I had with anyone were with those supportive of me. But they all told me horror stories of how I was the butt of everybody's jokes. If it weren't for these few cousins and second cousins calling and expressing their sadness about how things turned out, I would have never known anything happened. Yet, the mental images of the faggot jokes in every Kartaqi home and in the Kartaqi synagogue were more than I could handle.

I had to go back to work. Perhaps this would provide some distraction from the tough weekend events. All through the morning, I had email and Facebook open in the office.

Email

From: Laura (my 30 year old niece living in Israel)

To: Isaac

Date: 1/11/2010 1:19:21 A.M.

Subject: Hi

How are you holding out?

I guess the best tactic is just to ignore all those morons, and let them die in their own rage of jealousy how fabulous your wedding was. Just so you know, nobody is bothered by it here, we just have to be careful with your dad.

Email

From: Isaac

To: Laura

Subject: Re: Hi

really, if it weren't for all the supportive people calling and emailing I would not know that something happened. And I never see these people unless I go there for synagogue, which is like once in 6 months. So I can live without that too.

Email

From: Alon

To: Isaac

Date: 1/11/2010 4:26:12 A.M.

Subject: Surprise

who was it that said that one day you will surprise us?

so you did :-)

i see that google doesn't know you exist now.

how are you dealing with the crazy kartaqis, do they drive you crazy?

Email

From: Isaac

To: Alon

Date: 1/11/2010 7:48:17 A.M.

Subject: Re: surprise

I really don't have much of an interaction with Kartaqis these days. I used to go to synagogue like for Rosh Hashannah and Passover, and that's it. I don't see these people.

The only feedback is the supportive people who called and emailed saying they support the issue and they are upset the way the community invaded my privacy.

I then exchanged some instant messages with my cousin Alon in Israel. He told me that all weekend, most of my cousins and friends in Green Hills have been bombarded with telephone calls from other nosey Kartaqis who were desperate to find out how much my extended family knew about me and for how long. I was so preoccupied with myself, I had not even thought about others. My initial response was to be protective of Jenny and her kids, but I never thought about the bigger family.

I was crushed. Ultimately, I am responsible for my own actions. But the thought of others suffering or being harassed because of me was just too much to handle. It wasn't just me who was outed, it was everybody around me who was outed as well. And they could be subject to mockery or disdain based on how much they knew and how accepting they might have been. Suddenly, my own sorrow became secondary to the heartache of others. I needed to own up and apologize to those who might have been hurt simply because they knew me personally or are related to me. Just yesterday I thought I would never talk to these people or see them ever again in my life; today I need to gather the courage to contact them and apologize.

Email

From: Isaac

To: Thomas (second cousin, used to be very close friend)

Date: 1/11/2010 11:58:15 A.M.

Subject: Sorry

I am writing to apologize to you if my personal life has caused you and your family unnecessary headaches in the past few days. I know that many people have approached you, and were even less than kind to you due to our previous close friendship. My choices in life are not at all a reflection on you, and there is no reason you should be dragged into something that is not your fault. I am truly sorry for any hardship you have experienced.

Quite some time ago I realized that my life is not going to be compatible with the norms of our community. That's why I slowly withdrew myself out of the community and went my own way. I stopped coming to our synagogue, and have been attending other synagogues in the city. I also did not feel that I should burden any of you personally with information that may be too much to handle. It was best to live my life in distance, and in privacy.

However, many people who didn't even know who I am decided it was OK to pry into my life and invade that privacy. Yes, I did not take severe measures to protect that privacy, because I did not want to live in a bubble. My life has been open to all the Non-Kartaqi friends, work people, and my immediate family for quite some time. And all those people have been supportive.

Again, my apologies to you and your family. I am a big boy and can, and should, handle the consequences of my actions. Please forward any inquiries, gossip, or comments to me directly. I can take it.

Thomas called me right away. He said he had known about my sexuality for quite some time, but he decided to keep it to himself. He also said that there we indeed a lot of phone calls to him from all kinds of people in the community, but he managed it with cool and calm. He also told me that since he is familiar with the inner circles of the Kartaqi leadership, he imagines there will be some kind of policy statement about the matter, with a strong language of disapproval. He indicated that he will try to keep me informed of any negative consequences.

Facebook Message

From: Ron Namdar (second cousin)

To: Isaac

Date: January 11 at 12:07pm

Hi isaac....I just heard the good news, I am very happy for you . I wish you all the best . Give my love to your partner

Facebook Message

From: Isaac

To: Ron

Date: January 11 at 12:28pm

Thanks. We really appreciate your support. We are both very happy together.

Just in case any more yentahs decide to go to the wedding website, I changed it quite a bit. Check it out Mitchell-Namdar.com

It is too much???

Facebook Message

From: Ron

To: Isaac

Date: January 11 at 1:06pm

You won't win with these people. They are very backwards. but would like to talk to you about the site

I called him right away. He had attended services this past Saturday, and indeed there were tons of faggot jokes. There was a general sense of denigration and condescension among all those in attendance. My absence made it so much easier for everyone to reach a consensus of hate and disgust. Even though Ron was personally in favor of equality and respect, there was no room that day for such supportive language. I then inquired about the circumstances surrounding Jacob Namdar's involvement, and Ron promised he was going to find out about it. Meanwhile, I responded to Thomas.

Email

From: Isaac

To: Frank

Date: 1/11/2010 1:47:04 P.M.

Subject: Re: Sorry

It was great talking to you. Thank you for everything you have done to protect the interest of the family.

BTW, I changed the wedding website just in case some other yehtahs still try to go there. Check it our Mitchell-Namdar.com

Is it too much?

Email

From: Norman (second cousin, another childhood friend)

To: Isaac

Date: 1/11/2010 2:23:31 P.M.

Subject: Mazal Tov

Hi Isaac.

Mazal Tov for your wedding.

We wish you and Andrew a lot of happiness and a great life together.

We would love to meet Andrew one day, we wished you would have invited us to your beautiful wedding.

Ciao

Norman and Lydia

Email

From: Isaac

To: Norman

Date: 1/11/2010 2:33:19 P.M.

Subject: Re: Mazal Tov

Thanks so much for the warm wishes and your support.

As you know, my way of life is not compatible with the norms of our community. That's why I had done my best to withdraw myself as much as possible so as not to disturb the sanctity of the community. I had stopped going to the synagogue some time ago. Unfortunately, this also meant excluding all of you from my life, even though you are all very dear to me.

I was so saddened I could not share my wedding with all of you, and the few people who came all the way from Israel had to turn back and leave right away.

Hopefully we can all learn from this and move forward. I know that you had known for quite some time, and you chose to respect my privacy. You are a true friend.

Email

From: Rick (a stranger)

To: Isaac

Date: 1/11/2010 3:29:46 P.M.

Subject: Hello

hello Andrew and Issac
first and foremost i want say congratulations to you guys and wish a life time of love and happiness together. i don't know you guys and you wouldn't know me either i am part your community and i think is very sad and ignorant what they say about you i just want let you guys know their people in this community that respect and support you guys and i am sorry for not saying mazal tov to you sooner, me and couple other friends of mine would like to impose on you guys and meet you and Andrew for a coffee at your convenience. thank you

Rick

Email

From: Isaac

To: Rick

Date: 1/11/2010 4:19:55 P.M.

Subject: Re: hello

Thank you so much. It is really good to hear that there are those who have the courage to stand up and express their support.

I am actually handling the matter better than I thought. Didn't expect to find myself in a political situation, but I am managing.

The reason that you and many others don't know me so well, in a community where everyone knows or is otherwise related to each other, is that I had fully admitted to myself that my way of life is not compatible with the norms of our community. And in order to respect the holiness and preserve the sanctity of our community I had voluntarily withdrawn myself as much as I could. I elected to conduct my life entirely away, not out of fear, but out of respect. Believe me, it was very difficult to have a wedding, and only have three family members there among all my guests.

We would love to meet you and get to know you better. Perhaps it is best to let the dust settle from the current controversy before making any concrete plans, as I am dealing with this day by day.

I'll keep your email and get back to in the next couple of weeks.

And once again thank you for being so supportive.

By now I was starting to feel like a broken record. With every new email, Facebook message, or phone call from a friend, family member, or total stranger, I kept telling the same story again and again: I knew I was gay, I didn't want to disturb or disrupt the community, so I tried to keep a low profile and live my life in privacy. Each person approaching me surely felt they were doing the right thing. They needed

51

to reach out to express their good will and solidarity. There was some conflict, and they needed to tell me that they had my back. So many good-hearted people. I, on my end, needed to maintain my composure even though my life was becoming a cross between Twilight Zone and Groundhog Day. Same conversation again and again.

Email

From: Sharon (my 26 year old niece living in Israel)

To: Isaac

Date: 1/11/2010 4:02:22 P.M.

Subject: Update

So I heard all the yentahs are not minding their own business and sticking their long noses where they shouldn't...

How are taking it? Want me to come over and give them a little something...?? I will!!!

Now really, are you ok? It must hard. How was your talk with your dad?

You know this already, but still - We couldn't be more happy for you and Andrew, and couldn't have wished for a better addition to this family. no matter what shit everyone will put you though. we're with you.

Email

From: Isaac

To: Sharon

Date: 1/11/2010 4:06:24 P.M.

Subject: Re: Update

Thanks, I love you so much.

I am actually taking it decently well, thanks. And so many people whom I don't even know have come forward and expressed their support saying they feel horrible for how things turned out.

The talk with my dad was OK, he wanted to know WHY we made it official. So I explained to him in terms of the legality of how the government treats us is so different. Then at the end he asked if Andrew has any money anyways (thinking maybe Andrew is a gold-digger). So I told him he earns 10 times what I do, and his net worth is even more than 10 times. Then all of sudden he saw dollar signs. LOL

Email

From: Barry (another stranger)

To: Isaac

Date: 1/11/2010 4:23:46 P.M.

Subject: MAZAL TOV

HELLO ISSAC

I AM A COMMUNITY MEMBER AND I WOULD LIKE TO GIVE YOU AND YOUR COMPANION MY MAZAL TOV , AND WISH ALL THE BEST AND HAPPINESS IN COMING YEARS .

B.H.

Email

From: Ken (another stranger)

To: Isaac

Date: 1/11/2010 6:48:11 P.M.

Subject: Mazel tov

Dear Andrew and Isaac

I wanted to wish you lots of happiness and joy in your life. You guys are a beautiful couple and you deserve to have great life together.

Ken

I got home from a long, mentally exhausting day. As much as I needed some rest, my mind was racing. I got back on the computer again.

Facebook Message

From: Isaac

To: Ron

Date: January 11 at 7:13pm

Thanks for clarifying some things over the phone.

Jacob Namdar sent me an email from our wedding site, and since I did not know him, I didn't respond right away before I was going to find out who he was. But he decided to spread the information before he heard back from us.

Facebook Message

From: Ron

To: Isaac

Date: January 11 at 7:18pm

ok i will tell Jacob. He realizes he really messed up. Haha i never saw this guy so scared before. I guess the revised website worked.

Email

From: Keith (second cousin, husband of Rachel, who was first person to call on Saturday)

To: Isaac

Date: 1/11/2010 11:47:01 P.M.

Subject: Mazal Tov!

Dear Isaac:

Hope you're fine!

Despite what has transpired in the last few days and the unfortunate uproar it has caused in the community, I want you to know that me and my family still feel the same way about you.

In our eyes you are still the same Isaac we have always known. Someone who has always treated everyone with respect and therefore deserves to be treated back with the utmost respect as well.

It took a lot of courage on your part to do what you have done. The kind of courage that most people don't have. To be able to look inside you and recognize who you really are and to live your life in a way that to you seems like the normal way to live. The courage not to live a lie for rest of your life.

Many people are not blessed enough to discover true love with another person, no matter what their gender is. We are glad that you have been fortunate enough to find that kind of love with Andrew. The kind of love that makes you both truly happy.

We regret not having had the opportunity to participate in your wedding, and wish you both Mazal Tov and a happy, healthy and long life together.

We look forward to meeting Andrew and would love to be able to see all your photos and watch your videos.

All the best,

Keith

Facebook Message

From: Mark (a Zameeni cousin living is a different US city on the opposite US coast)

To: Isaac

Date: January 11 at 11:27pm

Hi Issac. Hope all is well and happy new year. I heard yesterday that some idiot or idiots from your synagogue acted disrespectfully to you, and it gave me a lot of ache and pain. I can not speak for them or be their guides on how to be a decent human being. Only let the Almighty respond to their vicious acts.

All I can say I still love you, and will always be proud of you to have you as my cousin, friend. you can not believe how much joy your presence brought last year at my son's Bar Mitzvah when you showed up here by surprise. You are a great man, doctor and human being and i am proud to have you as part of me, and I hope you do not abandon me and the rest of your good family members who will always love you for yourself. I hope you do not end up disappearing from our lives because of some other idiots in the community. Remember your joy is our joy and your pain is mine

Mark

Facebook Message

From: Isaac

To: Mark

Date: January 12 at 9:12am

That was so nice of you to write. And I guess news does travel the speed of lightning. LOL

Quite some time ago I knew my life is not going to be compatible with the strict Orthodox rules of our Kartaqi community. That's why I had voluntarily withdrawn myself from the daily activities there. I had also decided not to share with anyone there, since I did not want them to think their friendship or relationship with me would force them to be dragged into some situation they may not feel comfortable with. But some guy decided to look up info and shared it with everyone.

I know at least here, all my close family and friends have been bombarded with phone calls from all kinds of people trying to get more information. I am sorry if by any chance you or your family have become a target of harassment as well.

It really means a lot to me that you took the effort to make contact and express support. I can imagine you might have been surprised first, but nonetheless put your own emotions aside and reached out. I really appreciate it, and I am honored by your most kind words.

Hopefully one day we can all meet up and laugh about it. Let me know the next time you are in town.

Email

From: Frank

To: Isaac

Date: 1/12/2010 1:22:39 A.M.

Subject: Re: Sorry

Hi Doc:

I didn't get a chance to do much emailing at work today and at home, cable and internet is down since saturday. Although we already spoke today, I just wanted to thanks you for your earlier email. I read it after we spoke. As I mentioned, I knew about this for a few month so in a way I had some time to prepare myself for any questions and approaches I might encounter.

I didn't see the content of the email that went around, but this was very wrong of him to send mass emails about this. I am sure this whole situation developed into something much harder for you than you anticipated. As time goes by people who know you and cared enough to follow your life more closely would have learned about your choices sooner or later, and each would have dealt with it his own way. There was no need to drag the community and put you and your family in this difficult situation. Sorry if I may not make much sense, it seems that I am typing it with size 1 font on my phone and can't really tell what I am typing.

That night I was glued to the computer. There were a few more supportive messages like the ones above. I had to gracefully and thankfully formulate a response to each one of them. A couple of more phone calls too.

I was also monitoring what was going on at the wedding website. So far I had about 50 new visitors according to the counter on the site. People were still coming to look, and to read my response. Then a brilliant idea hit me. Maybe I need to expand the site a bit. Instead of just one page, let me give them some explanations, some material to educate them. I provided links to several web pages about Homosexuality and Orthodoxy. I wanted to let them see I was not the only one in this situation. There are thousands more just like me, and we are all struggling having to choose between our community values and our inner selves.

Tuesday, January 12, 2010

Email

From: Isaac

To: Keith

Date: 1/12/2010 8:46:25 A.M.

Subject: Re: Mazal Tov!

Thank you so much. Your wife also was the first person in the community to come forward and call and express support, much sooner than many others I have known for a long time and are more directly related to me.

Quite a long time ago I knew that my life is not going to be compatible with the norms of our community. That's why I had voluntarily withdrawn myself from daily life there and decided to pursue life separately. Although it was a tough conflict, I decided not to involve even those in the community close to me, because I did not want them to be dragged into it. Can you imagine if I had told a select few, and invited them to the party, and then their pictures would be discovered attending the party??? The Central Board would totally lose it...

I hope once all the dust settles, we can go back to our normal lives. I want to also apologize if the events of the past few days have caused you and your family any unnecessary stress. I know that many in our community have been relentlessly calling people close to me in order to get more info, and I regret if that made you the target of attacks as well.

Andrew and I would love to have you over at some point. Again, lets let the excitement pass before we can build new bridges.

Email

From: Avi

To: Isaac

Date: Date: 1/12/2010 12:38:29 P.M.

Subject: CONGRATULATION

HELLO ISAAC

THIS IS AVI

I HOPE YOU REMEMBER ME.

 I'M RON'S BROTHER IN LAW

MY WIFE AND I WANTED TO CONGRATULATE YOU ON YOUR WEDDING AND WISH YOU AND ANDREW ALL THE BEST,HEALTH AND HAPPINESS I ALSO AM VERY SORRY FOR THE TROUBLE SOME PEOPLE CAUSED YOU.

AS ALWAYS I HAVE A WORLD OF RESPECT FOR YOU .AND WE ARE VERY VERY HAPPY FOR YOU BOTH

I HOPE WE CAN STAY INTOUCH.

MY BEST:

Email

From: Isaac

To: Andrew

Date: 1/12/2010 12:50:57 P.M.

Subject: Meanwhile

Just so you know, you are also the newest celebrity. Everyone is referring to you by your first name like they have known you for years.

Email

From: Ron

To: Isaac

Date: January 12, 2010 1:49:31 PM

Subject: Re:

Hi issac...if you guys don't have plans yet, we would love to have you over our house friday night.

Email

From: Isaac

To: Ron

Date: 1/12/2010 4:50:46 P.M.

Subject: Re:

I think that is a wonderful idea. We would be so honored.

My one concern is that perhaps not enough dust has settled. I can imagine that the Central Board is in the process of putting together to have a policy statement like the "Green Letter" dealing with homosexuals in our community. Being that we are an Orthodox community, it is pretty obvious to me that they will declare such a lifestyle is not acceptable, and that all community members will be forbidden from interacting with people with this lifestyle.

Knowing fully that this would be the policy of the Central Board, I had gone out of my way not to bring my lifestyle into the community. If I start to show up to Green Hills less than a week into it, there goes my argument.

Perhaps it is best then if we all meet up in the city at some point, or we would be delighted to have you in our house in the country. We have a breathtaking piece of property; that is where we had the civil ceremony last summer, as you probably saw from the pictures and videos. Perhaps this Sunday or any other Sunday when you guys are free, you and maybe some others can come up for the day. Andrew is an amazing cook.

Let me know what works for your schedule.

PS. When they release the statement on basically excommunicating the gay people, they better also have a second statement about invasion of one's privacy, *Lashon Hara* (evil speech), and gossiping!

I was still preoccupied with the idea of people harassing my relatives for further information. I needed to clear the air with so many who might have been affected. I needed to call those relatives closest to me and apologize for any negative consequences they might have suffered. The main obstacle was that up until that point, I had not come out to them anyway, and now I had to call them and apologize for any harassment they might have suffered on my account.

Any homosexual person would normally come out to one person or a small number of people in any one interval of time. This makes the transition easier, and allows one to learn from the lessons of the first few conversations on how to make subsequent talks easier. Such was not my luck. An entire community of 5000 Kartaqis learned about me overnight. Judging how my Zameeni cousin Mark, living on the opposite US coast, learned about the news so fast, another 20000 Zameenis are the next in line in the chain of information. News was travelling, and fast. I didn't have the luxury of time to put my thoughts together. I had to act fast before there were more repercussions.

I called a handful of Kartaqi and Zameeni cousins and relatives to explain and apologize. Luckily, none of the Zameeni family had heard about my outing yet. It was better that they heard it from me rather than a third person.

This past Shabbat much of the buzz was among the congregants, and the leadership had not had enough time to formulate a response to the situation. I knew next Shabbat would be completely different story. Surely, the topic of my lifestyle will be the subject of the Rabbi's sermon. It was a foregone conclusion that a condemnation will be offered; we were not the kind of community that can tolerate an openly gay person amongst it. The medium of the weekly sermon would serve as a very strong enforcement vehicle to portray those views and solidify them in everyone's minds once and for all.

That night, I sat in front of the computer and contemplated what else I can do. There were a few dozen more visitors to the website. Unlike the Rabbi, I don't have a podium and a captive audience at the sermon who can hear my side of the story. The only thing I had going for me, or against me, was this website. By now I was seeing from the administrator's page that more and more people were coming to check out what I had to say. I had already left my email on the homepage, but not everybody might feel comfortable emailing me directly. I knew from when the site was initially set up for our wedding guests, there was a optional message board feature that allowed visitors to the website to leave messages for us. Those messages could automatically or manually be published for everyone to review. Being encouraged by so many relatives and strangers who approached me individually to express their support despite the collective damnation, I thought perhaps I could set up a Discussion Board to allow all people visiting the site to have an open discussion about their opinions on the matter. It would be a huge gamble, exposing myself to further criticism from those who surely would have more tact to contact me directly to curse me out. Yet I figured that things could not be much worse than they are right now. I might as well take the chance.

I opened a separate page within the site for the Discussion Board. I requested automatic email notification every time a new entry is posted. On the main page, I made an addendum at the bottom letting people know a Discussion Board is enabled, and that they can leave responses openly or anonymously. After that, it would be a matter of wait and see what happens. This was around 7 PM. And then, magic! By the time the night was over, there were already a few entries.

Discussion Board

Jane Smith ~ January 12th, 2010

I don't really know these guys, but I think the invasion of their privacy is totally unacceptable

Jon H. ~ January 12th, 2010

I agree with the previous comment. Especially for someone who was not at all involved in our community, just shared a last name with a few of us. Let him live his life in peace.

D.E. ~ January 12th, 2010

As a newlywed girl, I am actually jealous. Their wedding pictures were so much more fabulous than mine.

Me ~ January 12th, 2010

Although their way of life is not according to our *Halacha* (Jewish Law), they were very careful to keep their life away from the community.

Conversely, the idiot who told on them made the entire community guilty of *Lashon Hara* and gossip. Last Shabbat in Synagogue everyone was cracking jokes instead of praying. This idiot made us all sin. We all need to pray from now until Yom Kippur, and we all owe a big apology to these guys for what we have done.

Jane Doe ~ January 12th, 2010

How sad for the state of our community that I can't use my real name to wish you guys Mazal Tov and best of luck. Just know that for every loudmouth who gives you grief on your joyous occasion, there's someone like me who's secretly proud that you have elevated us from a backward moronic bunch to somewhat progressive! I consider you a pioneer. I hope you encourage more young people to embrace their own truth.

J. A. ~ January 12th, 2010

I saw from the pictures that the food was 100% Glatt Kosher although they were not planning on having anyone from the community at the wedding. And we saw in the pics that they presented the rings on a bed of *Noghl* (Kartaqi candy) on a silver tray, and they said the prayer for Jerusalem even though it was a non-religious ceremony.

This guy stayed so true to his heritage, even though his heritage betrayed and ostracized him as a decent human being.

Another Jane Smith ~ January 12th, 2010

You guys look so cute together. Mazal Tov!

Facebook Message

From: Isaac

To: Zach

Date: January 12 at 10:39pm

I guess I became a bit of a celebrity in the past few days. All of a sudden, all these people I don't even know came out of the woods and had messages of support and mazal tov. Then I told a few more Zameeni relatives, and now I am 100% out. Feels good.

One of these days we'll make plans to meet up.

Facebook Message

From: Zach

To: Isaac

Date: January 12 at 11:17pm

Wow sounds good. I wonder if you'll get any closeted gay kartaqis contacting you..

Facebook Message

From: Isaac

To: Zach

Date: January 12 at 11:23pm

So far it is only me and you. I think the others are waiting for the dust to settle before they take any action. I bet none more for a while. Many of them are also married with kids, so makes it so much more complex.

Someone told me the Central Board is going to have to come up with a policy statement. My guess is that basically they will excommunicate me and anyone in the future, and will strictly forbid any community members from interacting with us. Too bad. That is ignorant and self-destructive, and will cause unnecessary pain to so many others.

Email

From: Ellen (another second cousin, who lives in the city, and has ran into Andrew and I several times in the neighborhood)

To: Isaac

Date: 1/12/2010 11:35:51 P.M

Subject: Congrats!

Dear Isaac,

I wanted to personally congratulate you and wish you all the happiness that you deserve.

Although this was shocking news to almost everyone who knew you, I was aware of your relationship for the last few years and just didn't want to say anything to you. So, sorry to let you know that you didn't shock me :)

I could only imagine what you are going through with all the talks and disturbing messages and possible future lectures that will be going on in our little primitive shelter in Kartaqi Island. But knowing you, I'm sure you can handle everything very well without any one's help.

This was by far an introduction of a freedom lifestyle of any sort, to lots of people in our community who are struggling for, in which has been prevented to them for a lifetime.

I would love to make plans and meet Andrew once again, but I'll wait until you're settled with everything that's going on.

All the best!

Ellen

Email

From: Isaac

To: Ellen

Date: 1/12/2010 11:48:13 P.M.

Subject: Re: Congrats!

Thanks so much for taking the time to write. That is so thoughtful of you.

Yes, actually you have bumped into Andrew and me a few times, and although I might pass for straight, one look at Andrew and it is all out! LOL

Allow me also to this chance to apologize to you and your entire family if the events of the past few days have caused you any unnecessary headaches. I know that many yentahs have been bombarding anyone related to me with tons of phone calls and giving them a really hard time. I am really sorry if my personal issues were the source of any embarrassment to you all.

We would LOVE to get together. I have always thought of you as one of the more progressive ones in our family, and I admire you as a friend even more than as a cousin.

Lovya!

That night everyone was shocked to learn of the devastating earthquake in Haiti. The first reports estimated between 100,000 to 200,000 people dead, and still innumerable wounded. The devastation was horrible. There were images of utter chaos all across Haiti, which was already the poorest nation in the Western hemisphere. Who could possibly think how many orphans and widows were left behind? How many millions were now homeless?

Wednesday, January 13, 2010

Email

From: Keith

To: Isaac

Date: 1/13/2010 10:58:02 A.M.

Subject: Re: Mazal Tov!

Dear Isaac:

Thanks for your email. My wife and I totally understand your reasons for deciding not to involve those in the community close to you. It would have been very difficult to decide where to draw the line. Besides, inviting those people could have potentially caused a much bigger uproar during the happiest time of your life.

As far as me and my family are concerned, I want you to know that we have not been subjected to any annoying phone calls by the yentahs and no one really dares to attack me, Rachel or my mother about this issue.

So don't feel bad, everything is fine!

Hope to see you soon!

Keith

That afternoon, I checked on my website. There were a few more visitors, and a couple of new entries on the Discussion Board. I also discovered that after a new message is posted, I can go behind the scenes and attach a response as an addendum to the original text.

Discussion Board

Orthodox ~ January 13th, 2010

As an observant and orthodox man, I totally do not approve of their lifestyle. However, what the community did to them is so much worse than anything they ever did

Concerned Kartaqi ~ January 13th, 2010

BTW, does anyone know if the jackass who told on them has called them and apologized, or is he too chicken to own up to the disaster he created?

RESPONSE FROM US:

No, he hasn't called. And although we are upset about how things turned out, we wouldn't call him a jackass. He is another fellow human being. We all make mistakes.

F'gdabodit ~ January 13th, 2010

I just want to pose this question to Isaac, if you're proud of what you did, getting married and all, Why didn't you invite any of your friends to the wedding? why the double life, why the girlfriends in the past. Was it all an act going to synagogue on Shabbat. You quote the Torah, but the Torah calls your lifestyle an Abomination. Do you believe in what the nature has given you in your needs and wants, or do you believe in what the Torah requires of you? I envy you for your courage to go against your heritage and Do what you felt, but you also Lied and broke the religious laws. I want to know what the brilliant Doctor who is one of the brightest men in our community has to say for turning his back on it. I guess we are that scary as a group. Good luck, I know I won't be running into you in synagogue but I'm sure you belong to a more tolerant synagogue elsewhere already too.

Your friends were upset with you for not inviting them to your happy occasion I know that for a fact.

RESPONSE FROM ISAAC:

I really appreciate the criticism, but I'm conflicted about the tone of your comments: on the one hand you call it abomination, on the other hand you are upset how come I didn't invite my friends to celebrate that abomination with me? [BTW, I already explained the reasoning to them through private messages]

Firstly, let me state I never intended to be a pioneer or a spokesperson, for this or any other cause. Neither am I a politician, and my moves, like most of you, are not always highly calculated. I have probably made mistakes in the past, both regarding this matter as well as others, and I will probably make future mistakes too. All I bargained for was to live my life in privacy and peace. But the actions of others thrust me into a 'pioneer' status. My apologies if I don't perform the task as best as one could.

I will be very glad to share with you the numerous social and personal conflicts that affect me and millions of other people like me growing up in an otherwise mostly hostile environment. However, this is YOUR discussion board, not mine. Also, I opened up this discussion board to promote understanding and healing, not to exchange accusations.

If you want to have a more personal discussion, you can email me privately or call me. If you want to stay anonymous, just make a new gmail account and use that. Just recognize that even though thousands of people felt it was OK to go through every single detail of my life, you are still enjoying the privilege of staying anonymous.

Thursday, January 14, 2010

Email

From: Isaac

To: Jenny

Date: 1/14/2010 11:17:12 P.M.

Subject: Hi

Tonight I got a call from Rose (my dad's first cousin, an 82 year old widow). She started by asking something about her ear; she is a patient of mine and she has seen me in the office a few times. But I fully knew why she had called.

So I started first by apologizing if due to my story people have been bothering her. She was actually very sweet and said although she is old and from a different generation, she realizes that it my personal choice, and nobody had the right to be a yentah. She also said there is another gay Kartaqi she knows of, family of her husband living here, and another one who is family of her sister's husband in Israel. She even joked that her kids said finally there is someone with courage in the family who can live life his own way.

Altogether, she was very sweet and motherly. By her making the effort to call, that was her way of reaching out and saying she supports me anyway. She actually was not being nosey at all like I thought she was going to be. Her final question was that if I am happy, to which I said very much.

She deserves so much credit. She was really sweet, and she was the first one from that generation to try to tell me it is OK.

Discussion Board

didn't forget about it ~ January 14th, 2010

Responding to F'gdabodit:

The Torah mentions this abomination in passing, among a list of many others. So many of the other abominations we no longer care about so much, and so many commandments we no longer follow (when is the last time you performed a stoning, or a brother-in-law was forced to marry his brother's widow?)

For example, eating Hametz on Pesach, or not fasting on Yom Kippur are much greater violation, which are repeatedly mentioned all over the Torah. Yet we don't chase the millions of other Jews who violate these commandments out of town. Half of Israel eats Hametz, yet we celebrate them as war heroes and the pride of our government.

I think it is silly to pick on this single abomination so much out of proportion to everything else.

Bill Gates ~ January 14th, 2010

Can either of you two play softball? If not, perhaps the Namdar-Mitchell union wants to sponsor a team? Imagine the pride you'll feel when the 2010 Mitchell-Namdars are crowned as champs in June!

RESPONSE FROM ISAAC:

I was going to write something witty to go along with the joke, but Andrew said it will not be in good taste.

There were about 400 new visitors on the website so far. People were curious. Many more were looking than leaving messages. I added a few more links to some movies and books about gay people in the Orthodox communities. Somehow, I felt that given my new platform, I needed to educate as many people about tolerance as possible. I didn't know if people were actually checking out these links or bothering to learn from all this, but I felt the obligation to step up to my new platform as a spokesperson for equality and tolerance.

Friday, January 15, 2010

Email

From: Jenny

To: Isaac

Date: Jan 16, 2010, at 4:43 AM

Subject: Hi

I think this Jacob guy did you the biggest favor. Now you can live your life in peace and quiet.

Discussion Board

anony ~ January 15th, 2010

I remember reading in a Times article a few weeks ago that in the US, Jews have the highest level of support for same-sex marriage at 60%. That was followed by the Catholics with 50-something percent, and Protestants at 45%.

I guess our community has some catching up to do to that 60% level, or judging by the comments here maybe we're already there but can't openly talk about it.

Pamela ~ January 15th, 2010

Where is your gift registry?

OUR RESPONSE:

The little blurb about the gift registry was written in jest. We surely don't expect any gifts. But thank you for asking.

who cares ~ January 15th, 2010

Issac and Anderew.

congratulation and enjoy each other.

if i were in your place i wouldn't even care about all of this.

ignore everyone, live your life and put your website back on and get on with your life!!!!

in the closet ~ January 15th, 2010

i want to answer the one that called himself a secret proud.........How can you call your self PROUD and then be secret???its an oxymoron!!! if you have such strong opinions why dont you or who ever is in your shoes just face the facts and come out and live proudly???

Saturday, January 16, 2010

Today was going to be the big date. Last Saturday was too early after my outing for the Rabbi or the Central Board to have an official sermon or response ready for delivery. But a week later, the Rabbi will surely address the event in his sermon. It would be the "white elephant in the room" if he didn't. It was going to happen, like it or not. And I had no control in the matter.

I was sure he would use some very strong words against homosexuality. I was also sure that in his language, they would basically banish me from the congregation. And I was just powerless. It almost felt like I was waiting for my death sentence. Perhaps I'm being a bit dramatic, but the horrible feeling of knowing some doom and gloom awaits you, and you can't do a damn thing to change it, is the most miserable kind of anticipation. All I could was to sit home, wait for the services to be over, and for people to come home. Only then I could ask those still sympathetic to me how bad was the damage.

The most frustrating aspect was that the subject of the sermon – homosexuality - was *my* issue, not theirs. I didn't approach them with it, and I didn't discuss it with anyone there. As best as I could, I tried to shield them from it. My life and choices did not reflect on them one bit. I took full ownership of my homosexuality. Yet they are going to address it as though *they* own the issue, as if they know best. How could they possibly know anything about the long years of inner struggle I had to through before I came to terms with myself? Did they know if I ever contemplated suicide, as many in my situation would? Do they know if I had to see a therapist, or had developed a substance dependency, as so many other struggling homosexuals do? Am I in peace with myself now and can handle the Rabbi throws at me, or am I still a vulnerable individual on the brink of a breakdown? What gives them the authority to discuss an issue that is 100% mine in my absence and without consulting with me??? Had I already not suffered enough being gay in a very religious and unaccepting community?

When the Rabbi woke up today, intending to give a sermon about me, was he content with himself knowing that he was going to make life much tougher for another human being? Did he have to dehumanize me in his mind so that he can give that sermon and not feel guilty about it? Did I really make such a quick transition from an esteemed doctor to "that faggot" who needs to be singled out, isolated, and shunned from his congregation? Which words and imagery was he going to use to convey the same polarizing frame of mind to the hundreds of people listening to his sermon today?

Or was he going to rise above it all? Was he actually going to be a role model for proper behavior despite what the rest of the community had done to me this past week? Was he going to say more by saying less? Was he going to give a short few sentences about the obvious and well-known position of the Orthodox community on homosexuality, and then move on to something more relevant? The world just witnessed a huge natural disaster in Haiti: Was the Rabbi going to take advantage of this low hanging fruit given to him by G-d himself, and dedicate his sermon to the human aspect of this tragedy and diffuse the attention from my situation? Or did he need to be as petty as everybody else in the community and talk about me ad nauseam? Does he really need to go on the record to make a radical statement, further isolating the more liberal elements in our community from the conservative ones? Does he not realize that, at the end of the day, he is still technically my Rabbi too by the simple fact that I am a natural-born Kartaqi? Is he going to get up on the podium and fire me from being his congregants? Is he going to be a *mensch* (Yiddish word for person of integrity and honor), or is he going to be an un-*mensch*?

May you and your loved ones never be the subject of a public condemnation, especially one given from the podium of weekly sermon in a house of worship. May you and your loved ones never know the feeling that someone is planning on delivering an awful predicament about you, yet you are completely powerless to stop that and defend yourself and your honor. May you never know that loneliness of knowing there will not be a single soul in the crowd who would raise their hand and defend you from someone's evil description of you. May you never know how low I felt in those few hours of that Saturday morning as I restlessly awaited for my doom. May you never be that powerless in the face of adversity.

In the meantime, all morning I watched coverage of the Haiti tragedy on TV to pass the time. As bad as I felt for myself, I still thanked G-d for all he had given me: for my health, for having a shelter over my head all my life, and for granting me love and happiness. Nervously, I waited until 2 PM, and then I just had to find out what happened.

Email

From: Isaac

To: Frank

Date: 1/16/2010 02:20:29 P.M.

Subject: Hi

Any new gossip or news happened today? Or is it all yesterday's news?

Email

From: Frank

To: Isaac

Date: 1/16/2010 3:48:10 P.M.

Subject: Re: hi

Hey Doc,

There was not much talk as last week. Rabbi Levy mentioned it in his speech, He basically said that whatever people do in their private lives is their own business, but since the story broke out the way it did (i.e. people saw the site, pics, video) it became a public matter and they feel that they have to make a statement. He briefly mentioned the religion's point of view on this, and that some other synagogues might be ok and accept this, etc..

He was very careful to not attack you, not to mention your name or get into too much detail.

Facebook Message

From: Isaac

To: Zach

Date: January 16 at 1:23pm

BTW, I revised my website that had all the wedding pics on it and instead put up a one page statement, plus a place for discussion board. People have leaving all kinds of comments there. Check it out Mitchell-

Namdar.com

Facebook Message

From: Zach

To: Isaac

Date: January 16 at 3:31pm

I didn't even know u had a website, cool- ill check it out tonight. Out with friends now. Hope u enjoying the weekend, it's beautiful outside!!

Facebook Message

From: Isaac

To: Zach

Date: January 16 at 5:31pm

Yeah, we had a wedding website with pics and registry info. Some yentahs found it and forwarded it to everyone. That's how the news broke out. Within one day it went viral, and I become the most famous Kartaqi in town.

Facebook Message

From: Zach

To: Isaac

Date: January 16 at 5:38pm

Omg I didn't even know about this story. Whoever forward your web link must be an awful person. Btw are u planning on ever going back to the kartaqi synagogue? I'm still out and having trouble viewing your website on my iPhone, will check it out tonight when I get home

Facebook Message

From: Isaac

To: Zach

Date: January 16 at 7:40pm

Yes, that's how the story got out, not because I told anyone myself. It was all done behind my back. Almost 1000 website visits within a couple of days, that's a lot of yentahs.

Right now, it is too soon for me to even think about going back there. I was really going there 2-3 times a year anyway, so no big loss. Maybe in the future it will be different. I can just imagine all the faces if I showed up there.....

Facebook Message

From: Zach

To: Isaac

Date: January 16 at 8:25pm

1000 hits! You should sell sponsor spots ;) anyways... I don't think all the "attention" has been negative. My sister called me today and told me alot of her friends think it's "cool" and "not a biggie" and also the rabii at synagogue spoke today and said that if you choose to come to their synagogue people should be nice and respectful. My brother and his wife are expecting a new baby, I already apologize to them in advance and told them I will come visit them and the baby at the hospital and their home but I am not going to synagogue for the services. They totally understand.

Facebook Message

From: Isaac

To: Zach

Date: January 16 at 8:31pm

I hope you didn't decide not to go to the services on account of me and everything that happened to me. Some people are egging me on and saying that as a 'pioneer' I should not cut off ties and disappear, but try to show everyone that it is possible to keep in touch. I don't know if I have that much courage in me to show up there now, maybe in the future.

Facebook Message

From: Zach

To: Isaac

Date: January 16 at 8:46pm

My decision had nothing to do with you. I've never really been involved in the community, my bro and sisters are very much into the community. since they are super religious, my brother asked me not to come out in his community. In any case if I go to synagogue and someone ask me why i'm not getting married and I'm not allowed to reply "bec I haven't find the right guy yet" then I just rather go to other synagogues. It's probably wise for you to wait awhile before visiting.

Email

From: Albert (another stranger)

To: Isaac

Date: 1/16/2010 8:13:49 P.M.

Subject: Mazal Tov

Hello Dr. Namdar,

My name is albert and I am a member of Kartaqi Community in Green Hills. I am writing you this email to not only to congratulate you but also to applaud you for your decision. Do not get me wrong, I am 110% heterosexual, but am a firm believer in the fact that life is too short to deprive yourself of happiness for the sake of others. Wish you and your partner best of luck and many happy and healthy years together.

Mazal Tov,

Albert

Email

From: Isaac

To: Albert

Date: 1/16/2010 9:18:56 P.M

Subject: Re: Mazal Tov

We really appreciate your support and kind words. Although the week started a bit unexpected for us, the outpouring of support from members of the community such as yourself has been extraordinary. Thank you so much for taking the time to contact us.

Sunday, January 17, 2010

Email

From: Laura

To: Isaac

Date: 1/17/2010 12:36:10 P.M.

Subject: Re:

i just saw the new website.

Im sad that you felt you cant keep the old version, but i was happy to see all the good comments...

Facebook Message

From: Zach

To: Isaac

Date: January 17 at 3:16pm

I looked at your website this morning, love the background soundtrack :)

Very appropriate to what you've been going thru the last couple of week...

Facebook Message

From: Isaac

To: Zach

Date: January 17 at 7:41pm

I have half a mind of giving it another couple of days for the last of the nosies to get the message on the site, and then put back the original site with all the pics of us in the wedding. Let them watch and weep. Your opinion?

Facebook Message

From: Zach

To: Isaac

Date: January 17 at 10:56pm

I guess you need to do what you're comftible with... Keep in mind that if you repost your wedding pics and next week or 2 weeks from now Another yentah will check it out he/she will alert his/her fellow yentah to relog to your site. You might want to put a password on the site and just give it to your close family and friends. Unless you don't care about the yentah. Btw do u know who told on you? Were u friends with that person in the past? Did he know u in person? My sister came to visit me today with her kids and I told her your side of the story (I hope you don't mind) and she is absolutely disgusted by the yentah and what he did to you.

That night, I got a call from my sister Jenny in Israel. She said she received a call from Mrs. Jacobson, the wife of Mr. Jacobson, who is the President of the Kartaqi community in Israel. The Jacobsons, like most Kartaqis, are related to us as second cousins. But my sister and her late husband had grown close friends with them for the past few years.

Apparently, Mr. Jacobson had received an email from his counterpart here in the United States, giving him a full account of the uproar that surrounded my outing in the community. They got a full account of the details of my same-sex wedding. This was the first time that Mr. Jacobson, living an two oceans and one continent away had learned about my sexuality: from an official email from the Kartaqi Central Board. Mrs. Jacobson first asked my sister if my immediate family knew that I was gay and that I had married Andrew, or was it such a great secret that not even they knew about it. My sister reassured her that in fact my immediate family is very supportive, and had it not been for David falling sick, they would have all been there to celebrate.

Mr. Jacobson, however, was completely baffled about the intent of the email. Technically, I live in the United States, and I am not under his jurisdiction as a congregant in Israel. What is it that the US community wanted him to do with this information? Did they expect him to also get on the bandwagon and give instruction to the Rabbi there to excommunicate me? Did they want Mr. Jacobson to make a mockery out of my situation they way they had done in Green Hills? Did they want to make sure that the next time I go to Israel they would not let me into the Kartaqi synagogue? Were they being just gossipy, and a story this juicy was too good not to talk about?

It is amazing the efforts that some people go through to defame or isolate a person that has done them no direct harm.

Monday, January 18, 2010 (Martin Luther King Day)

Email

From: Jenny

To: Isaac

Date: Monday 1/18/10 9:32:15 A.M.

Subject: Re

Yesterday Rachel's two sisters who live here in Tel Aviv called to wish me mazal tov. It's interesting how the entire younger generation is so non-chalant about it and it's like someone opened the door for everyone.

Email

From: Isaac

To: Jenny

Date: 1/18/2010 10:12:47 A.M.

Subject: Re:

Look, it all depends how WE act. First, it is not like they saw me going to a dirty secret gay sex club late at night, but they saw that I am so totally comfortable with my choices that I am making it official by getting married and declaring my love to the world. They all saw in the picture all the happiness and love, not just between Andrew and me, but all the people around us. They also see how family and friends have been accepting and supportive.

So if they see that we are totally comfortable with it, they can also be comfortable with it. If we act like it is a big secret or a disaster or a shame, then they will act the same way too.

After all, we need to give more credit to those people than they we previously gave them. Of course there are tons of idiots there too, but no need to pay them too much attention.

Facebook Message

From: Isaac

To: Zach

Date: January 18 at 10:02am

I don't know the person, so I can only piece together the story from others. But the working hypothesis is as follows:

After our wedding, Andrew officially changed his name to Mitchell-Namdar. He also changed his Facebook name to the same. Then this guy called Jacob Namdar, who is not directly related to me, was doing a search on Namdar to see what he finds. Apparently he found Andrew's FB page, and started digging in to see who is this blond Namdar. From there he got to the wedding website, where we had pictures of our wedding and honeymoon posted for our guest to view. Since he didn't know who I was, he forwarded the link to a whole bunch of others, trying to see if they knew me.

From what I understand, it wasn't an outright malicious act, but just plain ignorant. Even though he may have not have known who I am, he should have recognized the sensitivity of the situation. Instead of forwarding the pics to ask who I am, he should have just asked by name who I am.

BTW, although I don't know you and haven't even spoken to you once, you have been a true source of comfort this past week. As much as Andrew is my soulmate and we complete each others' thoughts, he just is not familiar with the customs of our community, and can't provide feedback like someone who knows how things work with the Kartaqis. I really appreciate all your support

Facebook Message

From: Sarah (another stranger)

To: Isaac

Date: January 18 at 10:51am

Dear Isaac,

I wanted to introduce myself. My name is Sarah. I live downtown, and am married to an American. My parents are Kartaqi and live in Green Hills. I am not part of the community but do hear about some of the radical behavior that takes place. I have been very disturbed about some recent information I received and wanted to reach out to you. While I do not know you, i have heard great things about you and would love to connect.

Please let me know if you are open to a conversation.

Facebook Message

From: Isaac

To: Sarah

Date: January 18 at 11:07am

Thank you so much for taking the time to contact me and offer your support. Actually, we have been pleasantly surprised by the outpouring of support we have received from people we don't even know personally in the past few days. Many people have taken a personal mission of apologizing for the community's actions.

Well, I guess that makes both of us married to Americans. LOL. I have also been only peripherally involved in the community most of my life. Specifically, my lifestyle was not going to be compatible with the norms of an orthodox synagogue, and being fully aware of that, I had decided to seek my identity elsewhere. But as you heard, I was still the subject of much interest and curiosity, even to those who have never heard of me.

All that is in the past. I appreciate your compassion and sense of social justice (as seen in the Facebook pics of you with Obama).

Facebook Message

From: Sarah

To: Isaac

Date: January 18 at 11:19am

Dear Isaac, I am more than thrilled to hear from you. I would love to meet you in person. We are having an open house this sunday from 12-5 for Haiti Relief. Please stop by with your spouse if you can.

The issue is a lot deeper than just your specific case. We (as in our group of ex-kartaqi) support you. A law was passed on 10.28.09 that forbids discrimination against sexual orientation and gender. I feel the threat of a lawsuit could send a huge signal that these radical tactics are breaking up a community with many good people.

Facebook Message

From: Isaac

To: Sarah

Date: January 18 at 11:41am

Thanks for the invite. Let me see if it will work out with Andrew's schedule.

The lawsuit is an interesting point. Although my privacy was invaded, and tons of people gossiped behind my back, the information they saw was not password-protected, and nobody broke the law by looking into something that was otherwise public. I hadn't bothered putting a password on it, because I did not want all my non-kartaqi friends to think I live in a bubble.

As for discrimination, we have to think it out too. Yes, my life is not compatible with an Orthodox synagogue. They cannot deny me entry into a house of worship, but they don't have to be friendly either. Actually, from what I heard Rabbi Levy gave a sermon last Sat that these issues are a personal choice, and that if any such persons want to continue to attend services, the law forces them to be hospitable. So, again, no laws were broken (yet).

I agree that a whole bunch of social laws of decency and ethics were violated, but those you can't sue for.

Anyway, my best tactic at this point is to be the 'better person'. If I act in a way that I come across as a villain (suing the synagogue or its members), that will only further alienate me and others like me. If I keep the channels of dialogue open and allow people to be comfortable with me, it will soften everyone's mind to the whole topic.

The way the whole thing was discovered was when one particular yentah came across our wedding website of our pics and events, and he sent it to his friends, and it went viral. Since then I took the website down, and put my response for people to view. So far I have had 700 people checking it out, with many responding on the discussion board or personally to me by email. Check it out Mitchell-Namdar.com

Facebook Message

From: Sarah

To: Isaac

Date: January 18 at 11:46am

Wow - i thought that you were called and cursed out? Thats the story I heard. And many of my friends who heard the sermon said it was not hospitable at all. In any case, we are behind you and hope you come sunday to meet like-minded kartaqis!

i stand in solidarity with you. as reflected also by my FB status today. i am a huge activist, my profile info will give you more on that! where do you live in the city? what kind of medicine do you practice?

That day, Sarah posted the following as her Facebook status. Although up until now many had expressed their support to me in private, this was the first instance that a Kartaqi made a public statement in support. Amazingly, although many others would not have the courage to make similar public statements, they nonetheless aligned themselves with this view by 'liking' her Facebook status.

Facebook Posting

 Sarah On Martin Luther King Day and in fact on any day of the year, my family and I stand in solidarity with Dr. Isaac Namdar and his peers and the strong belief that nobody in this country should be discriminated against on the grounds of sexual orientation, gender and gender identity (verbatim from 10.28.09 hate crimes bill passed in Congress). Each of us has the right to chose how we live our lives in our democracy as long as we are law-abiding citizens. Please show your solidarity at www.mitchell-Namdar.com

Mitchell-Namdar.com
www.Mitchell-Namdar.com
January 18 at 11:55am • Comment • Like • Share
Jonathan, Rebecca, Veronica and 22 others like this.

 Janice
I second that emotion:)
January 18 at 12:07pm

 Joshua
Me too
January 18 at 11:39pm

Isaac Namdar
Sarah, Andrew and I stand in awe and amazement at your bold and courageous statement in the eyes of the world (well, at least Facebook). We salute you and your vision of equality for all, the very foundation of this great nation. We are honored to have you as an ally, and we hope that your wisdom will soon be the norm, not the exception. Again, a thousand thanks.
January 18 at 11:51pm

 Sarah
Isaac - Thank you for your discussion forum on mitchell-Namdar.com. I visited your site just now and read dozens of new entries. You have given people a forum they never had before. These people are desperate for Change.
January 19 at 9:25am

Facebook Message

From: Sarah

To: Isaac

Date: January 18 at 12:10pm

No, nobody called me, not even to apologize. Only kind people like you contacted to be supportive.

And as for the sermon, they ARE after all an Orthodox community, and the view of any Orthodox community is that homosexuality is a sin. If you and I don't agree with that view, then we can live our lives elsewhere where our views are accepted, as we have both done. What I meant 'hospitable' from the sermon is that it was mentioned that despite the firm stand of the Orthodoxy, the community was basically told to not prevent any gay persons from entering the synagogue and worshiping, perhaps more from a legal point of view.

Facebook Message

From: Sarah

To: Isaac

Date: January 18 at 12:12pm

my sense is that the gay population would be ex-communicated. that is one reason for my outrage. the other that the pulpit on saturday should have been used for haiti relief efforts as in hundreds of synagogues around the country. and then more and more issues i have

Email

From: Max (another stranger)

To: Isaac

Date: 1/18/2010 1:12:25 P.M.

Subject: Hi

Hi Isaac,

Congrats on your wedding. Don't let anyone take anything away from it. These guys are going to self combust in the next few years. I've been a target and I know how it feels. I recently was married and they interjected in my personal life. I told them that if they continued that it would force me to respond forcefully, and I would file harassment charges. They sort of backed down. They don't really understand personal space. I would say that you should probably put your website back up as it would do great things for the people that are in your situation but are frightened. I know of a few. I know that's not your job, but can you imagine if in the USA great people didn't take a stand, you wouldn't be where you are today. Just a suggestion, and its an easy move on your part, you're just living your life. I wouldn't bother having a dialogue with the leaders or threatening them as they don't get it. Anyway you sort of want them to cross the line and send letters out because then you'll have proof which is important if you decide to respond under the hate crime bill. I'm hoping they put the speech on saturday by the rabbi in writing. Again, best of luck with your marriage! Mazal tov!

Best,

Max

Up until now, I had gotten most of my information about the content of the Rabbi's sermon from Thomas, who told me that actually the sermon was very mild. However, I could now see that perhaps the speech was not as mild as Thomas told me. Perhaps Thomas was being kind, and tried to shield me from unnecessary heartache since I was going to keep away from the community in any case. Or perhaps, as he is a much more involved member of the community and abides by all the community regulations, to him the speech was mild, but it would not pass the standard of any liberal-minded person. The discrepancy had peaked my interest, and it became evident I should not 'defend' the speech solely based on what I heard from Thomas.

Email

From: Isaac

To: Max

Date: 1/18/2010 1:54:26 P.M.

Subject: Re: Hi

Thanks for taking the time to write and express your support. Actually, the outpouring of support from people just like you who may not know me, but still feel the desire for justice to prevail, has been impressive.

Two questions for you. First, you mentioned that they tried to intervene in your marriage, but didn't tell me on what grounds. Did you marry outside of Judaism or same sex or any other reasons? Why were you a target?

Secondly, I was obviously not there this past weekend, and did not hear the rabbi's sermon. But you referenced it. What was said? Besides the fact that we are an Orthodox synagogue and in the strict view homosexuality is not tolerated (no surprise), was there anything else said that would be hostile or inflammatory?

Isaac

Email

From: Max

To: Isaac

Date: 1/18/2010 2:19:45 P.M.

Subject: Re:

My wife is an orthodox convert, but converts are not accepted by the kartaqi as of 2008. As you may know the torah explicitly says you must welcome the convert as we were once strangers in the land of Egypt. Not to mention that there are money people who married non Jews in back in

Kartaq without converting and they are now kartaqi grandparents.

They have been downright nasty. They have been aggressively convincing through harassment and threats of not conducting ceremonies and walk-outs even my closest friends and family to not have me at their life events. They also sent out nasty speeches and anonymous letters to the community, calling my family and closest friends by a team of volunteer harassers who are organized by the rabbi and central board.

I wasn't there this weekend so until I see the transcript which I'm hoping they are stupid enough to send out, its all hearsay. But my understanding is that they said anyone who associates with you will be banned from the community. As I'm sure you're aware the implications and penalty for such a great mistake is potentially huge, that's why you sort of want them to continue to step in shit and publish it. Its all about proof. Putting your website back up may be enough to instigate them to make that mistake.-cheers

Email

From: Isaac

To: Max

Date: 1/18/2010 2:44:27 P.M.

Subject: Re:

I had the feeling that some form of excommunication is what they had in mind. Which is fine with me. Neither my livelihood nor my social circles are based on the community. So at the end it doesn't change much for me. If anything, it is liberating since I can now focus on my life and not be bothered to conceal something about me.

Email

From: Max

To: Isaac

Date: 1/18/2010 2:57:36 P.M.

Subject: Re:

agree it shouldn't affect your life, but its illegal to incite hatred under the hate crimes laws. Thankfully you have no risk of violence because the kartaqis aren't a violent bunch, but you never know and the speakers are breaking the law. if you feel like suing them later on, you'll have strong option as they bury themselves blindly with their hate propaganda and publish it. Remember its only a small minority who share their opinion, its just that there is no moderate voice, because its either to scared or its outside of the community like you, me or people like Sarah. sort of like what happens in Iran, Afghanistan or the PLO. that's how radicalization happens. but you're right, its really not our fight. life is just too short

Email

From: Jenny

To: Isaac

Date: 1/18/2010 1:39:59 P.M.

Subject: Re:

I got a call from the wife of the president of the Kartaqi Association in Israel, who is a good friend of mine. Apparently, that famous email even got to the people here. She wanted to ask if I knew about things, and I said yes.

Facebook Message

From: Ted

To: Isaac

Date: January 18 at 8:36pm

No sweat- I'm glad I can help...

In a couple of weeks the kartaqi yentahs will find something/someone else to talk about and you and Andrew will go on with your life.

Going forward you might be able to resume touch with more tolerant people from the community that you might have lost touch with in the last few years, and the less tolerant ones- well- who needs them!!

I hope you enjoyed your honeymoon! Btw when was the wedding?

Facebook Message

From: Isaac

To: Zach

Date: January 18 at 9:19pm

Actually the discussion board on our site is really getting heated. Apparently there is a big backlash about the whole excommunicating thing and ignoring more humane problems like Haiti. There were more entries today than any other day. Who knew I would become such a pioneering spokesperson?

Discussion Board

Kartaqi citizen ~ January 18th, 2010

I was reading through the comments, and it looked like at least a few days ago, the person who told on you had not come forward to own up and apologize.

We in our community have had an unspoken policy of don't-ask-don't-tell with regards to homosexuality. This allowed all members of the society to live at peace, without the need for any confrontation. By 'telling' on you, this person took the privilege of being as involved with the community as want away from you.

Allow me to apologize on his behalf.

Sarah ~ January 18th, 2010

I stand with you in solidarity to lead your life as you wish to in this free country. I apologize for any hurtful comments made towards you even though I am not part of the community myself. Where can I make a donation?

Kartaqi Citizen ~ January 18th, 2010

Mazal Tov and best wishes on your beautiful wedding. May everyone, straight or gay, share the love that you two share for each other. Love is a great thing, hate isn't.

The Jews are a very sophisticated, intelligent, compassionate people. Which is why it is so upsetting that so many Kartaqis are acting more like Muslims than Jews. They must have picked up their conservative, backwards views from living in Kartaq for so many years. What we hate about Muslim extremists is that they are so backwards, ignorant, and hateful. So why are we turning into them? We can't start acting like Muslim fanatics. We have to be more sophisticated and open-minded so we can maintain the integrity of our Judaism. Otherwise, we are just as bad as they are.

Unfortunately, the backwards, conservative people in our community are more vocal than the liberal, open-minded ones. Just like in the case of Islam, the fanatics are always more vocal.

The rabbi who recently preached hatred in our synagogue should be ashamed of himself for doing what Muslim mullahs do. They are just as bad as the mullahs. Preaching hatred is not a Jewish trait.

The Torah does speak out against homosexuality, but it also speaks out against eating unkosher, having sex before marriage, and not keeping the Sabbath. Are people who do those things evil too? Should they be excommunicated too? So should everyone that has had sex before marriage be excommunicated? If so, most of the *Shomer Shabbat* (observant of Sabbath) girls in the community would be banished.

We can't start becoming fanatical, like Muslims. The Torah is a beautiful thing that teaches love and compassion and respect. Let's learn to respect all members of our community.

T. N. ~ January 18th, 2010

What do you expect from the Central Board??? Their frame of reference is something that was written more than 3000 years ago, and was a perfect fit for nomadic desert life. As much respect and reverence we have for the Bible, we should be able to making it a living bible, not something that is frozen in time. For example, the bible also allows slavery, but it tries to do its best to make it as compassionate as possible. Does modern society allow slavery, even though the bible says it's OK?

Pissed off Kartaqi ~ January 18th, 2010

The Kartaqi community (out of fear of losing its integrity) is reminding me more and more of the Hasidic community. We may not look like them (yet), but we sure are beginning to act like them. Some radical Kartaqis have an irrational fear towards anything unfamiliar to them; so they make rules. Strict rules and unwritten social laws to keep 'unlike' people out and insiders obedient (typically enforced via blackmail). Rules that they don't realize are turning away many of the community's brightest people.

Very smart: Lets deny the fact that gays exist by banishing the ones that wish to live normal lives by coming out and threatening the others we know exist to remain quiet. Now we can take a similar stance to that of Iranian President Ahmadinejad. "The Kartaqi community has no gays".

Problem solved.

Congratulations and my deepest apologies on behalf of the idiots with a voice in my community.

Religious Kartaqi ~ January 18th, 2010

i saw on tv last week the big tragedy in haiti. i am 21 years old and haiti is the worst thing i've ever seen. i went to shabbat at the synagogue on Saturday and hoped our rabbi speaks to us about this terrible event. then i had to listen to bad tales about the gays. the next day and today i heard from my friends who are not Kartaqi that their rabbis spoke to them about helping haiti. i am *shomer shabbat* and now i never want to go back to the Kartaqi synagogue. i want to find a place where the rabbis and community understand the young people and that we dont want to live in a mental jail anymore. also i want to say sorry that we hurt you. thank you for letting us post here. All the best to you.

ANTI CENTRAL BOARD KARTAQI ~ January 18th, 2010

The Central Board was responsible for the Rabbi insults against gays. It was the worst speech from a Rabbi I have ever heard in the synagogue. The synagogue is a holy place - not somewhere to talk about hating. The men on the Central Board rule the Community like dictators. They have become dangerous to the young generation. My friends and me dream of leaving Green Hills. How can we if our parents listen to the Rabbi scare them. We are prisoners in this community and won't be let out until there is a young fresh central board that makes good decisions and not these fundamental extremist ones. I am grateful for this discussion board to release my anger after Saturday. I have relatives on the Central Board and am thankful I can post anonymously. Hopefully more will post. I know there are many of us that would like to speak out but are scared to. This is a good place to say things so others can hear us. Good Luck to both of you.

RESPONSE FROM ISAAC:

Since I did not think that coming to the Green Hills synagogue this past Saturday was a particularly good idea for me, would someone please let me know what was said in the speech?

Religious Kartaqi ~ January 18th, 2010

i read just now the message on the homepage. please do not take down the discussion board. we need to hear there are more of us that are feeling so much terrible pain from our community. maybe it will change something. Maybe

angry ~ January 18th, 2010

If the Central Board had any balls, they too would enable a discussion board allowing people to leave their comments so that the true feeling of our community could be heard without fear of consequence. How many of you think this time they really stepped over the line?

concerned citizen ~ January 18th, 2010

I heard about this visiting my grandmother on Saturday afternoon. I am already turned off by this community born and raised in it from birth. This for me was the last straw and has made me feel that I never want to step foot into the Kartaqi synagogue again. I want to wish you and your better half a long life filled with love, health, and happiness.

On a side note, being gay, lesbian or bisexual is not something one can control. It's not a mental illness or a genetic disorder, it is as natural as a man loving a woman or vice versa. This community needs to open their eyes to see the damage they are causing especially to the youth. I for one have decided when I have a family to not raise them in this toxic environment.

The central board is not better then Hitler, Hammas or any Middle East dictator. They treat the community like second class citizens. I think they forget and deny (the one they do best) that Jews were killed alongside gays in the holocaust and that hatred and prejudice is what drove the Kartaqis into America.

If you want act like a dictatorship but still reap the benefits of living in a free thinking, democratic society then please I'll personally buy you a one way ticket on Kartaqi Air and send you back to where you can from.

E.H. ~ January 18th, 2010

Thanks to Sarah for her Facebook status update today. Someone had to speak out loud on behalf of all individuals who are suffering by living a sheltered lifestyle in this community, where individual rights are prohibited. The younger generation will eventually rule this community and hopefully by then all individual rights will count and we could then be happy as a person and therefore as a community!!!

Paul Revere ~ January 18th, 2010

I see there is real momentum here. How do we make sure that the people behind these frustrated comments don't just give up and go back to their ordinary lives? How do we mobilize?

Kartaqi 999 ~ January 18th, 2010

By the way, is someone making sure that the Central Board gets to see all these comments? Are they sitting at home and feeling the pain with every new comment against them??

another gay kartaqi ~ January 18th, 2010

Congrats on your wedding!

As another gay Kartaqi I total understand what you had to go thru.

Thank you for putting up this discussion board, I think its important for people in the community to express their opinion without the fear of consequence.

Hopefully your action will pave a way for new more tolerant

community.

Mazal Tov and all the best to both of you :)

Although the story started by me being shamed in the face of an entire community, I was getting enough positive feedback to know I was not alone. I had put up a fight to change attitudes, and I was making some progress. People had come to the website by the hundreds, and even one just one voice of support was already one more than I could have ever imagined coming from members of the Kartaqi community. They were defying directions by the leadership to shun me from their lives. But I was also aware that there will be those that will use the Discussion Board to further criticize and shame me.

I decided I no longer need to portray the image of a victim in a paranoid state of shock. It was no longer necessary for me to be on the defensive; although I would not categorize my future actions as being on the offensive either. I decided to change the nature of the website a bit. I reloaded the original background song "Love is in the Air" by Tom Jones from when the website was first set up for our wedding guest. I also put one of our wedding pictures where I was lifting Andrew up in the air and kissing him as the main picture on the homepage. I changed the homepage message to a more festive tone, as follows:

Well, it's been a few months since our wedding, and it was time anyway to retire the wedding website.

For those of you who helped celebrate our joyous occasion with us, we would like to thank you for making our lives so blessed with your support and friendship.

For those who did not make the invite list (oops, sorry!), but nonetheless came forward to congratulate us and express your love, we are eternally grateful to you.

As giddy newlyweds, we can only wish that you and your children will have the kind of love and romance in your lives that we have experienced.   May every single one you be blessed with true love and companionship.

We have permanently archived our wedding photos on our Facebook pages. We have restricted online access to those whom we feel are within our circle of trust. If you believe you should be in that group, please contact us and we will release access to you. The rest of you still have an open invitation to come over for coffee and watch the album together [We think it is a sad state of affairs that in this day and age anyone would have to restrict access to their wedding photos, but we learned that the hard way].

If you still need to contact us, you can reach us at Namdar@aol.com

The Loving Couple.

Facebook Message

From: Isaac

To: Zach

Date: January 18 at 11:05pm

I just changed the website, check it out.

Facebook Message

From: Isaac

To:	Ron
Date:	January 18 at 11:06pm

I just changed the website to make it less defensive and more celebratory. But the comments from people are out of this world.

Facebook Message

From:	Ron
To:	Isaac
Date:	January 18 at 11:08pm

ohhh cmon dont change it......this is what they were asking for, is it the same address??? its the best thing that happened to kartaqis....they finally have a place to tell their views

Facebook Message

From:	Zach
To:	Isaac
Date:	January 18 at 11:13pm

Love it- you guys look sooo happy!

My family didn't tell me what the rabbi said. I think they don't want me to get upset. If you find out could you please let me know?

Facebook Message

From:	Isaac
To:	Zach
Date:	January 18 at 11:46pm

I am trying to get hold of the info as well, but judging by what people are commenting about the tone of it, must have been beyond the 'usual' excommunicating speeches.

Facebook Message

From: Zach

To: Isaac

Date: January 18 at 11:53pm

I'm sorry I can't help you with getting that info. My family will never tell me. Soooo- I love your disc board, been checking it every 5 minutes tonight :) hopefully things well start changing in synagogue but... U know...

Once u choose to go back to synagogue are u taking Andrew with you?

Facebook Message

From: Isaac

To: Zach

Date: January 18 at 11:57pm

At the moment I am not planning on that at all. Should there be a regime change (fat chance), maybe.

Despite being wrapped up in my own problems for the moment, I still knew that the most important story of the week was the human devastation in Haiti. Yet the elders of the Kartaqi community had decided to devote the podium of the Shabbat sermon entirely to an issue that was raised by my actions: homosexuality. They never contacted me, nor did they do any research into the human aspect of homosexuality before giving an entire speech in front of the whole community. They portrayed me as a non-human, as an agent of evil, and then they gave themselves permission to talk about my issue without my consent. I, for my part, needed to be an example of better behavior. I needed to refrain from lashing out, and instead introduce compassion into the debate.

The Orthodox Union (OU) is the umbrella organization of Orthodox Jews in the United States. I was able to easily find the link on their website that spoke of the Haiti tragedy, and made it possible to make online donations. I then created a link on my website to this page, and alerted everyone on my website's homepage to visit that campaign and make a donation. It took the Central Board of the Kartaqis another two weeks before they addressed the Haiti situation on their own website.

Tuesday, January 19, 2010

Email

From: Laura

To: Isaac

Date: Re:

Subject: 1/19/2010 11:56:00 A.M.

im reading the posts all day long and im just amazed.

really. it is so unbelievable whats going on there and im so sad to say that for the first time in my life im actually ashamed being a Kartaqi.

thats it.

Oh, and im so proud of you dear uncle Isaac, that you are you. you did a great thing. the two of you.

i really really hope that all the young people of the community, and not just them, will stand up and do something about it. and make a change.

cause they can.

Email

From: Laura

To: Isaac

Date: 1/19/2010 12:05:40 P.M.

Subject: Re:

can you tell me pls what that s.o.b rabbi said ?

do you have his speech ?

you weren't there, were you ?

Email

From: Isaac

To: Laura

Date: 1/19/2010 12:44:23 P.M.

Subject: Re:

Apparently the speech was so bad nobody has the heart to tell me exactly what he said.

I fully expected them to make some statement, saying that gay life is not compatible with Orthodox Judaism. If he was smart he would not make a big deal of it and move on.

But apparently he may have really gone all out. Some things like "legally we cannot prevent them from coming to our synagogue, but we all must encourage him to go find another synagogue"

Discussion Board

D. H. ~ January 19th, 2010

I really liked the Ahmadinejad comment before. It's true: Ahmadinejad said "we have no gays", and Rabbi Levy said "we have no gays". Same thing. Amazing!

recently married kartaqi girl ~ January 19th, 2010

I just recently got married and I am already being pressured by my family, friends and community to have children. My friends that have been married for only a few years all have at least 2 children and are constantly comparing themselves to each other and how many kids they have. Isn't it disgusting to use procreation as a means to advance your standing in a community? How does my story connect to this discussion?

The control/instilling fear factor goes beyond the central board. It has infiltrated and poisoned the minds of our grandparents, parents, siblings and friends. We are not taught to think for ourselves or do what is best for our families. Kartaqis are followers, not leaders unfortunately.

Who thinks it's normal to estimate how many children you want by what your mother in law says or oh my best friend just had her third, I need to catch up! No one is free to think for themselves as everyone has to add their two cents in to each others lives. Well it's my life and my husbands life, not my mother in laws, or the community rabbi's life.

As it is my right to decide how many children I want to have- it is your right to love who you decide to love, be it a man or a woman. I commend you on your courage and wish you both some much happiness and love.

Hoping this post gives all Kartaqis the strength to stand up for themselves and speak up for what you believe , its YOUR right not anyone else's.

AnonymosKartaqi ~ January 19th, 2010

I read everything on the board and couldnt wait to get my 4 kids to school today so I can write something. I come from a big kartaqi family with many cousins, aunts and uncles. I got married at 21. I finished my college degree but nobody let me do my studies well because my family told me everyday to forget college and marry. I married what kartaqis call a 'good catch', rich, from a wealthy kartaqi family, big house, good name. Now I am in a life where I have no feelings for my husband. My life is so empty it feels and I didnt want 4 kids. My husband pushed me into it so he can have as many kids as the others in his group. My husband travels every week almost and I think he cheats on me. I have the womans instinct to know. They say many traveling kartaqi husbands cheat when away but we have dont ask dont tell rule in the community. In this community men can do whatever they want and the central board allows it and the women have to be quiet. My parents give me no support and only want to show off to everyone that their daughter married a rich husband and they have many grandchildren. I cannot tell my feelings to the other wives in our group because I don't trust them. I even dont like any of the traditions. I get bad headaches every time I have to go to a wedding with so many people so my husband can show to his friends that everyone invites us. I admire your courage and wish one day I also can find true happiness like you. Many days I want to pack my bags and leave this life. I am glad we have this board now where we can share our feelings anonymously. I hope others come out too so changes happen. The Central Board and Rabbi should talk about adultery in synagogue and not hateful words to gays.

B. D. ~ January 19th, 2010

Pathetic! These nice guys here, ostracized by the leaders of the community, have posted a link for Haiti fundraising on their site, especially from the OU people, yet our own "OU" Central Board and all the "OU" Rabbi have said nothing or bothered to post their own links to address this great tragedy. Bravo!

Sarah ~ January 19th, 2010

Dear Andrew and Isaac, I am amazed at the entries on this discussion board that I just finished reading. I also commend you on your website Link to the Orthodox Union Haiti Earthquake Disaster Fund.

I clicked on the link and the first sentence says "Jews are described by the Talmud as "*rachmanim b'nei rachmanim*" a particularly compassionate people who are sensitive to the suffering of all, and we cannot sit by and ignore this terrible drama of human suffering and misery.

We know that what Israel did for Haiti has been remarkable and we know that many Jewish organizations and synagogues have dedicated themselves to Haiti relief this past week. The mere fact that the Kartaqi rabbi and Central Board did not use the powerful podium in synagogue this past weekend to speak to congregants about Haiti and instead spent time discussing your lifestyle is mind-boggling. These are not role models for young people. Haiti is one of the greatest tragedies in our lifetime, leaders in every community need to address their congregants in a timely manner as to how they can help.

john doe ~ January 19th, 2010

I was molested as young boy by an old kartaqi guy..years later i learned that it was well known amongst kartaqis what this guy does and so many like him. But he had a front row in the synagogue till the day he died....bec his sons were rich. so we close our eyes to this kinda behavior but excommunicate two great accomplished people who are honest and stand up people!!!!! what a shame, and we call ourselves THE BEST COMMUNITY IN THE WORLD

Curious George ~ January 19th, 2010

As a Kartaqi citizen I must apologize and wish you a Mazal Tov! The worst thing about our dictatorship and our Rabbi is that they ignore the essence of the Torah. They are just using religion as a political tool to achieve what they want. The Rabbi is the guiltiest because he should know better and stand up to their requests but he buckles because he is fearful and he wants his fat salary. He has sold out Judaism.

"...thou shalt love thy neighbor as thyself.", Leviticus 19:18

"What is hateful to you, do not to your fellow man. the fulfillment of this Mitzvah is the entire Torah and the others are merely an explanation." Talmud, Shabbat 31a.

There are some simple things we can do to organize-

1) organize a boycott of the Synagogue on the upcoming Shabbat, or at least of the Rabbi's sermon

2) Stop sending money to the Synagogue (this is how the Israelis and US government fight terrorists). Everything will crumble if don't have

money to pay the Rabbi's big salary

3) Organize a rally or a party that is anti-Hatred and anti-Central Board. Begin to fundraise to further ideas.

4) Petition for the rabbi's removal.

WE MUST BE THE CATALYST OF OUR OWN CHANGE. WE DON'T WANT OUR CHILDREN TO GROW UP IN THIS BACKWARDS HATRED.

Email

From: Sarah

To: Isaac

Date: Jan 19, 2010, at 12:13 PM

Subject: Your site

Wow – your discussion board has taken on a life of its own! Such heartbreaking stories. Please keep it going – it is the first real forum these desperate young people that don't have the mental strength as we do have to tell their stories.

How many hits have you had?

Email

From: Isaac

To: Sarah

Date: 1/19/2010 12:45:36 P.M.

Subject: Re: Your Site

So far 900 hits altogether, 150 in the past day. Thanks for 'advertising' the site.

Email

From: Sarah

To: Isaac

Date: 1/19/2010 12:48:03 P.M.

Subject: Re: Your Site

If you start getting the radical people posting nasty stuff (which you may start to get) I think you should delete the really bad ones (although I don't like censorship in any way but sometimes it is necessary to keep the integrity of the conversation) but by no means take it off!!! Its too important a forum

Email

From: Isaac

To: Sarah

Date: 1/19/2010 12:59:26 P.M.

Subject: Re: Your Site

I'm not going to censor it. If people see their comments were deleted, it will no longer serve a purpose.

Facebook Message

From: Ron

To: Isaac

Date: January 19 at 12:53pm

Your discussion board is on fire :)

Facebook Message

From: Isaac

To: Ron

Date: January 19 at 1:14pm

So much crap is coming out

Facebook Message

From: Ron

To: Isaac

Date: January 19 at 1:36pm

Yes... its a revolution, everybody was scared to talk

Discussion Board

Sarah ~ January 19th, 2010

Re: SHALOM MAGAZINE

Over the summer I received in my mailbox a publication called Shalom magazine addressed to me. It was a big glossy that took up a good part of my mailbox. Since we are still in the old Kartaqi directory I assumed that the mailing list was used to distribute this magazine. Given that it was called Shalom and had a nice glossy look , I spent some time flipping through it quickly realizing it had nothing to do with Shalom ie Peace and was the most disturbing publication ever to land in my home. Full of inaccuracies, harassment and hatred about individuals that don't comply with the Kartaqi lifestyle. I took the magazine to my office to finish reading it and to quickly remove it from my home.

Even though my twin sons don't read yet, I did not want such toxic material lying anywhere close to my kids. In the same vein that I do not want my kids exposed to any of the parenting values entrenched in the community like teaching your kids to exclude other kids so you can be in a specific group from birth onwards or raising them in an environment where kids learn that big houses, big wealth and being skinny and beautiful overrides being a good and empathetic human being.

Anyway, the magazine sat on my desk for a few days and one of our employees who has been working for us for over 10 years and is a well respected gay man in the industry was standing by my desk, and took it and started to flip through it: " Oooh I love the good looking people on the cover" he said. He started reading it and thankfully I remembered that on page 14 (or somewhere around there) there was a scathing headline article on Gays. Basically saying that gays are evil. I vaulted over him and grabbed the magazine before he could get to that page. He wondered why and in his wonderfully mild manner just assumed I was having a cooky moment. The magazine landed in the garbage, the content of it so shameful that I hope it was speedily recycled.

Before discarding it, I checked out the masthead and the only name mentioned was that of the Central Board. While they clearly do not assume responsibility for this material, the mere fact that their name is in the masthead means they endorse it.

If Kartaqis want to receive this type of propaganda then they need to make it subscription based. I have kindly asked to be removed from the mailing list as I don't want another one of these Shalom publications in my dear mailbox nor for my kids to ever be exposed to it as they start to learn to read (and they are already avid readers even with the minimal reading skills they have at age 6).

Shalom to me means Peace, peace amongst us and acceptance of our differences.

To George ~ January 19th, 2010

Responding to comments by Curious George: Hundreds of people have been de facto boycotting the synagogue for a long time. This only gives the podium to the radicals who show up and take us further to the extreme.

Instead, we need to actually show up in masses and storm the podium. We need to complain TO THEIR FACES, and let our point of view known. We need to take ownership of our synagogue. Is everybody with me on this?

PS, I loved the link to the Ahmadinejad spoof in the Videos section.

outraged kartaqi ~ January 19th, 2010

I think it is time that some one says something about the poor kartaqi couple that recently got married, the poor girl converted to judaism but still we spilled their blood on the street. this is worst that mullahs this anti jewish anti every decent person. That poor couple need an apology and a big welcome back to our community with open arms

BlaBla ~ January 19th, 2010

Listen, I have nothing against homosexuality, it doesnt bother me and I really couldnt care less. However, we are an orthodox community and it is against the torah to have relations with another man, no ifs no ands no buts, thats the law. Like it or not, its the law our community follows. I see people here bringing up other issues, and its fine, but just because there are other issues in the community doesnt mean that it is ok do change the Laws that have been passed down for thousands of years from out great forefather Avraham. I'm sorry, I wish you 2 the best of happiness, but it is not something our community can accept, no arguments.

very concerned Kartaqi ~ January 19th, 2010

Adultery, spousal abuse, child molestation, drugs, alcoholism etc.

THESE ARE NOT JEWISH VALUES.

Everyone knows this is happening behind closed doors in way too many Kartaqi homes. Dont ask dont tell is the way to go for this horrible behavior in our community. Just as it is in Kartaq under Muslim regime. Why do the Rabbi and the Central Board not say anything about it in synagogue? These people suffer in silence.

BlaBla and more BlaBla ~ January 19th, 2010

To answer your post BlaBla. You are entitled to your opinion and thanks for sharing it in a factual manner. But sex before marriage and eating non-kosher is also forbidden in an orthodox community as is showing massive cleavage in woman and still we do not excommunicate those members who all engage in that behavior. If we are to be a true orthodox community we must follow all rules not just those that please us and keep us insulated from the world around and terrorize anyone who feels differently from the masses.

Coup d'état advocate ~ January 19th, 2010

First and foremost - to BlaBla: I'm not going to make another analogy to justify homosexuality in our community. All I can tell you is to stop conducting your life strictly on scripture written thousands of years ago. You have to bend and re-adapt. If not, you may end up strapping explosives around your chest one day cuz you're being no different than a fundamental extremist. I am an observant man myself and I wouldn't appreciate you or anyone calling me out on one of my vices.

Back to the Coup d'état. Seriously, there are some really cloudy headed, egotistical people running around calling shots in our community. From what i've seen, our past community elections have been jokes.

Clearly, The community boards, leaders, and rabbi are reading this. I'll bet none of them will add fuel to the fire by commenting (as history shows - ruling gov'ts try to quiet uprisings by keeping mum). What must be done is to overtake the board (by election of course. I dont think torches and pitchforks are suitable today). If successful, maybe then we can gradually ease our community into the 21st century.

Vive la résistance!

BlaBla ~ January 19th, 2010

As i said before, yes there are other issues, but dont raise issues that our community has to defend others. Dont say that because most people in the community arent kosher and some feel the need to have pre marital sex it is ok for 2 men to get married, that does not justify anything. and to Mr. Coup D'etat advocate, explain to me how your brilliant mind thinks that comparing me to a terrorist justifies anything? Silly comments like this should be kept to yourselves.

Bla Bla and More Bla Bla ~ January 19th, 2010

Dear BlaBla, Most of us are not endorsing gay marriage on this board. It is a highly controversial and debated topic. Many non-orthodox Jews don't agree with it either. It is in fact a national debate. But we cannot harass someone who is gay. Isaacs website is his own property. He lives in a free country and as long as he follows the laws he has every right to celebrate his life through his website. He never came to the Kartaqis, they hunted him down to harass him. He isnt hurting anyone, he isnt campaigning for homosexuality. If anything, he is trying to help us understand how challenging his life has been and how he has wrestled with this for many years. Respect him and other gay men and woman for their human values and never forget that many go through years and years of pain and emotional suffering before they accept their homosexuality.

Judaism teaches us to 'love thy neighbor as thyself' not to just love your 'straight, orthodox kartaqi, fully community compliant neighbor as thyself'

Email

From: Jenny

To: Isaac

Date: 1/19/2010 1:50:42 P.M.

Subject: Re:

I'm glad to see there were so many positive comments as well. But you know, they are still not revealing their names.

Discussion Board

Coup d'état advocate ~ January 19th, 2010

Bla - Out of fear of turning this constructive forum into a name calling one, I apologize for the harsh comparison. I was trying to say that when people are overly passionate about something without bend, they can do irrational things that they may not realize greatly harm others with different viewpoints.

my bad. lets keep it clean.

kartaqi in high school ~ January 19th, 2010

I have been reading the posts for the past day and I am so happy to see people coming out and expressing themselves. I am a Kartaqi girl in my senior year of high school. I have been dating a Kartaqi guy (eight years older than me) for the last year. My boyfriend has already been pressuring me into getting engaged. As much as I care for my boyfriend I do not feel that I am ready to be with one person for the rest of my life, at least not now. I feel the pressure from my parents, grandparents and from his side as well. I desperately want to go to school to be a doctor. My family is against it and so is my boyfriend. I wish I had the strength to breakup with him but I know it will mean the end of my relationship with my family. My boyfriend comes from a well to do, big Kartaqi family as do I and I have been brought up to listen to my parents and obey them. I feel like the biggest decision of my life is being made by my parents and I feel like I am drowning. I will not have my parents support if I break this off and I am so scared to do so. I have other friends who are in my group that are in similar situations.

What do I know about life?. There is so much living I have yet to do. The one thing I won't give up on is my dream of being a doctor...I want it to much. I hope I can find the courage to stick up to my parents but honestly I feel like I maybe disowned simply for wanting to have control over my own life.

kartaqi mom ~ January 19th, 2010

In this day and age..do we have nothing better to worry about than what people do behind closed doors who do not bother anyone. Live and let live!

Congrats on your marriage and may you have happiness and joy for eternity

Me, Myself and I ~ January 19th, 2010

WOW, here I am thinking we are facing some tough times, recession, people losing their jobs, homes, people dying of cancer and sickness each day, 200,000 people dead in a matter of days and instead of people actually doing something worthy of their time, your all sitting here and stirring the pot, a pot that this community loves to stir up every once in a while when they are bored with their lives and have nothing better to do so they jump at the chance to take any little thing and exaggerate it to the above and beyond.

Issac and Andrew this is your life, your future, your journey, you navigate it any which way you both please. Whether I or anyone else agree with your lifestyle or decisions or not HAS ABSOLUTELY nothing to do with it. YOUR LIFE, YOUR JOURNEY.

To sit here and bash the central board or the rabbi, or the community for all the things going wrong in ALL of your lives is sad. This is a community, every community has its own way of thinking, living, preaching, teaching...

anyone who does not like it or agree with it, can walk away. Leave and don't look back. If you're going to so strongly advocate what you believe on this discussion board and speak so strongly against this community and its "leaders", be strong enough to stand true to yourself and not be anonymous about it.

You don't like what the Rabbi said on Saturday in synagogue, dont go to synagogue, you don't like your "group" dont go out with them, you dont enjoy weddings, SAY NO, you're not happily married or realized you married the wrong person, GET A DIVORCE- these are all things you can do if you want, there might be some bumps in the road along the way, but ultimately its YOUR LIFE, YOUR DECISIONS.

BUT- do not blame the community for having rules and traditions, and customs and establishing a way of life that they have built for generations, just because you may agree or disagree with them.

Every office has a boss, every store has its hours, every restaurant has its own menu, you cannot change the way this community operates or demands its community members to act, you can surely disagree but your only choice is to LEAVE and don't be a part of it.

Of course a Rabbi is going to speak against things such as homosexuality, adultery, intermarriage, its against the TORAH, its against everything they believe and learn and teach everyday. But why would someone who lets say is marrying a non Jew who knows its wrong to marry a non Jew when your Jewish but you could not control it, you fell in love, this is the right person for you, why would you need the support of a Rabbi and community members? This is not to say that people should track you down, harass you, threaten you or shame you in anyway, but do not expect to walk into synagogue a place of worship and G-D a week after you married a non Jew and have the rabbi and religious leaders welcome you with open arms.

Our community has a way of living and thinking, if you would like to be A PART of it, you must follow its "boss, hours, menu etc" and if you dont want to be a part of it, then there are plenty of other jobs, stores and different restaurants with different menus out there for you. At the end of the day being kartaqi does not define who and what you are, its what you make of your life, and your JOURNEY that defines you.

Don't wait till one day when you're about to die to realize you forgot to live.

By now I was first beginning to realize that the Discussion Board was entering a whole new dimension. While initially conceived as a tool of communicating with me anonymously specifically regarding issues pertaining to my sexuality and my outing, community members were now using it to interact with each other on basically any topic they saw fit. Some were expressing frustrations that they kept hidden for years, only now able to release it in an anonymous and safe way. Surely, I did not want to come across as an instigator, condoning chaos and revolutionary ideas just because I was personally wronged. I needed to distance myself from those advocating the Rabbi's removal or the resignation of the Central Board.

I inserted the above addendum at the end of that person's entry. I also created a disclaimer page, specifically stating that the opinions on the Discussion Board are strictly those of the guest bloggers. I did not know how much legal power my statement had, but I felt it was the right thing to do given some of the hostility expressed on these pages.

Discussion Board

Jim Carey ~ January 19th, 2010

Thank you, Me, Myself and I. You hit it right on the head. I completely agree with you.

To Me, Myself and I ~ January 19th, 2010

Appreciate your view but a community must represent the views of the people. Most successful businesses are run by a boss who takes into consideration the needs of his employees. Google, one of the most successful companies, has regular sessions I read asking employees to contribute ideas. This forum is not a waste of time. It is a very serious matter when a human being is harassed, especially one of our fellow Kartaqis, even if he is not an active member. We are not sitting around gossiping about who got married or engaged. We are addressing an alarming issue that has to with human rights. The human rights of a fellow Kartaqi. And as you can see, there are enough like-minded people in this Community that are voicing their thoughts. So let this be our platform. We may not change anything and maybe that's too ambitious of a goal given how radical the decision makers have become. But at least the minority and what is becoming a growing minority judging by this board, will realize there are others that feel like us: reluctant to give up our heritage, our religious commitment and determined to live in today's age and with respect for our peers around us.

Lets go green ~ January 19th, 2010

Perhaps one of the ways we can get our protest known respectfully and peacefully this coming Shabbat in synagogue is to all wear the same color. The Green Movement in the Middle East built an identity by all adopting something that makes a statement without yelling.

Not that I care much for green or the color of the mullahs, but a sea of bright green in synagogue would definitely make a shocking statement; blue just doesn't work because it blends in.

So lets have all the men wear green ties and shirt, and all the ladies wear green blouses in synagogue this Shabbat. Spread the word among your friends.

You completely got it backwards ~ January 19th, 2010

"Me, Myself, And I", you completely got it backwards. According to your own statement, with all the other serious problems out there right now, such as (to quote you), the recession, people losing their jobs, losing their homes, people dying of cancer and sickness, 200,000 people dead in a matter of days, then why is our synagogue and our Central Board focusing on homosexuality??? You made the case for me! Thank you.

Doesn't it seem silly to you that with all the other problems you mentioned, the Board is focusing on homosexuality? Where are their priorities? With all the other real problems out there, why focus on homosexuality, or two people being in love? Is it so bad that two people like each other? Is that such a problem for you, as cancer, or losing your home, or the devastation in Haiti?

The community should do something worthy with it's time, in these troubled times, instead of speaking out against homosexuality. That's the least of our problems right now, like you said yourself.

So leave these people alone. Why is it our business who they choose to love? According to you, they should leave the community. Well, HE ACTUALLY HAS. And he is still getting harassed. So what you said doesn't make sense. He did what you said, left the community, and the community is still not leaving him alone.

The Central Board should leave them alone and worry about the bigger issues we are facing right now. Let's learn to be good Jews, like G-d wants. G-d wants us to respect, help, and love one another, not put down and demean other Jews. That is very un-Jewish.

Respect ~ January 19th, 2010

Perhaps when we have a more representative Board and its puppet rabbi, we should invite Dr. Namdar back to our synagogue to apologize for what we have done to him. Not to condone or glorify homosexuality, but just to apologize. First, although he himself preferred to be non-confrontational and took his life elsewhere, we all invaded his privacy. Then we all cracked faggot jokes and, right there in Synagogue. Then we allowed our representatives to get up and demonize him right in front of the holy Torah.

I know Dr. Namdar and his family very well for several decades now. Although they didn't have a pot to piss in, Isaac paid his own way all through his education, all the while that his dad's peers in the jewelry district pressured him into making Isaac leave education and go sell jewelry. Now Dr. Namdar is a very well-achieved doctor in the city, with three office locations. He is definitely one of the top 10 smartest people in our community.

I never spoke to Dr. Namdar about it, but I am sure he must have undergone many many internal struggles to be able to cope with his homosexuality. He did not turn his back on us, we just didn't give him an alternative. Still, even though his dad probably thinks like all older kartaqi generation, Dr. Namdar fully supports his dad financially, even though he never got a dime from his old man. He is a model son and a model citizen.

concerned citizen ~ January 19th, 2010

To Me Myself and I..your views are your views and you are free to add to this healthy discussion. At no offense to you it seems like you are ailed with the same illness most traditional kartaqis have, its called denial. If you think it is ok to have a Rabbi address his community on Shabbat by ridiculing a man for making a choice to live his life against the norm, on Shabbat the holiest day of our week then I feel for you. It's immoral and disgusting. This is someone's son, a fellow member of this community and it is so out of line. The facts are all here written out by hundreds of kartaqis, this is not just about being traditional anymore, it about trying to control peoples minds and lives. Sending out a petition signed by the elders saying you cannot come to synagogue if you marry someone who decides to convert (who is jewish in my eyes) is only going to turn more people off to the community. I for one will not sit back and close my mouth anymore. I want nothing more than to feel comfortable and connected when I walk into my community synagogue. I feel so unconnected and so turned off that (g-d please forgive me) I might as well be sitting in a church. So to tell people to leave the community if they don't like how things are run is not the answer, its a cowardly thing to say. Instead, the central board should be listening to the alarming words on this page and try and work with their congregation to help the people who feel like outcasts to come back and feel like they belong to the community they were born into.

The Kartaqis take pride that they are the best community in the world. Well then let them start to prove that by listening to the voices of the people, instead of bashing them and casting them away as if they are garbage.

Green it is ~ January 19th, 2010

I second the motion to all wear green this coming Saturday. Lets all show up with the greenest shirts and ties we have, and let them see the old ways are outdated!

Concerned too ~ January 19th, 2010

"Concerned Citizen", you make an amazing point.

Humble ~ January 19th, 2010

In my humble opinion, I would have preferred if the events of last shabbat would have gone as below:

It is true that we are an Orthodox synagogue, which has values not compatible with homosexuality. I would have liked to see the Rabbi mention that more as a matter of fact, rather than with such antagonistic compassion. He should have followed that statement with saying that although gays may live their lives according to what they believe is best for them, it does not give us the right to interfere in their lives or ridicule them or make life any harder for them than it is. Then to make his speech perfectly well balanced, I would have jumped to talk about all the gossip and evil talk that ensued right after the story broke. To teach our people that what someone does in the privacy of their life is their business, but we need to better ourselves by avoiding *lashon hara* and by being compassionate. Alas, the speech was more Ahmadinejad than Mother Theresa.

Just see how eloquently and tactfully Andrew and Isaac expressed their opinions on the home page; none of US have that much tact even when we have been wronged.

Kartaqiator ~ January 19th, 2010

Why are you hiding behind fake names? The rabbi of our community and Central Board stand up week after week, show their faces and give their opinions. If you dislike this community so much, then state your name. You're just being cowards and hypocrites. You want change? Anonymously posting will get you nowhere. You're continuing the trend you dislike so much by "keeping quiet". As for me, I care about my reputation and the respect I'm given by my peers and elders because I build on it by doing good outside my home AND behind closed doors.

From kartaqi friends group ~ January 19th, 2010

Respect - thank you for sharing Isaac's life story with us. We feel proud to have a professional role model like him.

My friends and I just got back from school and heard about the board through a text message from my older cousin. The information is spreading virally to all the young kartaqis and expect to see us come on in big numbers soon. We are reading every entry together and want to thank all of you for sharing your voices with us. Especially for us younger ones who were born and raised in this country this board is the first ever opportunity you have given us to express our true feelings without upsetting our parents. Thank you so much.

concerned citizen ~ January 19th, 2010

To concerned too- thank you for your support. Just waiting for someone on the central board to get some guts and respond to our posts...

Shelly Norwick ~ January 19th, 2010

Whatever your beliefs are, treat people with RESPECT!

Curious George ~ January 19th, 2010

to me, myself and I. To say that the decisions coming out of the central board are the thoughts that embody even the majority of the people in the community is ridiculous. The Central Board allows only one viewpoint. that viewpoint can be expressed anonymously or with a name in publications like Shalom. Even if they spew messages of hatred. The other viewpoint can't be expressed anonymously or with a name attached. Hundreds of letters are thrown in the garbage that are sent to the central board. the ideology of a few is being passed on the majority through scare tactics, harassing barrage of phone calls, lies, rumors, threats of alienation and walkouts during joyous occasions, and non performance of ceremonies, etc. Why should we let our beloved community become hijacked and radicalized by a select few people who have nothing to do but instill their will and message of hatred on the people of the community. Should we let what goes on in Iran, Afghanistan, and Palestine happen to our beloved community because you're in some position of power. I don't think so. Your time is limited. It's just a matter of when. Just like the green revolution, it will happen.

j.g. ~ January 19th, 2010

I think that the kartaqi community has a problem in general with accepting people, whether it be gays, blacks, or any other race besides their own.

kartaqi mom ~ January 19th, 2010

I have been reading these comments..and the kartaqi in high school, my heart breaks for you! G-d give you strength in any decision you make..just know that, this man you are marrying should respect your wishes..as in all relationships..respect is the most important thing. In regards to the other posts, I feel there is a number of community members me included, that loves the people in this community and feel that we/us..disagree with some of the "edicts" posed by the central board. Perhaps a petition or some sort of statement made by kartaqi members who do not share in the beliefs of the central board could unionize and make a difference. We can reach out to those who feel isolated or alone or disconnected. Since, we love our families..we should have a synagogue that represents and respects ALL its "members." I have heard from many kartaqis that they would "leave" the community by extricating themselves if push comes to shove..and something has to be done about this. Rabbi Levy if you are reading this...fyi..many members will not donate this year. They do not want to affiliate or donate to a community that is racist and inhumane. It would taint anyone's reputation if they knew that they gave funds to an organization that preached hatred.

Jake ~ January 19th, 2010

AT THE VERY LEAST, 50% of our community is gay! No need to get all rouled up about one that hopped outa the closet last week...

Happy for you ~ January 19th, 2010

As a kartaqi woman...thank you for being you and standing up for what you believe in. ONLY GOD CAN JUDGE.

Just a Girl ~ January 19th, 2010

You know what I would like to know...how come NOW all of you are voicing your opinions, is this the first time the Central Board or

"Rabbi" have done or said something against most of your beliefs?

If all of you so called strong supporters and advocates feel so passionately about this issue and many others you pointed out, WHY HASN'T ANYONE ACTUALLY TAKEN A STAND BEFORE?

How come no one has actually gotten the courage to speak against these different views before? Its one thing to sit behind a computer where NO ONE sees you or knows who you are and write so passionately about your beliefs against the community, its another thing to actually do something about it. Put a face to words and do something about it in public.

The least you can do is actually learn from Isaac and Andrew who had the courage to actually stand up for their beliefs and embrace anyone who had questions or wanted to discuss issues further, even willing to invite those who are against them into their home.

You demand change, stand up for it PUBLICLY show your face and do something about it.

Takes more than just typing away on a keyboard....

just another girl ~ January 19th, 2010

Just a girl - why don't you share your name?

young girl stays anonymous ~ January 19th, 2010

Posting anonymous: It's the fear the community has instilled in our parents. My mother once told me that if I ever speak up about my true feelings I will not find a 'rich husband from a good family' so i need to keep my mouth shut. This in itself is another issue to deal with in our community. Most of us dont feel brave enough to stand up for fear of upsetting our parents and our extended families. We have been trained from birth to show a perfect face on the outside and never show anyone that anything is wrong with us.

I admire people who have the courage to speak up with your name.

Hoping your discussion board makes us realize that there are so many like us that it is safe to come out and identify ourselves. We are blessed with large families and the flip side is that we cannot say anything in public without it getting back to them. We wish that one day we can come out with our own identities but a lot of the scare tactics someone mentioned above need to be gone before that happens.

Response to 'just a girl' ~ January 19th, 2010

How come 'green' protesters conceal their identity while marching through the streets? Oh yea, I forgot; because they'll get murdered!! If i post my name, the rabbi may give a speech next week calling for my exile.

Silly girl

S-fan ~ January 19th, 2010

I would just like to say that it is amazing how this discussion board has allowed people to share the ideas they have repressed for so long- too bad we all had to wait for something like this to happen before we shared our thoughts.

Although I cannot say that I hate the central board and am totally against them, I can say that i am amazed that someone would choose a synagogue of all places to share the news of Issac's marriage to the community and i think his action alone is more disgusting than anything the central board has said or done. Yes, homosexuality is not in line with Judaism, yet neither is shaming a fellow man. How come community members are so vigilant about telling people to be more religious and eat more kosher and marry non-converted jews and not be gay and still have not taken a stand against disrespect and *lashon hara* between the congregants?

I am someone who is already active on the youth board and my silent protest will be to climb myself to the top leadership positions and start to move the community in a new direction, hopefully with the help of my peers.

WELL I AM SOMEONE ELSE ON THE YOUTH BORED AND MY LOUD
PROTEST WILL BE TO STOP YOU S-FAN AND NEVER TO LET ANYONE
LIKE YOU TO GET INTO A POSITION OF POWER

kartaqiman ~ January 19th, 2010

Mazal Tov to Andrew and Isaac. What a gorgeous couple.

I genuinely hope that you two don't mind that your site has become a
platform for a serious discussion about the value system in our
community, of which I have grown to become a staunch critic.

I am proud of my heritage. I love our traditions. I love my parents, my
siblings, my cousins.

But I am increasingly uncomfortable in a Kartaqi environment-not
least because of the way the community, so rich in heritage and
history, is evolving. We have been in the United States for 30 years,
and yet I feel that many in the community have regressed to pre-
Zameen times. And while I have much respect for the way in which
we Kartaqis have managed to stay together, I notice more and more
how much our mindset is akin to those Muslim fundamentalists that
we ran away from in the first place.

Those people who have suggested we critics stay away from
community functions/synagogue if we disagree with the protocol,
how about this idea. If it is so difficult to adapt to American values,
why not go back to Zameen? You can take your rabbi with you. I hear
their leader also thinks there are no homosexuals in his country (and
has those that are killed). Our rabbi should stand in solidarity with the
persecuted, not become persecutors. They have a moral obligation to
bridge the old and new worlds in a compassionate, inclusive way.

I sometimes look at Zameeni Jews with envy; their zest for education
and opening their minds is inspiring even as they have their own

issues too.

We have so many reasons to be proud to be Jewish. Our traditions, our compassions, our ability to bond with other minorities who have also been persecuted through the ages.

I hope our rabbi and the central board read this and take this to heart. There is no place for hatred, not now, not ever.

Again, Mazal Tov to Isaac and Andrew and I genuinely wish you two happiness. And if you desire, may G-D bless you with beautiful children!

rona ~ January 19th, 2010

unfortunately the kartaqi community thinks is " untouchable" but it is not, real problems come out in modern time..it takes time to really comprehend them, can't be overnight

The entries on the Discussion Board were getting posted with increasing speed. Each time a new entry got posted, I received an automatic email notification from the wedding website server with the entire content of the message. Initially I thought this helped me keep up with developments without myself having to log on to the site constantly. But now so many new entries were coming in at such lightning speed that just reading those emails was becoming a full time job, let alone digesting them. The debate was also shifting into a much wider spectrum of social issues than I anticipated.

Discussion Board

SOUTHERN MAGNOLIA ~ January 19th, 2010

WHATS FUNNY IS THAT MOST PEOPLE WHO ARE WRITING AGAINST THE CENTRAL BOARD, THE RABBI, THE COMMUNITY, THE CLIQUES, THE CASTE SYSTEM, THE POLITICS ARE THE ONES WHO ARE ACTIVELY INVOLVED IN IT. THIS IS HYSTERIA

Love over Hate. ~ January 19th, 2010

I'd just like to say congrats to the happy couple who seem to be genuinely in love. Good for you. I am proud of you for living your lives truthfully, being honest to yourselves and to others.

Being gay is not something you can help, choose or change. I'm sure there are many gay, unhappy married men out there (who might cheat on their wives), and that is much more sad to me than two men who fell in love, were not ashamed, and got married.

Each and every one of us deserves the equal right to love, whether that makes others uncomfortable or not. I'm proud of some of the comments I've seen here. I hope all of you continue to take a stand in what you believe in and hopefully this community will change for the better.

Anonymous ~ January 19th, 2010

People that have been persecuted for their faith should think twice before attacking others and promote hatred.

anonymous ~ January 19th, 2010

Whys everyone making such a big deal? Let them hop each others pogo stick in happiness.. I would be more concerned when a kartaqi girl gets tired of hooking up with guys and wants to settle down and marry a donkey... (give it 10 years)

concerned citizen ~ January 19th, 2010

To tabernacle- it is the close minded judgment you just posted that will keep our community in the gutter forever...times will change just look at the posts here. We need more people like s-fan to climb the ladder and overthrow this fanatic ruling regime. It's about time.

tabernacle ~ January 19th, 2010

LISTEN CONCERNED CITIZEN, WHY DO YOU KEEP SAYING WE ARE IN THE GUTTERS, IS THERE SOMETHING WRONG? WE ARE AN ORTHODOX JEWISH COMMUNITY WHICH DOES NOT ALLOW 2 MEN 2 GET MARRIED, IM SORRY IF THAT OFFENDS ANYONE. IT ISNT CLOSE MINDEDNESS, IT IS WHO WE ARE. IT WOULD BE SAME IF SOMEONE MARRIED A NON JEW.

need to speak up kartaqi ~ January 19th, 2010

Tabernacle - if you have a point to make please do not use capitals. It sounds like you are yelling and while you probably feel very angry, this is a civil board. Most of us do not advocate gay marriage. we are critical of harassing an individual who left the community and lived his life as he wishes. this is a free country and we are lucky to live here. if we are orthodox then we should deal with this issue in a human way and not through harassment. Thats the orthodox and jewish way.

murdered ~ January 19th, 2010

I am asking all the married gays (to the opposite sex) please express what you are going through, what a horror to be married to some one you are not attracted to and lie and cheat and fake...if you have any guts left, share it with everyone so maybe we dont encourage getting married to an opposite sex while you are clearly gay, we just want to sweep you guys under the rug. Its about time you spoke

Hailey Hoffman ~ January 19th, 2010

Congratulations to you both and BRAVO (all caps) for following your path. Kudos for choosing to embrace the way G-d created you. May you have a blessed and happy future as a family!

concerned citizen ~ January 19th, 2010

Hi Tabernacle. I don't mean to offend you and I am sorry if I did. The reality of the situation is that we are in the gutter and digging the whole deeper with every decree that comes out of this community. I understand that we are an "Orthodox community" but its time to wake up and smell the reality- this community is as far from orthodox as possible- the only thing we have adopted from the hassidic or orthodox is their fanaticism. This forum is nothing to do about 2 men getting married..it started b/c the way this issue was addressed was morally wrong end of discussion. They were ridiculed in front of everyone on Shabbat- that is as unorthodox as it gets. Sorry for the dose of reality. I can get into more detail if you would like---ie drug abuse within our youth, premarital sex, letting your cleavage hang out in synagogue, or and *lashon hara* that goes on every week in synagogue when our dear rabbi is trying to preach to us about how to be orthodox! Are all those things listed above characteristic of being orthodox!?!! I THINK NOT!

Mini Cooper ~ January 19th, 2010

Tabernacle- It's not "who we are". You represent a voice in the community and an interpretation of Orthodox Judaism. Clearly from the voices on this bulletin board, your voice is not the only voice in the community. You're going to have to accept that fact. Orthodox Judaism has been interpreted many different ways and almost all interpretations allow the family and individuals the dignity to deal with these sensitive issues in the context of the family. They avoid embarrassing, ridiculing and harassing to achieve their goals as that is clearly prohibited in the Torah and also not acceptable in modern society. The Torah itself on multiple occasions makes it a point to treat others well and says this is the only real message of the Torah. It also goes further to say that we must treat converts, jews, slaves and non-jews with respect as we were once strangers in the land of Egypt. Your interpretation of Orthodox Judaism throws out the primary messages of the Torah and instead allows you to hide behind your last name and your veil of observance. Your opinion and that of the board is not necessarily that of the community. There is clearly a disconnect. You shouldn't let this anger you, it's just a fact that change is on its way. So please take off the caps as noted above.

Let's see ~ January 19th, 2010

I wonder if Scrolls, written and edited by the youth of the community, will feature any articles pertaining to everything that happened? Should they print some of the comments posted here? Should they ask Dr. Namdar to write an article telling the rest of us everything he had to go through?

proud kartaqi ~ January 19th, 2010

our great grandparents were stubborn and steadfast against majority Muslims. they were not cool at the time. thanks to their stubborn ways we are here and not Shiites in Kartaq.

what any individual does in their privacy is nobodys business but as kartaqi jews we have to protect our traditions and values as a community. i did not hear any gay bashing or intolerance by CB or our rabbi so i just dont get the rage.

issac i wish you healthy happy life.

youngdad ~ January 19th, 2010

i actually see kartaqis as a whole as role models for other societies. i see incredible tolerance by having hasidic, orthodox, secular, nonbeliever under same roof and same families. i see kartaqi parents sacrificing their lives for children as opposed to american society of divorcing for snoring. i see moderation and unconditional love of israel. i see when a family stricken with tragedy the whole community weeps with them .

dont get me wrong we are far from perfect but as whole i know i rather live in this group than any where else.

Proud Kartaqi too ~ January 19th, 2010

to proud kartaqi from another proud kartaqi: we only hear what we want to hear. my interpretation is different, there was a bitter undertone of harassment. obviously something ticked all of the people posting on this board off. how else can one explain the pages and pages of entries since yesterday. it is an indication of much bigger issues than just Saturday's message. the issues need to be addressed as i am just as proud a kartaqi as you probably are but do not tolerate the rules brought on to us by a handful of signatures of the central board. we all need to be heard. proud kartaqis of all shapes and styles.

Fun in Kartaqi Jewish Center ~ January 19th, 2010

Hi everybody,

And most importantly, hello to my Kartaqi Jewish brothers and sisters.

I am writing here as a witness to Rabbi Levy's speech on Saturday, January 16, 2009. It was actually one of the quietest lectures Rabbi Levy gave, as nobody was speaking that day. In my opinion, Rabbi Levy is a mouthpiece of the Central Board of our community, and as the leader of the community and the recipient of the community's paycheck, does not always entirely express his views. That doesn't mean that his words were insincere on Saturday. It's just some food for thought, my friends.

Rabbi Levy likes to make analogies. He made the following argument through this analogy: if someone had abnormally high levels of testosterone and raped women, would their actions be justified? Absolutely not. Therefore, if someone likes to sleep with men, does that justify his gay act? First of all, since when is a gay act tantamount to rape?

Secondly, Rabbi Levy made the assertion that our holy ancestors in Kartaq did not know of such things, for there was no pornography at the time! Alright, so why did my righteous and truly religious Kartaqi grandfather tell me that his friends frequented brothels often in

Kartaq? Is that holy? Also, Gharwim, the city from which Kartaqis originated from, is known for the preponderance of homosexuality among its population. Please, let's not mention that men living in close quarters with men and (and women with women) did not prompt such an activity.

Rabbi Levy progressed to talk about two schools in Psychology relating to homosexuality (if this was the case, science and the field of psychology would be regressing by now). Rabbi Levy spoke about the "sleeper effect" in relation to homosexuality, basically stating that repeated exposure to gay pornography will prompt one to not only be more comfortable with homosexuality, but that he/she will also come to like it, to accept it as normal. He didn't give an alternative to the sleeper effect, or state that it may just be natural to be attracted to sexuality in general. The theory of "omnisexuality" was not discussed.

Then, while saying all of this, Rabbi Levy said that many have confided in him that either they or their children have these tendencies (which may, in my opinion, mean that deep down he is acknowledging that people struggle with this). It's fascinating that at this point, he doesn't say, "We are not in this community by birth, but by religious affiliation." (one of the most wonderful things about our community is that we are born into it, and this decree is most antithetical to the ecumenical nature of our birthright). Rabbi Levy distances himself from the "sinner against God," as written in the Bible. We have excommunicated the sinner. Why do we, as Jews, let go of the biblical commandment of stoning but decide to keep a commandment that outcasts others?

teenage kartaqi ~ January 19th, 2010

to young kartaqi dad- I would also like to see the Kartaqis act as a REAL role model for other Jewish communities to follow not just preach that they are the best. I know first hand of Kartaqi families just eating up their hurt anger and frustration and not getting divorced for the sake of their children, this is not always the best situation for a family. Please don't put down American society, there is so much that we benefit from living in this society such as being able to practice our religion in peace. Unfortunately I have seen the community adopt the negative aspects of American culture and looked past the positives such as education, such a vital thing for every youth in this community. And as for your last comment when a family is stricken with tragedy, yes the community does rally around the family but it is only temporary and mostly always for show. Where are they when the going gets tough? Kartaqis are notorious for jumping the boat when things get tough- they only want to be around happy things! I would love to walk around with my head held high and say I am proud to be a Kartaqi, but unfortunately with circumstances such as these I am afraid I cannot.

collegeboy ~ January 19th, 2010

teenage kartaqi. i have to be fair. for orthodoxy he was extremely mild and soft and there was no condemnation or hate at all by rabbi. of course this forum would attract more people who are younger and kind of against order. that is in youth nature.

love the safety net and community belonging that we have. i wont change it for the world.

No Fun in Kartaqi Jewish Center last Shabbat ~ January 19th, 2010

Dear 'Fun in Kartaqi Jewish Center',

I was there as well and have a slightly different view as to the tone and the congregations full on gossip mongering and I certainly was not having fun at all.

There is a documentary called 'Trembling Before G-D' that was made several years ago. Maybe it is a good idea to view this movie as it accurately depicts the challenges of being gay in the hasidic and orthodox community and that it is not a choice to be gay nor is it affected by your environment/pornography/living in close quarters with other men.

It is an award winning film and gives realistic insights into the complex lives of gay orthodox Jews.

I remembered seeing this movie many years ago when I was still struggling with sexuality. Although it was an eye-opener, I could not at that time relate to those characters. They were all Ashkenazi (European) Jews. Somehow they seemed foreign to me. I now realize that those characters and me have a lot more in common than I was ready to admit to myself back then.

Immediately after reading this posting, I added the link to the website of this movie and a few other ones with similar topics. I put all those links in a separate page with the title "Orthodoxy and Homosexuaity," an intentional juxtaposition of terms.

Discussion Board

teenage kartaqi ~ January 19th, 2010

to collegeboy- I am not against order- I am into reality and that is not what this community is into. Stop trying to hide behind a veil of lies...there is no safety net in this community- it is a false reality we are fed from birth. Backstabbing, hypocritical *lashon hara* speaking is more along the lines of the truth. You don't have to change it for the world, but for the pissed off people on this forum change will come no doubt about it.

yentah ~ January 19th, 2010

I second the idea of inviting Dr. Namdar to have a feature article in the next Scrolls. I'd like to hear from him too. Although at this point, I am not sure if he wants to have anything to do with us. Thanks for letting us use your site, by the way.

collegeboy too ~ January 19th, 2010

Our rabbi is anything but mild. He connects through people by playing on their fears. The fear that their child might be exposed to gays and therefore become gay, women exposed to temptation at the gym and have sex with their male trainers, go away to college and marry a non jew, daughters go away to college and lose their virginity or marry non-kartaqi. These fears are played on through analogies and tale tales. This is the true hysteria. He and whoever tells him what to say are the true instigators. We're guilty of allowing him to play us, but not everyones eyes are open yet.

teenage kartaqi ~ January 19th, 2010

collegeboy- Are you trying to say that instilling fear is going to keep our youth from doing what they are going to do? Being gay is not something one can help- a display such as last Saturdays will not do anything accept make people angry. Trying to keep our youth in a bubble, talking down to them and trying to control their minds and lives with threats will not help the situation, only worsen it. We can only teach our youth the beauty of our religion and heritage and hope that they make the right decisions. And on a side note- our youth is finally opening up to marrying outside the community (not the worst thing in the world) and the virtue of remaining a virgin till marriage has been lost with the new generation...so obviously the current tactic is not working

newly young dad ~ January 19th, 2010

Most orthodox rabbis try to stay away from the topic and don't go on and on about gay people, harassing and targeting anyone who associates with them. If asked they might say something like the strict interpretation of the Torah doesn't endorse it and leave it at that. They would never do what transpired on Saturday, because its unnecessary and cruel. Issac and Andrew so sorry you had to even hear segments of that nasty speech.

Email

From: Isaac

To: Hailey

Date: 1/19/2010 9:21:41 P.M.

Subject: Thanks

Thanks for the warm wishes you expressed to us on the Message Board.

We also really appreciate you taking the courage to do so with your real name.

Isaac & Andrew

Email

From: Isaac

To: Sarah

Date: 1/19/2010 11:51:57 P.M.

Subject: Re: Your Site

Do you think you can use any of your contacts to get the transcript of the rabbi's speech? Or the accompanying policy statement from Central Board? I am so intrigued to hear what he said, the little tidbits and interpretations from people on the Discussion Board are contradictory, I want to be able to judge for myself.

Email

From: Sarah

To: Isaac

Date: 1/19/2010 11:54:02 P.M.

Subject: Re: Your Site

Yes, of course. Will get on it. Some great stuff today. I am impressed. I just love tracking this stuff as for years I have been the recipient of confidential calls of outcries by young people and now this forum, finally a therapy for them and a place they can have a voice. Thank you!

Wow! What a day it turned out to be! The Discussion Board totally took off into unchartered territory. Which is actually typical of how Kartaqis do anything. Once one Kartaqi develops interest in a new vacation spot, trendy restaurant or bar, new shopping venue, new sporting event, or anything that is considered the 'it' thing to do, the rest just follow. They always do everything en mass. And they quickly migrate from one novelty to the next. Ten days ago the 'it' thing was to look into my wedding website and check out all the pictures and crack faggot jokes. Today, the new 'it' thing has become to get on my Discussion Board and air out their frustrations about the leadership. Although that was not the aim of my blog, you just can't stop the Kartaqis.

The one feature I did not expect is the amount of time it was taking me to go through such a multitude of entries. The website host continued to send me email notifications with the content of each new entry on the Discussion Board. I kept getting new emails all day long, and I felt compelled to read every single entry right then and there. I also felt the obligation to make sure that the content did not contain any language that was not appropriate, and that the discussion remained civil.

Wednesday, January 20, 2010

That morning, I checked on the Discussion Board as soon as I woke up. I was surprised to see that there were a couple of hundred more visitors all night, and a handful of more entries were posted all through the night.

Email

From: Sarah

To: Isaac

Date: 1/20/2010 7:16:15 A.M.

Subject: Re: Your Site

I am trying to get the speech but it seems they are not releasing it because of lawsuit fear. One of the posts says the speech was mild because of lawsuits

Email

From: Jerome

To: Isaac

Date: Hi!

Subject: 1/20/2010 11:11:20 A.M.

Dear Isaac

I don't think we have ever met, but I just found out about your wedding site, and have been following the discussion board. I wanted to send you a quick message to congratulate you on your wedding to Andrew.

I am gay and live with partner in the city. All my friends know about me and are very accepting, but for whatever reason --chalk it up to my lack of courage, my fear of disappointing my loved ones or plenty of other reasons I am sure could keep a shrink in business -- I haven't been able to come out to my immediate family. I am sure they know. It's so difficult, and really impacts my relationship adversely.

I just wanted to let you know that I was so happy to find the web site and so inspired by you - even as we don't know each other I hope I meet you and Andrew in person soon!!! I think I know your father...I used to see him in the synagogue. I believe our fathers are friends. I hope he is doing well in Israel.

Best wishes, and thank you!!!

Jerome

Email

From:	Isaac
To:	Jerome
Date:	1/20/2010 11:38:48 A.M.
Subject:	Re: Hi!

Thanks for writing to me.

I do remember seeing you with your parents as our fathers chatted in the synagogue. Intuition, but my gaydar went off on you right away. LOL.

Glad to hear you are happily partnered. As you know, Andrew and I took the extra step and got married.

The main lesson I have learned from this is that more people have been hurt by me not telling them soon enough, rather than telling them outright. I got lucky that my sisters and their families have been so supportive, more than I ever imagined. But dad, I am sure he went to the same knucklehead school as your dad and all the elders of our community.

Would love to make more of a contact with you and learn about you and your partner. You can also call me 678-555-1212

PS, tonight I am meeting another gay Kartaqi living in the city that I just got to know about after the whole hoopla started. Networking!

Discussion Board

family ~ January 20th, 2010

Did you all know that all of Isaac's immediate family lives in Israel, including his dad and siblings and all his first cousins? He only has second and third cousins here. So in a sense the community is the ONLY family he had here. And now the community singled him out to be the subject of forced and mandatory alienation. Are these the Jewish values we all grew up with? Now even his third cousin is prohibited from inviting him over for Pesach or Rosh Hashannah??? Really? Is that a very Jewish thing to do, to let him be with nobody on the holidays or shabbat?

NotSoGreenHills ~ January 20th, 2010

First, I am not in favor of what Mr. Namdar does. Nor am against it. In fact, I don't care. And why would I care? However, what I do care about is not being exposed to patronizing speeches about how life in the 21st century is ought to be lead. I don't need to be told what I ought not to watch on TV, I don't need to be told what my children ought not to watch, and I don't need to be told that "our wives" should not have male tennis trainers. [For those who remember that speech.] Do we really need all these parental speeches? Aren't some of those speeches tantamount to an insult to our own abilities to live an adult life? Similarly, we do not need to be told that the gay lifestyle (or any other lifestyle) is good or bad. Besides, please remember: Nobody will turn gay by watching Project Runway & Co. Nor will a gay person turn straight by being restricted to TV shows from the 80s. I don't want to overstate the obvious, but: There was no TV at Mount Sinai, and yet we were instructed by the Torah that the gay lifestyle is bad. What's the reason for that prohibition? Obviously because homosexuality was prevalent already then. In other words, it's a myth that the "American Media" is supposedly producing homosexuals.

Second, regarding the speech, in response to those who say it was a mild: it was expressly stated why the speech was the way it was, namely for fear of a lawsuit. So let's keep that in mind when giving too much credit.

Third, and I think this is the biggest issue: The increasingly irreversible trend of Green Hills's turning into an ultra-religious ZIP. What comes to mind is the recent outburst of Rabbi Klein from our sister Zameeni community during a private house party because it was allegedly held in violation of a Jewish holiday. [Some may have heard about this.] I know people who don't dare eating in non-kosher restaurants in Green Hills for fear of being "caught." At this rate, there will come a time where certain people won't dare being "caught" driving on Shabbat. What is next – an edict against parking your car on the Synagogue's parking lot on Shabbat?

Are all the edicts (as I see more coming) worth the long-term collateral damage that is being done to a previously all-inclusive community?

city ~ January 20th, 2010

It is so nice to read all your posts, I am also glad that someone posted Rabbi Levy's remarks - they are even more outrageous than what I expected. I cannot believe he actually said those things. Really shameful. I hope he will apologize or at least address it in synagogue.

D. H. ~ January 20th, 2010

I was looking online for some info on Orthodox Judaism and its policy on gays, and I found the following editorial from Rabbi Tzvi Hersh Weinreb:

> While the sources irrevocably forbid homosexual relationships and overt homosexual behavior, there are other issues that are more nuanced and must be clarified. One has to do with the attitude toward homosexual individuals

prescribed by Jewish tradition. Here it is critical to adopt the distinction, already implicit in numerous rabbinical texts, between the sin and the sinner; that is, between the person and his or her behavior. Given the nature of our times, it is impossible to formally condemn people who violate Jewish norms. Orthodox Jews and Orthodox synagogues display various degrees of tolerance and acceptance to individuals who are violators of the *halachic* (Jewish Law) aspects of the Sabbath, or individuals who flagrantly violate the *kashrut* (kosher-ness) laws. The tolerance rightly shown to these individuals by no means condones their behavior, but accepts them as people who may be misled or uninformed. While tolerance for individuals who manifest homosexual tendencies is certainly a Jewish value, there is a great difference between tolerance for an individual and recognition of a movement which wishes to turn something clearly wrong by Jewish standards into something not only tolerated but normative

Sarah ~ January 20th, 2010

On October 15, 2009 I lost my closest and dearest friend to complications from the swine flu. She was a remarkable woman on many levels but there is a story to share which is relevant to this discussion. Miriam was diagnosed with Hodgkin's disease in 1998 at the age of 25 and had to undergo a bone marrow transplant (BMT). A BMT is a brutal procedure where large doses of chemotherapy destroy your immune system and are then replaced with fresh cells. It requires you to stay in an isolated hospital room for several weeks and visitors need to wear protective gowns, gloves and masks while in the patient's room. This procedure as barbaric as it was, gave Miriam 12 years of a full and vibrant life until she was diagnosed with the swine flu in late August.

The reason I am sharing this story is that Miriam spent every week of those 12 years visiting other patients that were undergoing BMTs at the hospital. Last summer she went every day after work because she felt such a need to help these people. Every time she walked through the BMT unit she relived the experience of her own trauma just to help others see that they too can come out alive from this procedure and live a healthy life.

I personally know one member of the community that is as committed to helping the sick as Miriam was but wont publicize it to anyone because in her own words 'Kartaqis don't care about the work I do since it's not about Kartaqis, so why tell them and aggravate myself. I did tell a few of my friends and they said: 'Why do you waste your time helping a destitute'.

I am sure there are many individuals like her in the Community but we rarely hear of them because they don't have a forum that makes them comfortable to speak up.

By intimidating individuals like her who commit themselves to helping the needy and the poor of the general population (not just the Kartaqis) and demonizing Dr. Isaac Namdar who has dedicated his life to medicine and helping others, the most important of Jewish values are sadly being overlooked, regardless of your personal interpretation of Orthodox Judaism.

extremely liberal ~ January 20th, 2010

Since we are all being so open minded...Isaac tell us, whos the pitcher and whos the receiver? How does it feel getting it up the ass? I've never tried it but if you say its good I might think about it since everyone on this forum is praising you...you think I can get your Rabbi's digits to marry me and my boyfriend as well??

RESPONSE FROM ISAAC:

Firstly, I would like to thank all the posts with messages of support.

Secondly, we all have tried to keep this discussion civilized and mutually respectful. The above entry is way off any acceptable social behavior. Pure example of intolerance.

Third, what happens in the privacy of my bedroom in no more anybody's public business than what happens between YOU and your wife in the privacy of YOUR bedroom.

Please try to keep your comments polite and respectful.

will become family ~ January 20th, 2010

In response to your statement 'family', I don't believe anyone who is a friend of Isaac or a relative of his should disown him for the freedom he had chosen to live his life in. Many in this community are starving for a free lifestyle of sort. I have a lot of respect for our Rabbi and central board but I will take charge in inviting him and his lovely partner to our holiday gatherings and events if no one else does. So thanks to 'family' who brought up this issue!

will become family too ~ January 20th, 2010

I dont know Isaac but I heard today that Isaac lost his brother-in-law to cancer a few months ago. Does that mean we would not allow him to come and sit *Shiva* (mourning period) with his family at the Synagogue? Giving him and his family comfort during such a hard time. The sense I and many others got on Saturday is that openly gays are not welcome to the Synagogue. Even if they attend, we are not going to welcome them. We cannot let that happen, that is inhuman.

Dear Isaac - my deepest condolences to you for the loss of your brother-in-law and sorry you have to deal with all this during your time of grief

Role Model ~ January 20th, 2010

I think Isaac should be praised...I always wanted a great role model for my kids to follow. My husband is wayyy too heterosexual, now that we have Isaac Namdar I can show my kids how every man should live their life!

psychologist ~ January 20th, 2010

I think everyone should leave the happy couple alone and they should leave the community alone.

I also think that a lot of you need a lot of help. If you are unhappy with your lives it is NOT because you are kartaqi. And if you are so unhappy to be kartaqi please do what you like and disassociate yourselves. If you are so unhappy being Jewish then go marry a non Jew...

if you need a divorce or dont know if you should marry your boyfriend go see a shrink! Leave poor Andrew and Isaac alone, this is their wedding's message board...did any of you even bother getting them gifts off their registry? If not then dont write here!!

Medium of making money ~ January 20th, 2010

Adding to Sarah's note. I am a female living in this community and I know Isaac's friends and relatives. I would like to add that Dr. Namdar makes most of his money by performing surgery on his patients and knowing him through people who had visited him and the way he runs his practice, surgery is the last thing he proposes to his patients, only when all other options are not helping. Let's not talk about how certain others make their money in this community. So thanks to Sarah for your beautiful story!

serious psychologist ~ January 20th, 2010

Dear Psychologist, you make it sound so easy to disassociate yourself. Not everyone has the mental strength to do that so we try hard to be part of the community we love and stay close to our families. Some of us dont have it in us to just get up and leave, we are looking for an alternative within our community and not asking for much, just some tolerance for respecting our individual space as most modern orthodox communities do.

Maybe the Community needs a psychologist to handle those that are so fearful of public opinions expressed here.

psychologist ~ January 20th, 2010

Dear Serious Psycho,

I already dissociated myself. I actually still live in Green Hills believe it or not and have my own non kartaqi friends and life. Although Green Hills is Kartaqi infested you can live your own life here, but if you feel you cant, then just get up and move to the city or elsewhere

Salisbury Steak ~ January 20th, 2010

I have just read every single thread on this forum and just wanted to say a few things. Isaac, you do what you have to, but if you believe this community is going to accept who you are, you are wrong. As much as people want to say we are not an orthodox community anymore, you are downplaying the most important part of the community, and that is our customs. Rabbi Levy's speech on Shabbat was 100% accurate, there is nothing more or less he could have said. Of course the community is anti gay marriage, it is fully against the torah. He said very clearly no one should harass or make Isaac and his partner feel bad, but at the same time we can not welcome them into our holy sanctuary, and he is very right, there is a temple a few miles away called Temple Emanuel and they would gladly take you 2 in. But we can not, I am sorry and there really isnt any argument.

Gate ~ January 20th, 2010

Well said salisbury steak...

NotSoGreenHills ~ January 20th, 2010

Salisbury Steak, why do you say "But WE can not?" Shouldn't you be saying "I cannot?" Please let every adult make his/her own determination as to what can or cannot be done.

As I have said before, we ought to stop giving patronizing (even if well-intended) advice to each other. It's just not healthy for a community

Enlightened ~ January 20th, 2010

Thank you Salisbury Steak. Everyone else, please go set up a meeting in Temple Beth-El to argue the Kartaqi stance. That's a very suitable place for your ideology.

Jewish Father in late 50s ~ January 20th, 2010

Salisbury Steak (and Gate), I am assuming you are also advocating writing another edict forbidding Isaac and anyone gay to enter the sanctuary or participate in our prayers.

If that is the case please give us advance notice so I do not purchase paper towels for that week as you will supply the paper for my wife and I to wipe our kitchen counter.

The green letter you so successfully mass mailed to all Community members regarding another group you do not agree with was insulting enough.

To create rules for us without asking for our vote is not right.

You have masterfully prevented those you do not see eye to eye with or who do not lead the perfect Kartaqi lifestyle from being part of our community even though they are very dedicated to the Kartaqi Community. Many of them very smart and accomplished individuals who we should celebrate with pride.

If you want to keep the peace in the Community, I strongly advise that you have members vote on such important issues and not have a handful of elders and rabbi sign off on it and put them into law. We all have a right to vote on the future of our Community and even if our vote isnt the majority, it is still the democratic way to make such critical decisions that affect our future and those of our kids. You probably will win in the end but at least you have given your entire Community a chance to have a voice.

Use your power wisely because at some point you will be forbidding us to talk to strangers, woman to wear pants, kids to go to public schools, watch TV, etc etc

Your scare tactics have worked so well and it is terrifying to many of us what more you will do.

So please consider this as a polite and genuine request to stop the imposition of laws on all the Community. Give us a chance to speak up.

I am a orthodox, *shomer Shabbat* Kartaqi Jew myself and do not want to be excommunicated from this Community because I disagree with your approach. I do not come from a wealthy or recognized family with a name to be able to get myself on the decision making bodies of this Community to make this change so only my voice can bring the change I would like to see.

city ~ January 20th, 2010

Dear Salisbury Steak,

Just the fact that you say there is no argument, proves how closed minded you are. All these posts prove exactly that an argument can be made. And I find it very rude of you to offer temple emmanuel to them. Why don't you let them make their own decisions and stop muddling in other people's lives

kartaqi teenage mom of 3 ~ January 20th, 2010

One of the girls in my clique of friends told me to read the posts on this page. I am finally finished reading every last one and I have to say it's about time!! I was married at the age of 18 to man 13 years older than myself. I did not come from a well do family and for this reason my parents insisted that I marry him due to the fact that he could advance our families standing in the community. I wanted to go study journalism and psychology and instead by the age of 22 I already had two small girls and was basically a child raising a child. Now at the age of 26 I have finally starting going back to school for my dream (though I have to keep it a secret from my husband's family)! As a 26 year old woman I can look back on my life so far and say that I would never forsake my children and say that I don't love them or regret having them but living in a marriage where there is no love and compassion and I am merely treated like a doorstop every morning and night is a nightmare. My husband never once acknowledges all that I have sacrificed for him to live behind a perfect Kartaqi veneer. In a way I am not any different then Issac. Instead I was ridiculed by my own parents who forced me into a marriage that I am miserable in, but this is the answer I get today "You must stay in it for the girls ".

My advice goes out to all girls who feel they have to be pressured into marriage at a young age- particularly Kartaqi in High School. Stick up for yourselves- if you are with someone in high school then wait a few years until you know who you are, if you have aspirations to have a career then go for it and if your boyfriend/spouse can't handle it they are not for you and more importantly too coward a person to see you be more successful than them! We Kartaqi woman are the brightest in the world and have so much untapped potential. Do not let this community stomp on your dreams and talents, they did that to me and now I am regretting it all- all expect my daughters.

common sense ~ January 20th, 2010

Jewish Father....it is democratic, you vote for the board, they make the decisions....stop crying. Did you vote for the health bill being imposed on you, or any other law you follow in this country? You vote for people to represent you, and they make decisions...

Salisbury Steak's view point might not me politically correct, but he's correct in the notion that we are a small community with customs. Eating unkosher is a sin, you don't see someone bringing a cheeseburger to synagogue?!?!

He's also very correct on his interpretation of Rabbi's speech. I truly

don't care what Isaac and his partner do with his life, and i felt the
same way coming out of synagogue that day. Rabbi very clearly said
do not go after them, do not say anything negative towards them. I'm
wondering how many people on this discussion board actually heard
the speech?? And how many of you are just using the Rabbi as a
scape goat for your own agenda's??

abc ~ January 20th, 2010

suck cock Jewish Father and everyone else who agrees with the Gay
ways

Granny ~ January 20th, 2010

my grandchildren call me granny am 78 years old but they show me
computer and internet and i reading everything here. my englishe it is
not so good but i want to write to you all i am from old school kartaqi
and love my community. i born in kartaq and live many years in
kartaq. i dont like what happening in synagogueh on shabbat this
weekend.

now you tell us go to tempele emanuel if we dont like synagogueh
rules. i want to stay happy in kartaqis. i dont know tempele emanuel
and nobody in there. if i dont like it the new kartaqi laws then i must
go there?

response to common sense ~ January 20th, 2010

common sense - I heard the speech as did many of my friends and we
left the synagogue in shock. This forum is not for our own agenda. We
want our voices to be heard and never to let another Kartaqi who
committed no crime to be hurt in such a way and ridiculed behind his
back. It is also what the congregants did after, with one faggot joke
after another. Even people related to Isaac were ridiculed i heard.
You can spin it any way you like, there is a reason for our outrage

enough ~ January 20th, 2010

Can this please stop being a forum for people talking about their problems...no one cares about how unhappy your marriage is. This forum was meant to discuss a different situation

concerned kartaqi mother of 3 young kids ~ January 20th, 2010

to enough - this forum started because of a situation but it seems that there are deep stemming problems that no one addresses. if they are not addressed then we will continue to use this forum as our outlet. The episode with isaac has brought up much of what many of us have bottled up and what the central board successfully got away with. i would like to hear everyones personal story here whether it is related to isaac or not so we can make our community one where everyone is respected and can live peacefully. so everyone, use this forum as a place to pour your heart out but remain kind and civil. we have all waited too long for this type of forum. thank you Isaac

Disgruntled Kartaqi ~ January 20th, 2010

To all you suggesting disappointed Kartaqis leave, I have this to say: I AM NOT LEAVING. We live in a democratic society; and while not entirely, we try to maintain a democratic system within our community (needs work). Up until now, our central board elections have done little to educate us on the candidates beliefs and intents. We've been voting for the wrong reasons (wealth, popularity, friends, family).

Judging by the outpour of feedback on this board, I think it's safe to say we've reached the tipping point. Come time for the next elections, things will certainly change. There will be more transparency with the candidates. And there will certainly have to be a form of checks and balances set in place (this discussion board unfortunately, is the only platform we have to go against the leaders).

My thoughts on how the community should be are clearly more

159

liberal than yours. But it is only through a healthy, honest, and fair hierarchy system (if you guys in the CB are reading, remember you were elected to serve us) can we reach a happy and healthy medium the majority of us agree on (there will always be the few on the far left/right).

And when this change happens (notice i'm not saying 'if'). I will not request that you leave our community because you are upset about something. The ruling party will listen to you (rather than ignore which they've so effectively done so), and try to work with you.

Extremism, in any direction is bad.

concerned citizen ~ January 20th, 2010

Why are all the posts that come from the anti-liberal side so defensive and out of line? ABC please do not use such vulgar language to get your point across . Salisbury Steak- how would you feel if I told you to relocate to a new synagogue? Running away is not the answer. I propose that the central board along with our community rabbi hold an open mic night with a Q & A session to let these important topics be addressed. Please don't send out another drawn out signed document telling us that we now cannot allow same sex couples into our homes. This community cannot be run by tyrants anymore- it needs to stop for the sake of the future of our community.

kartaqi teenage mom of 3 ~ January 20th, 2010

To enough- How dare you suggest that no one cares about my unhappy marriage! Maybe you don't care! But I CARE! My voice will be heard for everyone woman who is miserable in her marriage and can't speak up for herself. You are probably a disgruntled person who doesn't want to accept the fact that there are real issues that need to be addressed here. This is now a platform for all voices to be heard in a peaceful way. Thank you.

enough ~ January 20th, 2010

concerned citizen - If you are going to a modern orthodox synagogue then you should understand they have to have modern orthodox rules. The fact that the parking lot is open on shabbat is enough leniency. No one is telling you to run away, but if you do not accept the religiosity of your synagogue then maybe you should go to a reform or conservative sanctuary. Our synagogues are modern orthodox and will never change.

concerned citizen ~ January 20th, 2010

enough- I am not asking people to change or stop living as religious pious jews- there is nothing wrong with voicing your opinion I think you are just scared that the truth is starting to leak out and that people have a voice. It is cowardly to tell us to leave a beloved community. The higher ups in the community cannot dictate life- end of story and hide behind people's desperate plea to be heard. Brushing problems under the carpet is not going to get us out of this predicament...listening to peoples real plea for help is a start.

p.s. ~ January 20th, 2010

Concerned Citizen-- Because they are dictators, don't you know by now what kind of language or tone of voice dictators use to get their point across?

My head was exploding. New entries were coming in at such a rapid pace. I knew that like any community, we had our own share of issues. And being so tight-knit, those issues often cannot be comfortably discussed publicly, which just makes it easier for them to multiply. However, having kept a relative distance from the community for many years, this whole experience of the Discussion Board was such an eye-opener for me.

Discussion Board

fat kid loves cake ~ January 20th, 2010

Forget homosexuality, the biggest problem our community needs to address is ANOREXIA!!!! why is every girl pressured to be 90 lbs or else they wont get married. What about the fat girls? Don't they too deserve a chance at love no matter their size?

Here is an idea, why dont we try to be completely different and adapt to some of the ways of African Americans- the bigger the ass the better!

Kartaqi Girl ~ January 20th, 2010

Why is our community beginning to sound more like Muslim fundamentalists than Jews?

concerned citizen ~ January 20th, 2010

finally some jokes- alleviate the tension a bit! anorexia is another huge problem-- needs to be addressed.

impossible ~ January 20th, 2010

I took a look at this board a day or two ago...can't believe how its blown up since then.

Anyway, I thought I'd throw my 2 cents in. I don't think that there is any way to handle this situation and make all sides happy, it is Impossible. Gay rights are an extremely controversial issue similar to abortion, not just in the Kartaqi Community but also in this "free" Country. I understand the Central Boards and Rabbi's concerns and fully respect them but I also understand the concern of the opposite side.

HOWEVER being treated inhumanly and not welcoming someone to a synagogue to pay respects to a family member who has passed is wrong on many levels, spreading hate and telling people (sometimes even threatening) not to associate with someone outside the norm also crosses a line.

WTF ~ January 20th, 2010

this forum is a joke thank you Dr Namdar for making the community a joke, I'm sure now we'll accept you and your "husband." Unbelievable.

Kartaqi Mom ~ January 20th, 2010

It seems like our rabbi has more in common with Muslim mullahs than they do with Jewish people. These extremist views should not be tolerated. Judaism is the most beautiful religion that preaches compassion and understanding. Some tyrannical, backwards leaders in our community are distilling these values, and turning us into nothing more than the very Muslim fundamentalists we ran away from in Kartaq. These leaders remind me more of Ahmadinejad than any Jew I know. Considering we ourselves were persecuted, we should learn not to persecute others. There is so much prejudice against Jews, we should learn not be prejudiced against others. What kind of values are our rabbi and leaders teaching our children? To be close-minded, talk bad about an innocent person in front of everyone in synagogue and in front of G-d, and talk *lashon hara* in synagogue? Shame on you rabbi. This is not the Jewish way. Jewish people are much better than that. That is why we are the chosen people. Why are we being forced to adopt views that are identical to Fundamentalist Islam?

kartaqi teenage mom of 3 ~ January 20th, 2010

agreed kartaqi mom! best post to date. i back you too.

It became evident to me that the Discussion Board was fulfilling a much needed niche within the community, one that actually did not have much to do with my circumstances. People were using my site to air out laundry and express frustration, and they felt comfortable doing it on my site since to them I represented the new face of the opposition.

I didn't know much about moderating a discussion, but judging by the last few entries, I could see that not everyone knew how to express themselves eloquently and respectfully. I needed to lay down some ground rules for respectful discussion. Any type of content denigrating one group to make your point, as seen in the examples of people comparing the leadership to Muslim fundamentals, could not be accepted. I inserted the entry below to maintain civility in the discussion.

Discussion Board

ISAAC NAMDAR~ January 20th, 2010

A NOTE FROM YOUR WEBHOST:

I AM WRITING IN ALL CAPS NOT BECAUSE I AM YELLING, I JUST WANTED THIS ENTRY TO STAND OUT AS YOUR WEBHOST. PLEASE, NO ALL CAPS IN THE FUTURE.

Although the Discussion Board was initially started for a different reason, I respect that many people have used it as a medium for exchanging opinions. Freedom of speech is what this great country was founded on.

However, I have noted some profanity and derogatory language in some of the entries. As the host of this site, I will not tolerate any language that is less than respectful. I have made a point of not getting involved or censoring anybody's opinions, but profanity and belittling will not be welcome here. Please feel free to express your opinions, as long as you keep it respectful (and this respect includes people of other religions, people of other synagogues, people of any beliefs that may be different than yours).

Jerome ~ January 20th, 2010

I have thought about this discussion board for the last 24 hours or so (ever since it was brought to my attention) and how to respond to it.

I am completely inspired by Andrew and Isaac's bold move, and by many of the subsequent postings, as I feel that the moderate voices in this community have been squelched by religious diktats coming from a place of fear. And trust me, that is not a very pretty place. In fact, it is a very dark place to be, and not a place that can co-exist with the beauty of our religion and my father's rich heritage.

I am downright outraged by the disrespectful tone taken by some of our community members (see abc for instance), and I find it hard to believe that our rabbi would endorse such behavior.

I missed the rabbi's speech this past weekend, only because I have decided long ago that I don't feel spiritually at home in this synagogue, even though my family, whom I love more than life, is very actively involved.

When I do attend, I do so out of respect for them, but there have been instances when I was very disillusioned and uninspired by some of the things the rabbi said, or downright offended by the silly comments I got from random community members.

Synagogue should be a place for us to celebrate our similarities and our culture, rather than a haven for people that enjoy pointing out our differences and thereby triggering some sort of witch-hunt. That is surely not what G-d has in mind.

I know that homosexuality is a heated topic in orthodox circles (see the recent controversy over a panel at Yeshiva University). But everyone who is filled with such hate should know that being gay is not a choice — how could it be? It is so much easier to be straight, particularly in a community so driven by marriage and procreation.

I'd like to stress that the importance of unity in our community. In relative terms, it is a very small community, but even so, there are sure to be differences among us. I hope that my generation and future ones will realize that without acceptance, understanding and kindness, the community as a whole will get smaller and smaller and more radical, until there is nothing left to fight for.

Kartaqi Guy ~ January 20th, 2010

I'm an observant, semi-religious guy in my twenties. To me, what Rabbi Levy did was much worse than what Isaac Namdar did. What Rabbi Levy did was incite hatred against another Jew. Isaac never incited anyone to hate another person.

Is it so bad to post pictures of you and your loved one on a web-site? (If you don't like it, don't look at the web-site). Or is it worse to embarrass someone, and talk about them behind their back in front of a whole synagogue? That goes against everything that is Jewish.

I wonder how G-d will judge both of these people. Someone as harmless as Isaac Namdar, who is a doctor and helps people every day and whose only crime is to love another person. Or someone like Rabbi Levy who talks *lashon hara* behind someone's back, and makes a whole synagogue mock and ridicule a person? Ultimately, G-d will judge.

It is so sad, because Rabbi Levy is such a nice person when you talk to him in person. Maybe it is our dictator-like leaders on the Central Board who are forcing him to do this. And out of fear of losing his very high-paying lucrative job, he has to do what they say. But this is no excuse. Ultimately, he cannot talk bad about another Jew, who is so harmless.

I feel like our community is losing our Jewish values, by becoming more extremist and more backwards.

Young guy ~ January 20th, 2010

Everybody, stop worrying about gay people. With all the difficulties that are going on in the world right now, the rabbi has nothing better to do than talk about than homosexuality?

There are so many more problematic things going on in the world. Who cares if someone is gay? This isn't Kartaq. Are the leaders in our community worried that people are gonna see someone that is out and gay, and decide to become gay too? Don't worry, nobody is going to turn gay. No straight person will turn gay, just like no gay person will turn straight. If they could, don't you think gay people would turn straight and avoid all the problems, harassment and difficulties they have to endure.

Trust me, no matter how much I'm exposed to gay people, it won't make me gay. I always liked girls, hot girls. Being exposed to a million gay people won't turn me gay. I LOVE HOT GIRLS. Stop worrying, you old-fashioned people. Gays are harmless. And they are actually very nice people. Let them lead their lives in peace, with who they love. It's none of our business.

Why should that offend any of us? Grow up people. And rabbi, please start talking about more relevant problems in synagogue. Gays are not a problem.

Ron Namdar ~ January 20th, 2010

I know Issacs family ever since i was a child and i am very fond of them. I know and remember that he was raised in a family full of love and peace. Maybe thats the reason he became such an honest and decent human being. I know that for many years Issac used to leave his great apartment in the city and spend shabbat with his father in Green Hills, accompany him to the relatives homes on friday nights , then taking his dad to the synagogue on saturday , and then spending the whole day with him. He was by his dads side all the time he supported him and still does in everyway, took him out on every occasion , until his father decided to move to israel. When i had the privilege of spending time with the DR. at family events... i remember thinking this is one of the smartest selfless , polite humans i even known. As you can see on this board there is not a single negative word about this great man. I only hear and read and remember good things he has done and all the charities Issac and Andrew are involved in. So I for one would never disassociate myself from this couple , i would actually celebrate them. No matter who decides what about them .

Irony ~ January 20th, 2010

Kartaqi Guy, G-d will judge you for saying that about our rabbi, too.

ISAAC ~ January 20th, 2010

REMINDER: Please choose your words carefully and eloquently. Maintain respect even for those whom you don't agree with. This respect should definitely be extended to our Rabbi, the Central Board, and all community servants, even if you don't agree with them.

Despite my previous instructions and pleas, there was one profanity-laden entry that got posted by an anonymous person, clearly intended to shock and evoke disgust. My initial reaction was to go the administrator's page and delete that entry altogether. This permanently erased all records of the entry ever being posted. Although I still believe that I had to do something to maintain the integrity of the Discussion Board, I regret acting instinctively and erasing the entry in such a way that it seemed it never existed.

I later learned how to selectively "beep out" profanity by only replacing any curse words with a placeholder like "[profanity]", yet save the remainder of the entry on the server for review and documentation. This allowed for much more transparent moderating of the discussion.

Facebook Message

From: Isaac

To: Ron

Date: January 20 at 2:00pm

Thanks for the very very sweet post.

Email

From: Janice

To: Isaac

Date: 1/20/2010 3:02:43 P.M.

Subject: Scrolls

Dear Dr. Namdar,

My name is Janice and I am an associate editor of the Kartaqi community's quarterly magazine, Scrolls, with which you may be familiar. As you are aware, recent events in your personal life have become a subject of public debate and have spurred a wide spectrum of opinions, including some that have never before been voiced. I am wondering if you would like to contribute your voice, as a community member who has broken the mold, in the form of a letter to the community or an article for Scrolls (the next issue should be going to print in about one month). It is my duty to objectively provide people with the diverse opinions of the community, both liberal and conservative. I hope you are willing to share your experience and thoughts. If you are interested, please let me know. Thank you.

Sincerely,

Janice

Email

From: Isaac

To: Janice

Date: 1/20/2010 3:12:17 P.M.

Subject: Re: Scrolls

Thank you so much for contacting me. That is very thoughtful of you to want to include comments about this topic in your upcoming issue.

As I am contemplating my response to your request, I have a couple of points to make. Firstly, as you know, I have been banished from the community by the Central Board and our Rabbi. I am sure giving me a voice in a publication sponsored by the CB would be a direct contradiction of that edict.

But even prior to my banishment, I had voluntarily and willingly withdrawn myself from the community due for my respect for the norms of the our society. If I submit an article, many may perceive me as a 'troublemaker' that just won't go away.

Please take a moment to go through the above considerations before we agree on my response to your request. Please notify me when you have discussed this with the editorial board.

Respectfully, Isaac Namdar

Email

From: Jerome

To: Isaac

Date: 1/20/2010 3:16:25 P.M.

Subject: Re: Hi!

Thank you so much for getting back to me, and for your kind words of support. It's definitely hard, and even harder for me because sister and her husband are ultra-orthodox, and also very involved in the community. He is, in fact, on the central board. I don't know how they would react but I fear the worst.

My partner and I would definitely like to meet you and Andrew in person. You have my email, and my cell is 456-555-1212.

I actually posted something on the site earlier, using my real name. I am quite shocked at some of the commentary on the discussion board, but at the same time, surprised by the warmth and support of so many others. It's nice to know that there are people out there who care about our struggles, and who, ultimately, wish us all happiness regardless of rules and religion.

Meanwhile, on a totally different note, my partner and I are looking for a synagogue that we can feel comfortable in the city. He grew up reform, and you pretty much know my background. Do you at all belong somewhere?

I much appreciate your time and hope to meet you soon.

Discussion Board

Cable Car ~ January 20th, 2010

Dear Fellow Kartaqis - Thank you for expressing yourself. I followed this board ever since my sister mentioned it to me yesterday.

I have read every post and am shocked that it took so long to have a board like this for our opinions.

You see, our Community does not allow us to express ourselves if our views differ. It had come to this point and this board clearly shows it.

I remember growing up and whenever I said anything critical then my parents would say "keep quiet".

I thought very hard if I should post and what I should post. How can I post when there is so much I have wanted to post over the years and I had to keep it all inside. But I want to post one thing that really bothers me inside.

I am a Kartaqi young man who recently got married. Did I want to get married? Not really, but it was easy thing to do because all my friends were doing it. I come from a family with good reputation so I got married to a nice girl from the community. She did not show her true colors until we got married. She pretended when we dated that she is a modern women and wants to have different things in her life than her friends.

The minute we got married she turned the tables and I did not recognize the woman I loved so much and married. She wanted everything her friends wanted, shoes, bags, house, vacations, miami, jewlery etc. For example if her friend got a new bag from her husband she would come home and yell at me and why did I not buy one for her and that I don't love her. If another friend bought a house she also wanted to have the same size house. If her friends went to a vacation in Miami, she got angry if I said I like to go to Israel instead.

I often sit on the train and look at other woman and wonder if they would be nicer to live with than my wife. I know my non-Kartaqi wives of my friends who have much more respect and understanding for their husbands.

I cannot tell my wife how I truly feel because she would get her parents involved and I dont want to be on the bad side of her parents. The reason I feel I can write this and remain anonymous is that a few of my guy friends are in the same situation and probably many more guys in the Community are.

I am not happy so I try to stay away from my wife and my home as much as I can. I am scared to have kids with her too.

Divorce would make my parents disown me so I cannot do that. I am not a brave guy that way and I dont now if I can hurt my parents feelings by leaving my wife. It is scary for me to feel this way as a newly-wed.

Isaac I admire you that you are so brave to live your own life. I wish we can all be brave and do what makes us happy.

Thank you that you are all sharing stories of your life on this board. It helps us know we are not the only ones that suffer quietly.

Mathematics ~ January 20th, 2010

Wow: 1600 plus hits to this discussion so far in 24 hours. That is a big percentage of the Kartaqi population. Isaac, what a wonderful service you have done for all of us, young and old who needed this discussion board.

Let's spread the word so all our Kartaqi friends young and old know we are here

yentah ~ January 20th, 2010

Does anyone know if the Rabbi or the CB has seen what is going on here? Do you think they will post their reaction here?

RESPONSE FROM ISAAC:

The Rabbi and the Central Board have their own websites, and I respect their wishes if they refrain from this board, or wish to post their response on their own sites, or not respond at all. However, should they want to use this forum, I will extend them the courtesy and post their response on their own dedicated page so it does not get lost in a sea of other comments. My email is Namdar@aol.com.

Young mom ~ January 20th, 2010

I'm a young, Kartaqi woman and I think the rabbi and the community shouldn't be speaking bad about gay people when there are so many real problems in the world right now. Gay people have done nothing wrong. Speaking bad about gays is a very un-Jewish thing to do because Jews are supposed to be some of the most compassionate and accepting people in the world.

Look at what the Israelis are doing in Haiti. I saw reports on CNN and Fox News that showed that Israel was the first and only ones there providing medical care, and helping the Haitians.

Being Jews, we should have compassion...for gay, straight, and all kinds of people. We should not act like the dictators from Zameen. We should act like Israel.

I cried when I saw the video of the Israelis helping the Haitians. It's all over Facebook, if you want to take a look. Let's remember that, as Jews, we are a kind, compassionate people. We should be kind to gay and straight alike.

nik ~ January 20th, 2010

First of all Congratulations and Mazal tov! Girl, that took balls! Very proud of you. I work for a group Kartaqis, and my guys are very cool, and we looove the woman, they're just too fabulous! (and how cute are the boys???- hold me hostage!) take no bull from any of them, most of them are a bunch of self righteous, hypocritical, backwards (and they prob take it in the back!). stick to jockeying camels and leave good people alone!

XOXO nik

26marriedguy ~ January 20th, 2010

With all due respect to Dr. Namdar, I'd like to state my opinion on this matter.

I believe that homosexual attraction, as Jerome said, is not a choice; but what is a choice is acting on your attraction. Although I believe homosexual actions are wrong (much like eating unkosher or adultery), it is within your right to live your life the you want. However, when you are part of a community that has sustained itself for generations through its values and customs, and you make a PUBLIC decision/statement (i.e. gay marriage, eating a cheeseburger in synagogue, walking hand-in-hand with your mistress in synagogue) that goes against this value system, you are not only endorsing your actions, but encouraging them as well. Obviously I don't speak for all Kartaqis on this issue, but I was at Rabbi Levy's speech last week and I couldn't agree with him more. Our Kartaqi Jewish community is on a path, set long ago, made of certain traditions/customs/values. If you want to stray from this path, it is in your right within the privacy of your own home. If you want to stray PUBLICLY from this path, please do not be a part of this community. I commend all those people who have certain urges/attractions that go against our Torah, and are disciplined enough not to act on them.

I'm sorry if I offended you Isaac. I wish you and your husband all the best.

RESPONSE FROM ISAAC:

I am fully aware of the traditions of our community. I decided to take my life and lifestyle elsewhere when it was obvious this would contradict the community's values. I did not make a display for the community, and nobody from the community was invited. The posted pictures were for American friends only. The clash happened only when another member of the community, un-invited to the website, got in and disseminated the information. Analogy to the cheeseburger story: as long as anyone decides to eat a cheeseburger in the privacy of their home - nobody's business; but if they bring the cheeseburger to synagogue, then it becomes public display. My marriage was kept far away from the community, and I never demanded any attention for it. The only PUBLIC part of this ordeal is when the community decided to make it public and dedicate an entire Saturday sermon to it.

I now know that making analogies in a debate is completely wrong. The minute you make an analogy, you are debating the merits of your analogy, not your original topic. Andrew and I keep a completely kosher home, and would never even think of eating a cheeseburger. It was wrong of me to put myself with the same group of people who deliberately and intentionally eating non-kosher foods. Being gay is neither intentional nor deliberate.

Discussion Board

Plain Task ~ January 20th, 2010

People, everyone has problems, im sorry nothing is perfect. But you shouldn't come on this meaningless discussion board and start airing your dirty laundry for everyone to know. Have some respect for yourselves. This board is disgusting.

Also, lets start another board so that The MAJORITY of this community can get their voices heard without Isaac going trough and deleting the comments he deems as "disrespectful"

anonymous ~ January 20th, 2010

I'm glad your parents risked their lives and persecution to move to America for you to open up about your homosexuality. You are getting the attention you have been craving all your life. I hope I die before you just so I have front row seats when g-d judges you.

anonymous ~ January 20th, 2010

do everyone a favor and move to Haiti.. Go help the ones that will appreciate you more than anyone here..

shamed kartaqi/proud jew ~ January 20th, 2010

I am going to express what it think the route problem is, as well as being open minded by criticizing both sides of the argument, but bear with me since this is going to be kind of long.

The biggest problem of our community is that we lost our identity, being Kartaqi is not what it used to mean, especially going back centuries to see that we were built on the opposite values/standards of life we have today. For the women who post that they are unhappy in their "forced" marriages and preach "be happy at all costs, even if being gay makes you happy, so power to you"! Every community has gays, and Rabbi Levy was right to say society desensitizes people, but the problem is that all the leadership the CB appoints (cough*controls*cough) is basically going to be politically correct and approach this the way the CB decides, which is to blame society, which is only a small part of the big picture. But nobody has the balls to blame the real issue, and that issue is the parenting. In a few years when more Kartaqi homes get foreclosed and people close down their businesses because these same parents spoiled their kids to the point where their kids are not equipped to survive in the real world on their own, and they cannot maintain this competitive material lifestyle, something worse will happen: we will have more criminals, mischief's, gays, drug addicts, atheists, assimilations, etc than ever.

Another extreme is the overexposure that every Kartaqi feels like they are followed by a paparazzi when they want to just go buy food, yet most of them love it and live for the attention and drama, so they are hypocrites (yes I'm talking to you too, self-righteous Yentah reader!). We are overexposed to each other, hence the low marriage rate. Facebook, making 500 lavish engagement parties and after-parties, and clubbing together just makes it worse. People know too much about the materialistic outer shell of their Kartaqi "friend" and label them as such, yet barely know this "friend" deeply by treating them with true care. I say "friend" in parentheses because hanging out, competing, slandering, and jealousy within EVERY "clique" doesn't constitute friendship. If you want to see real friendship, then go talk to soldiers in the Israeli army who risk their lives for their fellow soldiers and people.

My personal belief is that Homosexuality should not be shoved down people's throats, but neither should heterosexuality. That is why our sages command us to keep laws of 'Nida' (separation), not just at home, but even outside we should not take part in public displays of affection with our significant other. This is a private thing, and all that can come out of that is jealousy from people who don't have that. I respect the liberal position to speak their minds; however I am upset that these same liberal people are bringing up how people speak "Lashon Hara", and claim everyone is a hypocrite for breaking the torah in other ways i.e. driving on Shabbat, keeping kosher etc. (which are all valid points, by the way). But Judaism isn't an all or nothing religion and we cant start nitpicking who keeps what and who doesn't, because we should all start changing from within before trying to change others. That being said, if a homosexual is using the torah to support his argument then color me confused.

Now to my last and MOST IMPORTANT point: the biggest problem facing our community is the rampant "Lashon Hara" being spread. This very thing, along with "Sin'at Chinam/Hatred of Fellow Jews", destroyed our temple (Beit Hamikdash) and put us in exile. And now history is repeating itself.

"Lashon Hara" is responsible for the lack of values and downward spiral the community has taken, but what upsets me is that the closet gays and liberals are the same people who love the juicy gossip, love spreading "Lashon Hara" and ruining people's (even their own "friends") reputations and lives. A lot of these people that are complaining have many reasons to be upset that they cannot be open, however its not because of fear of tarnishing their reputation, in fact most inner circles already suspect or know who's gay, but its these same gays and/or liberals who hide behind a computer screen and bash the community for its negative traits while they are too cowardly to speak out in person, are the same ones who should be held responsible for bringing down the once positive spiritual energy of our community. Their real fear is that they will lose their social status and cliques a.k.a. avenues for gossip and slander. There is no other fear besides that, because having a traditional family with kids is not the priority for them anyways: Which brings me to these women who complain about their forced marriages by parents.

No matter how much pressure your parents put on you, you still made the decision to marry young for riches and status and it's in your hands to decide to leave, and if you have kids you are responsible to do what's best for the family. Give your husbands an ultimatum to change or you will leave them, but you must also change, especially with your demand for money and material and also if you flirt/sleep with other men. Its easy to blame parents for everything , and in this case its warranted, but you ultimately made the decision to get married and finally a few years later you realized you are living a life devoid of meaning and happiness (maybe your husband wasn't as rich and popular as intended by your premeditation), you choose to blame others. Yes they were wrong and have a backwards way of thinking, but people you must "make the bed you sleep in".

At least this Namdar guy moved away and had the balls to make his own decisions. I do not condone those decisions, but they are not mine to make, and if the community has bylaws that's normal and should be respected (but you still have free speech), a line should be drawn somewhere because eventually this will lead to other things such as marrying Christians and forcing us to accept them as community members. The institution of marriage is of holy matrimony intended for having children, whether or not you believe in G-d, I cant remember the last time a baby came out of a guy, clearly getting married is unnecessary, its just a way to rub it in. but again, its his right because the country allows it and nobody should slam him. He may have put up this site but it's his property and he did not intend to get ratted on by some gossiper who did not think before he acted so "zealously" (but he is a Jew and we must forgive him and not slander him as well).

For the record I think the community has more pros than cons, but we've lost our way. And to prove this isn't a one sided opinion, I mostly blame the parents and older generation that paved the superficial way for us. Even the right wingers are to blame. You send your kids to public schools, mock spirituality, teach competitiveness, spoil your kids, name them 'Tristan' or 'Mason', and then one day that child wants to marry a goy you freak out thinking "what will my Clique say?!" and try to convince this child that marrying Jewish is important. Umm, at what point did you make Judaism important to this child? Judaism has nothing to do with going to Synagogue to socialize. Most people are breaking not some but ALL 10 commandments. Speaking any form of *lashon hara* is the biggest form of jealousy and the worst sin since our sages teach us that "Derech Eretz Kadma Le'Torah/Proper Behavior Must Come Before Torah" and the fact that jealousy is one of the 10 commandments (along with KEEPING SHABBAT), that suggests the level of importance it has (more so than keeping Kosher, going to Synagogue and putting on Tefillin, since they are not on that list of 10). These ritualistic and symbolic things we do, known as *mitzvoth* (good deeds) are mainly done as reminders that a form of action must follow beliefs and values. So in my opinion learn-it-up should be every night and the only thing learned should be "Shmirat HaLashon/Guarding Your Tongue" by the Chafetz Chaim, until it's ingrained in the ENTIRE communities heads! I know none of you have the balls to ask for forgiveness to those you have slandered, because in many cases it has spread to far and deep. But you will answer to the Judge of this world one day, so at least start by making this change and sticking to it, while teaching your children the same, and having the courage to stop others from gossiping when you see it, since it is an equal sin to hear it.

To finish my point: Everyone gives their sons "Brit Milah" (circumcision), the *mitzvah* (good deed, commandment) symbolizing the importance of keeping the sexual organ pure from sin. Yet the words in literal Hebrew mean "covenant of words/speech" and it is the 1st thing we implement on a newborn, implying that all sin of impurity starts and ends with self control of desires, and the main 2 parts of our bodies we sin with are the mouth and sexual organ. This is a kabalistic concept that will take hours to delve into, but Google it if you want. The point is that EVERYONE needs to look themselves in the mirror and not wait for the CB to clean up the mess of our predecessors, but the changes must come from each person. Kartaqi is just a temporary title, when you all figure out that we are Jews first and identify yourselves as such, maybe then you can start criticizing others. But for now, the only thing to do is dropping everything and committing ourselves to AVOIDING "LASHON HARA" AT ALL COSTS!!!

Kebab House ~ January 20th, 2010

Plain Task: We hear the voices of the MAJORITY of the Community in email blasts, magazines, more magazines, more newsletters, more letters, on shabbat, in fact 24/7.

Isaac has not deleted comments but if you use profane language as some of the posts indicate you receive a warning so we can maintain this board civil.

The MAJORITY of the community doesnt give us the board to share our views and stories we have held in for so long.

We will support this board regardless of what the MAJORITY threatens to do. Insult us, threaten us but you cannot make us go away.

Isaac is generous enough with his time to manage it so the board is civil and support it through what originally was his own private site. So thank you to Isaac.

Disgruntled Dad ~ January 20th, 2010

For those of you that say the Torah says homosexuality is an abomination, well, the Torah also allows for stoning and slavery. Do you also believe in stoning people or slavery?

The Torah was written thousands of years ago. You have to adapt it to current day. Not live in the past, like radical Islamists. You can't take it too literally. If you do take it literally, you should also believe in stoning and slavery.

You should just understand the general message of the Torah: to treat your family and others with respect and love, and to be a good person and a good Jew. This means, not being prejudiced against other people. You should have already learned this since us Jews have been the victim of prejudice ourselves.

Kebab House ~ January 20th, 2010

Anonymous: That is a horrible comment. You say you want to die before Isaac so you have front row seats when G-D judges Isaac. The rifts in this Community are far worse than I thought. Words like yours will finally break this Community down. You owe your fellow Kartaqis and especially Isaac an apology. Keep this board civil please.

Isaac ~ January 20th, 2010

Just take down this board and forget everyones stupidity. All this is doing is tainting the first few months of your union. While I may not agree with your lifestyle choice, I believe everyone deserves happiness. Reading the slanderous drivel that most of our Kartaqi "brothers and sisters", have been throwing your way, I commend your fortitude doc. But I still think you should take this site down and live your life unencumbered by these people and their opinions. G-d bless you, and the best of luck to you.

Isaac ~ January 20th, 2010

and I'm another Isaac, not Isaac Namdar in case that wasnt obvious.

Harold ~ January 20th, 2010

Bottom line is this community has a body of rules and guidelines which must be maintained or slowly but surely there will be complete chaos. You wanna be gay and get married....great congratulations....there are plenty of reform synagogues that will accept that behavior. What's next tattoos and piercings to be justified also??? You made a decision now stick to it even though there are consequences. Live your lives fruitfully and joyously. Our synagogue is an orthodox synagogue...with orthodox rules. You can't have your cake and eat it to my friend.

mazal tov,

L'chaiim

Kebab House ~ January 20th, 2010

Another Isaac: you cant demand Isaac to take down this board. There are so many Kartaqi people that have logged on the board. Accept criticism, the Community is not perfect and there is finally a place to say whats on everyone mind here. And do not try to bring down the board by getting a computer hacker, which I am sure is being discussed by those that have posted profanity and insults. This is a civil board. Keep it civil

realist ~ January 20th, 2010

Hi Everyone,

I have to agree with 26marriedguy. The community has an obligation to protect the Jewish Religion. It is against the Torah to do certain things, for example committing adultery, eating non-kosher and gay marriage. We must preserve the values of the Torah as we are an orthodox community. Yes, many members of our community eat non-kosher, and cheat on their wives. But nobody would dare bring a cheeseburger into the synagogue or bring their mistress to services.

182

What you do on your own time is up to you, but when you publicly go against the Jewish Religion than there is a problem.

Many of you are saying times have changed and people have changed. People who want to change the religion can go to a reformed temple. The reasons why Jews still exist today are because of the people who have preserved the Jewish traditions. And for everyone who says we have to adopt the American way, are wrong. Look at history, anytime we have adopted the cultures around us and got too comfortable, we have been exiled or faced persecution.

TO ISAAC:

After reading a few of the posts on this board I can see that you are definitely a respectable and commendable person. I have no doubts that you are a good person. Unfortunately, you went against something our Religion stands for and our community has to protect our religion. I can see you tried not to involve the community and I commend you on that. But please understand why our community has taken certain action. We have to make sure our community knows right from wrong according to what we believe in, The Torah. We definitely could have handled it differently to avoid so much *Lashon Hara*, and we need to own up to that as well.

isaac ~ January 20th, 2010

Kebab House, did you see a demand on my part? I saw a suggestion to Isaac. Not to you.

And maybe you could visit Dr. Namdar for that little paranoia issue you have going. Happiness in a pill or something....

please discuss ~ January 20th, 2010

i'd like to pose a serious question. all joking aside, if in 10 years, a kartaqi person decides to marry his/her dog, should we embrace this person and "adapt to the times" regardless of our values, or should we ask said person to disassociate from the community and privately live their life however they want?

i am not trying to equate homosexuality with bestiality, but i can't rule out its possibility...

thoughts?

Beau Bridges ~ January 20th, 2010

Anonymous, Harold, and realist, great comments, I couldnt have said it better myself.

Donut ~ January 20th, 2010

Realist: I just found out about this board and read every entry. How many times does Dr. Namdar have to say that he did not come to the public. Read for yourself that he stated it many times.

Someone in the Community got into his website and spread the rumors. In the same way someone would invade a home to see if a Kartaqi was eating a cheeseburger or lying in bed with his mistress.

yo ~ January 20th, 2010

yo donut, Marriage is in itself a public statement!! none of this wouldve happened if Isaac decided to have a gay relationship behind closed doors

Really??? So many marriages happened that same day in July. Those marriages, some of them also between same-sex partners just like ours, were just as public as my marriage. Yet the Kartaqis decided to make a public debate and analyze only my marriage to the fullest, simply because of our ancestral link. The controversy and the ensuing chaos occurred not because I made my marriage 'public' to the Kartaqis, but because they shared between themselves a piece of information which they were not yet ready to handle. Besides, why should I have to live my life behind closed doors more than any other person? Why should I go out of my way to isolate myself, while others can share their love without any fear?

David ~ January 20th, 2010

Hello............... I want to let you all know that this blog is probably one of the most amazing things I have ever read. I got a brief background of what went down to get this started and let me just say mitche (isaac) you're a freaken genius. You went for something you believe in whether ppl like it or not and look at what is coming about.

You are making people realize that life is about chances and risks and this is absolutely perfect in every way shape and form. Anyone who bashes or has anything bad to say about these 2 ppl are retarded and need to get a reality check.

They caught the whole community in something that they thought was wrong and made this into something that much larger.

Well done!!!!!!!

Me, Myself and I ~ January 20th, 2010

shamed kartaqi/proud jew: I dont know who you are, but you're the only person on this board that expressed yourself true to what you believe, respectfully and tastefully.

It's easy to use others as a scapegoat for your personal problems (which most people on this board are doing) it takes much more to look at oneself and acknowledge that each of you (myself included) have contributed to most if not all the problems in our community that we are speaking against here on this board. You demand change, start by changing yourselves.

I would love to see if this week in synagogue we were to hold a platform for everyone to voice their opinions and you had to stand up and publicly say a lot of what you all posted here, would you? And yes even if it meant being ridiculed or embarrassed or spoken about behind your back for being "different" just how you compare it to the people in Zameen who would be murdered if they showed their face, but still you so strongly believe in CHANGE, would you publicly stand

185

up and join others who thought like you or differently from you?

realist ~ January 20th, 2010

to Donut. If you read my whole post you would see how I commended him on keeping himself distant from the community and not going public. I was simply trying to state my opinion on why it should not be tolerated in our community.

Again this is nothing against Isaac as he did not come to the public. Sorry if I was unclear.

Jessica ~ January 20th, 2010

David i could not agree with you more. They basically took a community that bashed them and turned it around and made it into the community's issues.

I think Green Hills has the problem not you guys.

kartaqi dad ~ January 20th, 2010

this is in response to Kartaqi Guy and kartaqi mom ~ January 20th, 2010..... how DARE u Belittle the rabbi of our community, they only speak the truth... if your want to be gay then by all means do it, but behind closed doors... all of your who spoke "lashon hara" about our rabbi should be ashamed of yourselves

hopeful ~ January 20th, 2010

This is my first visit to the site and I surely haven't gone through all the comments. From what I've seen thus far, I feel compelled to ask, even URGE the people posting to ask themselves: what constructive value will my criticisms have on this board. Of course you're defending the religion, who wouldn't? But are Isaac and Andrew going to change their minds, after coming this far for something they believe in? Sacrificing this much? Imagine it was your child. Hurling non-constructive critiques at your children will do nothing but agitate them, turn them off from your stance, and make you look like an ineffective zealot. Put your passion about this situation into something effective- talk to you kids, tell them the importance of Jewish values, strengthen those practices you CAN strengthen: do not condone *lashon hara*, imbue them with the moral standards of our culture and our religion but also practice them before your children's eyes, set examples, and set them on the path that we believe is the Jewish way. Isaac and Andrew may not be living according to the moral standards of our community or our religion as we know them on this specific element, but they're still deserving of our respect as humans. Who are we to put them on the slaughtering block; do we ostracize every member of our community that commits adultery (no matter how you define that), steals, lies to a court, or humiliates their fellow in public? We have to put things in perspective, and work on ourselves rather than putting our efforts toward changing one or two individuals. It's much easier to critique others; will we use this as a wake up call to turn and look into ourselves?

RICHARD SIMMONS ~ January 20th, 2010

ALL OF YOU TAKE YOUR LIBERAL....

[Note from ISAAC: As much as I never thought I would have to do this, the profanity in this comment was so vulgar I just could not leave it. A thousand apologies to 'Richard Simmons', but please do not use MY website for hate messages]

carlos ~ January 20th, 2010

Can we stop with the cheeseburger analogies? Homosexuality is not a choice. Eating a double bacon cheeseburger is.

FACT: homosexuality is genetic. Just like having blue eyes or red hair is linked to a certain gene, so is homosexuality.

With that said, being a moral (gossip free), mildly religious man; I cannot go to sleep at night knowing my community wishes to exile its own members based on something they cannot control. Forcing them to live a life in solitude (or hiding) is also morally unjust.

To those making analogies, please think them through. Or at least read a science magazine on occasion.

MESSIAH IS COMING ~ January 20th, 2010

to SHAMED KARTAQI/PROUD JEW: That was by far the MOST accurate, well said, and enlightening thoughts I have ever read about the problems in our community! You have inspired me to another level and deeply introspect how I can change MYSELF. You nailed it right on the money. I recommend everyone to read the blog of SHAMED KARTAQI/PROUD JEW. You changed the way I think and hopefully the way I will act!!!

yo ~ January 20th, 2010

yo carlos, just because you start a sentence with "FACT:" doesn't make what follows a fact..there is no evidence whatsoever that homosexuality is genetic (FACT)...if it was, it wouldnt exist because gays dont procreate!!!!!!!!!!!!!!!!

sweet justice ~ January 20th, 2010

I read through all of the comments on this board and then called my parents and thanked them for raising my sister and I not to spew hate and mask it as religion. I keep shabbat, and *kashrut*, and believe in the importance of observing Judaism, but I do not believe in hate mongering or slander. That is not what Judaism is about. When we start throwing rocks at adulterers (and lets not pretend like adultery [for men] is not an openly accepted reality in our community), then I will start accepting the religious edicts against homosexuality.

My parents are pious people, who have never hurt anyone, and even though they do not accept homosexuality, and believe it is against the Torah, not once did they deride their children for having gay friends. They opened their homes to our friends, regardless of sexuality or affiliation because Judaism is about kindness and decency. You accept people because they are people, not because of who they want to have sex with.

The only thing that happens when a Rabbi stands at his pulpit and decries homosexuality is more closeted homosexuals.

yo idiot ~ January 20th, 2010

Gays do procreate. Not everyone lives a gay lifestyle. Many are in the closet with a wife and children up until the day they die.

Young Kartaqi Mom ~ January 20th, 2010

Angry Kartaqis, what the hell is in your DNA that you cannot have a civil conversation when others disagree with the Communities leadership. So far everyone on this board, even those that disagree with the comments made have been respectful. It is ok to disagree but your problems seem to be rooted very deep if you use such a harsh and insulting tone. Get into anger management class or learn to see the other side of the picture in our community. We are all not like you. We cannot all be like you. So stop insulting Isaac and stop insulting the people that take the time to write so passionately on this board.

50 Cent ~ January 20th, 2010

David...the only retarded is you, you are a fool and have no life. Enjoy.

Ja Rule ~ January 20th, 2010

"the only retarded is you" ok 50 Cent.

yo ~ January 20th, 2010

yo "yo idiot", if the gays who are in the closet do procreate, then i guess the whole gay marriage phenomenon is the demise of the gay population! its taking all the closeted gays out of the game!!

Ru Paul ~ January 20th, 2010

DOES ANYONE ELSE HAVE THE CRAVING FOR A NICE JUICY HOT DOG RIGHT NOW....OR IS IT JUST ME???

yeah right! ~ January 20th, 2010

wow!!!! "SHAMED KARTAQI/PROUD JEW", your statements are the most powerful and true. we all live a lie of some sort and forgive ourselves by judging others. i think we should heed your advice (YOUR ESSAY SHOULD BE READ OVER AND OVER AGAIN BY EVERYONE). ALL your words ring true, and i like that you seem to come from an unbiased perspective, by defending/criticizing each side of the argument and being the only one to offer a valid solution. sign me up for Chafetz Chaim!

Anything for Salenas ~ January 20th, 2010

I agree with Yeah Right! I just read that and "Shamed Kartaqi/Proud Jew" was by the most amazing blog I've read through this entire site

Vince McMahon ~ January 20th, 2010

A question to all the LIBERALS who decided to express their opinions. If i decide that i want to have a sex change next week to become a woman....do i sit in the men's section or the woman's section of the sanctuary??? And can i use the ladies room....its my right isn't it?? LETS GET WITH THE TIMES PEOPLE.....you people are so primitive...who has one wife these days...lets serve pork next week after services, what's the big deal, we have to adapt to the "new times"

carlos ~ January 20th, 2010

to Yo,

The field of genetics is very complex. I'm not going to pretend i'm an authority on it. but one thing thats very clear is that gays do not have to procreate to pass on their genes (is that the argument you were making?). You and your significant other can have gay offspring (it doesn't make any of you gay, relax). Whether or not homosexuality is genetic is not a question. Defining the genes and how they are triggered is.

yo ~ January 20th, 2010

to carlos - touche

to vince mcmahon - right on brotha!

Teenage Kartaqi Girl ~ January 20th, 2010

Those of you who unlike me did NOT attend Shabbat last week at the Synagogue and are wondering what went on , you are able to see the mockery and insulting jokes made about Isaac and gays as you read some of what is going on the board right now. I am sure these are part of the many people that made all the horrible faggot jokes after the service.

It will give you a taste of what was going on in the Synagogue. And this mockery went on for much longer than the Rabbi's speech. And is the reason I dread going to synagogue again although I go every single week. This is so upsetting to me.

I am 16 years old and hope even though I am a teenager that you believe that what I saw and heard is true.

confused ~ January 20th, 2010

im a lil confused...if being gay is genetic, can someone explain to me how there are hundreds of sets of identical twins, who have the same exact genetic makeup, and consist of one gay and one straight

Najva ~ January 20th, 2010

I have a brief suggestion: if the synagogue wants to take a stand against what is prohibited in the Torah and bring the offenders into the public eye then there should be a consistency.

Any theft, in business or otherwise should be brought into spotlight on a Saturday making sure that all know who the guilty party is. No exclusion based on the wealth of the guilty.

Adultery, child molestation, cheating in business should also receive a spot light.

Joshua ~ January 20th, 2010

First off, you're all a bunch of spineless twits for hiding behind fake names.

Numbbehr Second: I don't know what everyone is complaining about. If every successful, good looking, well dressed doctor in this community went gay, well dammit I'd be the happiest man on Earth. I'm thrilled that he married a man, that mean I have a better change of scoring a great girl to be my future depressed kartaqi wife with three young children (see earlier posts if you don't get the joke).

Joshua ~ January 20th, 2010

And yes I saw my typos in the last post. I don't need to impress you people!!

Simply Ethical ~ January 20th, 2010

Excellent Post Naiva, I could not agree more. How can we tolerate adultery, child molestation, cheating in business, drug abuse, alcohol abuse? I always thought its a dont ask dont tell. And it happens behind closed doors and nobody comes out because of shame.

carlos ~ January 20th, 2010

to 'confused',

Like I said earlier, I am not an authority. If you wish to dig deeper, the Royal College of Psychiatrists and the American Academy of Pediatrics to name a few have done extensive studies.

To address the case of identical twins (which I recall the rabbi also brought up on saturday), It is true that there are identical twins (identical genes) that differ in that one is gay and one is not. One study done, showed that roughly a bit more than 50% of a gay identical twins sibling was also gay. At first glance, this would clearly imply that there is no direct genetic link to homosexuality (even though 50% is a very high number). But, a second study was done along side the identical twin study with fraternal twins (dissimilar genes); and the results showed that a bit more than 20% of a gay twins sibling was likewise gay. This difference implied the genetic link.

The study was done by "J.M. Bailey and R.C. Pillard" in 1991 - "Twin studies and homosexuality"

Email

From: Sonya

To: Isaac

Date: 1/20/2010 4:18:16 P.M.

Subject: Thank you

Dear Dr. Namdar,

My name is Sonya, I am not Kartaqi myself, but my husband is, and therefore I guess I belong to the community.

I just wanted to let you know that we stand in solidarity with you and your partner and that we wish you a great life together.

I have been reading the posts on the blog, and I find it fascinating - thank you for that.

However, could you please remove the obnoxious ones about eating hot dogs, and so on - I find that it is making a mockery of the situation. I know you are not trying to be a moderator, and I am sure you a busy with your life, but these comments are just rude.

I wish you the best,

Sonya

Email

From: Isaac

To: Sonya

Date: 1/20/2010 4:21:19 P.M.

Subject: Re: Thank you

Thanks so much for your support.

Just reading the posts is becoming a full time job, let alone editing and commenting. I will try to keep it clean there.

Email

From: Sarah

To: Isaac

Date: 1/20/2010 5:35:11 P.M.

Subject: Re: your site

Isaac, my fanatic religious relative told me they are terrified about the forum and will try everything to have you shut it down. Everyone who knows I speak with you begged me to tell you to not give in. There are also posts on the board pleading for that.

Email

From: Isaac

To: Sarah

Date: 1/20/2010 5:42:08 P.M.

Subject: Re: your site

Don't worry, I'm not going to shut it down. At the same time, I have more important things to do than to sit here and be a moderator for the internal conflicts for a community that excommunicated me. Which is ironic, they have to come to the place they excommunicated to be able to talk to each other.

Email

From: Sarah

To: Isaac

Date: 1/20/2010 5:47:08 P.M.

Subject: Re: your site

Yes I know but I would keep it up for now. It may slow, it may not. If it doesn't, then another site is an alternative. But its good to be an agent of civil change for those not brave enough

Email

From: Ellen

To: Isaac

Date: 1/20/2010 5:54:22 P.M.

Subject: Re: Congrats!

Isaac,

We have a lot of catching up to do...

Meanwhile I've been asked by several people who are writing on the discussion board to keep it running at least for few more weeks. There's too much anger in this community and too many unhappy people that never had the chance to give their opinion about anything.

This is bringing awareness that something must be done about this proposed lifestyle in this community.

I had several posts since yesterday and I'm also talking to Sarah who's encouraging people to post their opinion.

Email

From: Janice

To: Isaac

Date: 1/20/2010 6:43:18 P.M.

Subject: Re: Scrolls

Hi again,

I truly regret to inform you that our community is indeed as backwards as you suggest. Some other people involved in the magazine feel that our hands are tied; our funding comes from Central Board, whose views are not in line with yours, and thus, we are forbidden to represent something that they do not endorse as a community value. In my opinion (as a journalism major), this is censorship at its worst. I actually was asked to contact you by a few young community members who felt your voice should be heard, but unfortunately, authority got in the way. I truly wish you the best and I hope that one day the community will be controlled by people who are at least willing to give people the right to speak, despite their personal views. Sorry again to disappoint. Thank you.

Email

From: Isaac

To: Janice

Date: 1/20/2010 6:48:09 P.M.

Subject: Re: Scrolls

I thought it would be the case. However, as a true journalist, please feel free to mention in the next issue the same exact facts: that idea was raised to ask for my input, but due to political climate and 'censorship', you were not allowed to proceed with freedom of speech. I think just that statement alone, for which they cannot fault you, would be much more effective than anything I could have written for you.

Email

From: Sarah

To: Isaac

Date: Re: your site

Subject: 1/20/2010 7:09:04 P.M.

Central board has asked a friend to take over site and move it to Kartaqi.org. Please don't let that happen. They will censor it. Its their way of wanting to quiet it down. If anything it gets moved to independent place. These people have become terrified of the outburst

Discussion Board

Salazaar Slytherin ~ January 20th, 2010

The post by I donno why everyone is praising the blog by was absolute garbage and I dont know why everyone is praising it. Anyways, homosexuality will never be accepted in our community, so sorry for your choice.

***Isaac stop taking down our posts, we have a voice too.

RESPONSE FROM ISAAC:

I have only deleted the profanity of ONE post. No other posts have been deleted, although many have asked me to do my best to maintain a civil discussion. If you don't see your post, it is because people are posting at such lightning speed that by the time you click 'submit', there are 10 more ahead of you. LOL

Salazaar Slytherin ~ January 20th, 2010

sorry meant the post by Proud Jew/depressed kartaqi or whatever it was

davidkhan ~ January 20th, 2010

I am completely shocked at some of the comments here. I always knew that many members of our community lack intelligence. After all, education is not exactly considered paramount in the average Kartaqi household, and I don't think that our rabbi does anything to promote it.

The inability of some to express their thoughts in a dignified manner, however, is just further proof that these people cannot be taken seriously, let alone be charged with making decisions on behalf of the community.

In order for this community to survive, we need change, and we must open our hearts and minds to the future, not be held back by the past.

I too stumbled across an issue of Shalom magazine last summer. The fancy photos piqued my interest, but the deeper I got into the publication, the more upset I became by various articles, ranging from the one about the supposed virtues of the Syrian community (perfect timing, really, considering that many prominent Syrians including their chief rabbi were arrested shortly after) to all that nonsense about maintaining the jewish identity pure. They made me wonder whether the editor has been reading "Mein Kampf" a little too closely. The verbiage and content painfully harkened back to fascist literature. And don't get me started on the piece about homosexuality. I vowed to hunt down the editor and confront him, but I was told of his personal pain, and so I refrained and now pray for him and his family.

We should lead as an example of humanity, not one of hatred.

On a very different note, I am tired of all this talk of Temple Emanuel this and Temple Beth-El that, and this fear-mongering against conservative/reform synagogues. Kudos to them for their open mind, and we as a community should celebrate them and many of their members. They have done a lot for Jews in America and for Israel. Their members' contributions have built the hospitals that most Kartaqi women give birth in. I'd like to see a Kartaqi couple pictured in that row of photos at Green Hills Hospital.

And when was the last time you saw a Kartaqi name grace a cultural institution?

We are all Jews and G-d will make no difference. We should all get along and learn from one another.

Truth ~ January 20th, 2010

So your taking down people's post that you dont agree with huh? Or the ones that have a voice that differs from yours?

All your "this is a friendly board and we welcome ALL and everyone's different opinions" is bullshit!

Coward

I assure you that no posts have are getting deleted. Just remember that this webhost was designed to cater to wedding pictures, not to serve as a blog for an entire community. I am not sure if they can handle that kind of traffic, but once again all comments are respected and maintained. My only objection is to profanity.

By now I was realizing that the freedom of speech of this public board was too easy to abuse. Since there were no pre-stated rules of use, and I had not set up any mechanism for quality control, any comment could be entered and posted immediately. Not only could people express their radical opinions on both ends of the spectrum, but they could post frivolous profanity to degrade the conversation altogether. I knew that censoring was completely inappropriate, but I could not tolerate profanity. As seen in the following entry, I made a point of substituting the profanity in all subsequent postings with "[profanity]", yet kept the title for reference.

Discussion Board

hot diggity dawg ~ January 20th, 2010

[Profanity]

real truth ~ January 20th, 2010

Hey so called truth...if you knew the Dr. even remotely , you would know that he would never do that!!!! maybe its your twisted low class mind that would do that if it was you. thats why YOU are a coward and dont say your name

peter pan ~ January 20th, 2010

I just read this blog that everyone seems to be raving about (PROUD JEW/SHAMED MASHADI) and I couldnt agree more!!!! Very well said...

peter pan ~ January 20th, 2010

I dont get what Salazaar Slytherin is talking about...

shamed kartaqi/proud jew ~ January 20th, 2010

to NAJVA: i understand your point of view and agree with your idea to bring other peoples sins to the spotlight as well. the only issue with that is we dont need a rabbi to do that, in fact you and most of your brethren take part in vilifying those closest to you. all kartaqis do is talk shit about each other. just because you hear a rumor, doesnt make it a fact to reveal to the spotlight, the only way to do that is if there was a legal conviction and the subject was proven by guilty by the civil court system (i.e. leave it to the court judge and The Judge Upstairs), otherwise it is slandering.

if you read my previous post, i broke down all sides of the coin and call it what it is. the difference in this case is that there is no arguing the fact that Mr. Namdar came out, he admits it. others are less likely to come out and admit they are child molesters and cheat in business. so i agree with your stance that if someone is 100% proven guilty of these charges the Rabbi should condemn it, as i'm certain he would anyways. but lets be real, thats never going to happen. but Mr. Namdar has come out, its his right, i disagree with his lifestyle, but his openness lends itself out to public discussion.

you also mentioned that "no exclusion based on the wealth of guilty". i agree that our community, and most others, respect the high rollers and overlook their misdeeds. which brings me to my next point.

we are capitalist democrats as americans but must revert to socialistic (to some degree) methods of running the synagogue, not in the sense of "big government", but specifically regarding donations

201

and where people sit. the people sitting the closest should be the oldest and have assigned seating, even if it means not being next to friends. the argument will be made: "but they will stop coming to synagogue altogether". well my answer is TOO BAD! they set a bad example for their kids already by molding them to be part of specific groups from a young age, so them not coming anymore shouldnt be a threat.

the one thing that upsets me is that when they auction off the prayer for honorable income, it goes to the highest bidder. basically, the rich get richer, which is messed up.

my solution: do as the Ashkenazi do, charge everyone for membership and thats it, those who can give more should give more behind closed doors, those who cant should give what they can.

any truly pious Rabbi (hard to find) knows and should teach that if the torah had to be summed up into one thing, as the ultimate goal of humanity, it is SUBJEGATION OF THE EGO. once we allow our ego to control our lives we have broken every law that Judaism stands for. im not an expert in money management, but if this system of membership is implemented with all the kinks ironed out, i think its a good start, to show we are all equals.

All kartaqis need to look in the mirror and ask how they live with themselves considering that i have not met ONE kartaqi who likes all the people in his/her circle, yet still hang out all the time with a fake smile.

99% of us are full of it, a bunch of hypocrites who feel the need to slander others to mask their insecurities. like i said before the only solution to our communities problems are teaching and ingraining the laws of "lashon hara". otherwise this is all a waste of time, this topic of gays will be a laughable problem in 5-10 years when the avalanche finally hits the ground, since this issue is just 1 out of many this community is facing, yet choose to only criticize but not have the balls to lead by example.

who's down for change? if you are, stop trying to change others, start looking within yourself first.

and for those who commented on my previous post, i'm glad you were moved and hope we are going to continue to move in the right direction. if you woke up today it means G-d wants you here and there's still work to do.

concerned citizen ~ January 20th, 2010

This comment is in response to Shamed Kartaqi/Proud Jew. Your comments are one of the first to come from a place of constructive thought out words and I agree with mostly all you have said. I have to add that there is a great sense of fear inflicted on the Kartaqis to stand up for themselves. It is just recently that woman that are not happy in their marriages for serious reasons, not just "I am not in love with you anymore", I am talking about abuse, being cheated on- these few woman have taken that step to free themselves from abusive lives. This is not an easy step to do, especially when your own family doesn't back you or the CB (who listens to peoples problems) tells you to "dont' ask and don't tell". This community is in desperate need of leadership that works with the people, not against them. A community that enables people to have a voice and let that voice be heard. Do you want to know why do many of our youths have fallen into drug abuse? Why do so many of our young girls not live up to their true potential? Why young men feel burdened to take a wife who expects everything from the sun to the moon? Why our youth is adapting to the negative points of American society and not following the good? You are right once this recession really takes hold- the future of the youth will seem very dim when they don't have the necessary education to compete in today's job market and Daddy's business goes to the cleaners and the big house Daddy bought for him and his wife is reposed by the bank. These are all real stories from real kartaqis. So the voices that have been raised to shout out to be heard are screaming out for a reason.

That reason is fear, that reason is being ill educated, being talked down to, being brainwashed from birth. Hearing sermons in Synagogue about how Kartaqis are above Zameenis, above Americans a self righteous mess. It's about showing off, it's about competition, it's about excluding children who come from not so rich a family, its about a last name.

It's as far from being Jewish as possible. Look at the Zameenis, they are light years ahead of us. They were sending their children to become lawyers and doctors back in Zameen, it's pitiful to see our youths minds wasted and underused.

I mentioned this before if the board will hold an open mic night, I will personally come myself and defend my words above. I am not scared. Sometimes it only takes one person to give strength to people, if your own leaders can't do that then I will.

peter pan ~ January 20th, 2010

THIS IS RE-POST FROM "SHAMED KARTAQI/PROUD JEW":

> I am going to express what it think the route problem is, as well as being open minded by criticizing both sides of the argument, but bear with me since this is going to be kind of long.
>
> The biggest problem of our community is that we lost our identity, being Kartaqi is not what it used to mean, especially going back centuries to see that we were built on the opposite values/standards of life we have today. For the women who post that they are unhappy in their "forced" marriages and preach "be happy at all costs, even if being gay makes you happy, so power to you"! Every community has gays, and Rabbi Levy was right to say society desensitizes people, but the problem is that all the leadership the CB appoints (cough*controls*cough) is basically going to be politically correct and approach this the way the CB decides, which is to blame society, which is only a small part of the big picture. But nobody has the balls to blame the real issue, and that issue is the parenting. In a few years when more Kartaqi homes get foreclosed and people close down their businesses because these same parents spoiled their kids to the point where their kids are not equipped to survive in the real world on their own, and they cannot maintain this competitive material lifestyle, something worse will happen: we will have more criminals, mischief's, gays, drug addicts, atheists,

assimilations, etc than ever.

Another extreme is the overexposure that every Kartaqi feels like they are followed by a paparazzi when they want to just go buy food, yet most of them love it and live for the attention and drama, so they are hypocrites (yes I'm talking to you too, self-righteous yentahs reader!). We are overexposed to each other, hence the low marriage rate. Facebook, making 500 lavish engagement parties and after-parties, and clubbing together just makes it worse. People know too much about the materialistic outer shell of their Kartaqi "friend" and label them as such, yet barely know this "friend" deeply by treating them with true care. I say "friend" in parentheses because hanging out, competing, slandering, and jealousy within EVERY "Clique" doesn't constitute friendship. If you want to see real friendship, then go talk to soldiers in the Israeli army who risk their lives for their fellow soldiers and people.

My personal belief is that Homosexuality should not be shoved down people's throats, but neither should heterosexuality. That is why our sages command us to keep laws of 'Nida', not just at home, but even outside we should not take part in public displays of affection with our significant other. This is a private thing, and all that can come out of that is jealousy from people who don't have that. I respect the liberal position to speak their minds; however I am upset that these same liberal people are bringing up how people speak "Lashon Hara", and claim everyone is a hypocrite for breaking the torah in other ways i.e. driving on Shabbat, keeping kosher etc. (which are all valid points, by the way). But Judaism isn't an all or nothing religion and we cant start nitpicking who keeps what and who doesn't, because we should all start changing from within before trying to change others. That being said, if a homosexual is using the torah to support his argument then color me confused.

Now to my last and MOST IMPORTANT point: the biggest problem facing our community is the rampant "Lashon Hara" being spread. This very thing, along with "Sin'at Chinam/Hatred of Fellow Jews", destroyed our temple (Beit Hamikdash) and put us in exile. And now history is repeating itself.

"Lashon Hara" is responsible for the lack of values and downward spiral the community has taken, but what upsets me is that the closet gays and liberals are the same people who love the juicy gossip, love spreading "Lashon Hara" and ruining people's (even their own "friends") reputations and lives. A lot of these people that are complaining have many reasons to be upset that they cannot be open, however its not because of fear of tarnishing their reputation, in fact most inner circles already suspect or know who's gay, but its these same gays and/or liberals who hide behind a computer screen and bash the community for its negative traits while they are too cowardly to speak out in person, are the same ones who should be held responsible for bringing down the once positive spiritual energy of our community. Their real fear is that they will lose their social status and cliques a.k.a. avenues for gossip and slander. There is no other fear besides that, because having a traditional family with kids is not the priority for them anyways: Which brings me to these women who complain about their forced marriages by parents.

No matter how much pressure your parents put on you, you still made the decision to marry young for riches and status and it's in your hands to decide to leave, and if you have kids you are responsible to do what's best for the family. Give your husbands an ultimatum to change or you will leave them, but you must also change, especially with your demand for money and material and also if you flirt/sleep with other men. Its easy to blame parents for everything , and in this case its warranted, but you ultimately made the decision to get married and finally a few years later you realized you are living a life devoid of meaning and happiness (maybe your husband wasn't as rich and popular as intended by your premeditation), you choose to blame others. Yes they were wrong and have a backwards way of thinking, but people you must "make the bed you sleep in".

At least this Namdar guy moved away and had the balls to make his own decisions. I do not condone those decisions, but they are not mine to make, and if the community has bylaws that's normal and should be respected (but you still have free speech), a line should be drawn somewhere because eventually this will lead to other things such as marrying Christians and forcing us to accept them as community members. The institution of marriage is of holy matrimony intended for having children, whether or not you believe in G-d, I cant remember the last time a baby came out of a guy, clearly getting married is unnecessary, its just a way to rub it in. but again, its his right because the country allows it and nobody should slam him. He may have put up this site but it's his property and he did not intend to get ratted on by some gossiper who did not think before he acted so "zealously" (but he is a Jew and we must forgive him and not slander him as well).

For the record I think the community has more pros than cons, but we've lost our way. And to prove this isn't a one sided opinion, I mostly blame the parents and older generation that paved the superficial way for us. Even the right wingers are to blame. You send your kids to public schools, mock spirituality, teach competitiveness, spoil your kids, name them 'Tristan' or 'Mason', and then one day that child wants to marry a goy you freak out thinking "what will my Clique say?!" and try to convince this child that marrying Jewish is important. Umm, at what point did you make Judaism important to this child? Judaism has nothing to do with going to Synagogue to socialize. Most people are breaking not some but ALL 10 commandments. Speaking any form of *lashon hara* is the biggest form of jealousy and the worst sin since our sages teach us that "Derech Eretz Kadma Le'Torah/Proper Behavior Must Come Before Torah" and the fact that jealousy is one of the 10 commandments (along with KEEPING SHABBAT), that suggests the level of importance it has (more so than keeping Kosher, going to Synagogue and putting on Tefillin, since they are not on that list of 10). These ritualistic and symbolic things we do, known as mitzvoth are mainly done as reminders that a form of action must follow beliefs and values. So in my opinion learn-it-up should be every night and the only thing learned should be "Shmirat HaLashon/Guarding Your Tongue" by the Chafetz Chaim, until it's ingrained in the ENTIRE communities heads! I know none of you have the balls to ask for forgiveness to those you have slandered, because in many cases it has spread to far and deep. But you will answer to the Judge of this world one day, so at least start by making this change and sticking to it, while teaching your children the same, and having the courage to stop others from gossiping when you see it, since it is an equal sin to hear it.

To finish my point: Everyone gives their sons "Brit Milah", the mitzvah symbolizing the importance of keeping the sexual organ pure from sin. Yet the words in literal Hebrew mean "covenant of words/speech" and it is the 1st thing we implement on a newborn, implying that all sin of impurity starts and ends with self control of desires, and the main 2 parts of our bodies we sin with are the mouth and sexual organ. This is a kabalistic concept that will take hours to delve into, but Google it if you want. The point is that EVERYONE needs to look themselves in the mirror and not wait for the CB to clean up the mess of our predecessors, but the changes must come from each person. Kartaqi is just a temporary title, when you all figure out that we are Jews first and identify yourselves as such, maybe then you can start criticizing others. But for now, the only thing to do is dropping everything and committing ourselves to AVOIDING "LASHON HARA" AT ALL COSTS!!

Lentil soup ~ January 20th, 2010

To all those homophobes and haters on this web site-I am so sorry for you. I hope *Hashem* (Hebrew for G-d) will forgive you.

Here's a thought. Maybe you should stop buying Chanel bags, because, guess what, Karl Lagerfeld is gay and so is most of his design team. Or Louis Vuitton, because, hey, Marc Jacobs is gay and Jewish (and, actually, looking to marry his partner - Mazal Tov!!!).

And Valentino is gay and Dolce & Gabbana are gay. So are the designers of almost every major fashion house, surely even designers of "modest dresses" if you scratch the surface hard enough.

I don't want to stereotype gays as there are plenty of gay doctors, lawyers, writers, economists, business men and, yes, jewelers.

So think twice about what you post here before you, or your wife, rushes out to the next sample sale for the next circus wedding.

The designers won't be missing you.

yo ~ January 20th, 2010

yo lentil soup, your point irrelevant and meaningless..none of your aforementioned gay designers are kartaqi, and our whole discussion is about a kartaqi who came out of the closet

I hope G-d will forgive YOU for being an imbecile

question for Isaac ~ January 20th, 2010

Isaac, I dont want to get personal but I am just very curious to know how your family reacted to you marrying another man. Did your father support you or cut off connection with you. The reason why I am asking is to see how the older generation kartaqis react when homosexuality becomes part of their family lives. Please feel free not to answer if you think its too personal. I was just curious.

RESPONSE FROM ISAAC:

My father knows about it through a series of graduated discussions with him. Not surprisingly, people of that generation don't have the same view of life as we do. He prefers not to talk about it, but our love and respect for each other is so great that not even this will break our father-son bond. My siblings are very supportive. My nieces/nephews think it is the coolest thing to have a gay uncle.

Lentil soup ~ January 20th, 2010

Dear Yo, I know it was a rather light-hearted comment on a rather serious issue.

But if you can accept the work of these people in your house, at synagogue, at your weddings and other functions, and use it with the hope that it will help you maintain status, then how can you refuse a gay man from coming into the synagogue to pay his respects to his family, or to the deceased, for example?

Dr. Namdar has done nothing to offend anyone in the community. He has chosen to go down his path, and find his own personal happiness. What was offensive was for community or religious leaders to single him out and make it a case for ridicule in a holy space. That was the sin.

And by the way, I don't like being addressed as "yo."

High Schooler ~ January 20th, 2010

I shared this site with my teacher at school and she was so impressed by passion about our community. I would like to write my senior thesis about the struggles of being different in the Kartaqi Community. I hope Isaac that I can reach out to you. Thank you for giving us this discussion board. Especially for us high schoolers it is amazing to see another side of the story we are trained to hear.

Despite my pleas, people were getting increasingly confrontational in their debates. Inflammatory language, name calling, and occasional profanity were diminishing the quality of the discussion. Some were using the anonymity of the Discussion Board to express years of frustrations towards others in the community. More importantly, I realized that the Discussion Board was becoming a liability for me. People might mistake the views expressed by others as mine. Otherwise, they might think that the Discussion Board was a way for me to lash out at the community for the way they invaded my privacy. I needed to clarify the mission of the Discussion Board and define its scope.

Discussion Board

ISAAC NAMDAR ~ January 20th, 2010

MESSAGE FROM YOUR HOST:

This website was originally put together for us to share wedding photos and stories with our supportive friends. Since then, through a series of events, it has morphed into a community Discussion Board.

Please keep in mind that this site is OUR personal property, and you are welcome to visit it as our guests. If you choose to leave a comment, we request that you strictly refrain from profanity. Any profane language will be deleted, but the original heading will remain for reference. We also ask everyone to leave your comments in a constructive manner, with the fullest possible respect for other community members, our Rabbi, Central Board members, any community servants, other communities, denominations, minorities, religions, or anyone whom you may not agree with personally.

Since the Discussion Board has morphed into something that at times is beyond the scope of this site, we would be glad to look into transferring the forum to another location that is not under our auspices. If anyone has any suggestions, please contact Namdar@aol.com to discuss options. However, since many of you have personally pleaded for the survival of this service, we will keep the site open for the time being.

Jen ~ January 20th, 2010

You know the difference between you and other gay men in our community? They marry women! (I guess it's much better to make 2 people miserable.)

Teenage Kartaqi Clique ~ January 20th, 2010

Isaac my friends and I beg that you do not take down this site. And it is what it is because you are supervising it and you make sure it stays inline. Please dont move it and please dont shut it down. You are the best coach for this site. We need this board so badly. If it has an official kartaqi title nobody will post and we will lose all previous posts that are so important to us young people to read. Long Live mitchell-Namdar.com

95b03 ~ January 20th, 2010

Hmm, can i start to advertise on your website??? it'll be sure to make lots of money in pay-per-clicks!

greenmovement ~ January 20th, 2010

I now realize how the people of Middle East must feel. Ruled by dictators and intimidated by religious authorities. Unable to accept and embrace people who are different, and who like to speak their mind freely. They are sent to the prison.

I am beginning to feel like we Kartaqis need to start our own Green Movement.

Iron Sheik ~ January 20th, 2010

I love the gay people, I respect the gay people. But the ones I dont like are the dumb ones. And the dumb ones are the Ultimate Warrior....and Eric Simms.

papito ~ January 20th, 2010

nobody seems to be focusing on the deeper issues or offering sound advice and solutions besides SHAMED KARTAQI/PROUD JEW. your second post is also right on the money

Hailey Hoffman ~ January 20th, 2010

In kind response to "Vince McMahon," if Judaism did not adapt to the times, it would now be an obsolete religion. The Rabbinic Judaism that we practice today is derived from Pharisaic traditions, which came about as a result of the Jewish Diaspora. If were still practicing the original form of Saduccaic Judaism, we would still have high priests (in white robes), only 1 temple, we'd be making animal sacrifices, and would have not a Talmud (or its contents)in existence, among other things. The fact that Jews traditionally have only one wife is due to adapting to a more current society. And the fact that we do not have slaves, like our biblical ancestors, says something about our ability to adapt as a Jewish society.

Historically, it has been Judaism's malleability in interpretation and adaptability to surrounding cultures that has allowed our ancient tradition to survive centuries.

What yours or my personal social preferences are is not entirely the point here. The point is humanity and democracy. You and I have both chosen to follow a humane religion and live in a democratic society.

I hope whatever direction the community leaders steer us in involves kindness and longevity.

Impartial ~ January 20th, 2010

Let's all keep in mind that Rabbi Levy and the Central Board only want the good of this community and our children. We respect Isaac as a human being and he is entitled to his way of life, but his private way of life is not respected in this community and should stay private.

Headache ~ January 20th, 2010

I thought you guys were supposed to be good at designing. This message board gives me a headache. Give it some structure!

K-Fed~ January 20th, 2010

Isaac, PUT THE PICS BACKKKK UPPPP......WHAT ARE YOU ASHAMED OF????

KENNY G ~ January 20th, 2010

are you guys gonna have children??

BJ ~ January 20th, 2010

were you born gay or did you just get sick of women after a certain point??

WantingaBetterCommunity ~ January 20th, 2010

Impartial: In my mind Rabbi Levy and the Central Board behind him has done nothing but damage to our Community. And I say that with the utmost honesty and respect. Rabbis are not perfect as you saw in the Syrian case so we are entitled to be critical of our Rabbi. He may be a wonderful guy as an individual and I am sure individually there are some nice folks on the CB too. But as group leadership they have failed a solid part of the Community. And maybe Rabbi Levy is merely a parrot for the Central Board. I dont know that but whatever is going on, it is not working for a good part of the Community.

Look at where we are today. A divided community that is becoming more polarized by the day with this poor leadership. We were never this divided when we moved to this country.

Great leaders see the needs of their Community and think outside the box - think Gandhi. Rabbi Levy and his CB team think what is good for them is also good for us (especially the youth) and keep us all in their mental prison.

Again, it is not sacrilegious to criticize rabbis and religious leaders for anyone that might be alarmed right away. It is our duty to hold our religious and community leaders accountable. They have failed us and they know it. Their response will be to shut us up and keep us quiet. Wont happen now. Too late. The momentum for change is there.

concerned citizen ~ January 20th, 2010

To Jen- The reason our gay kartaqi men marry woman in the first place is b/c of the fear they feel to be themselves and obliviously it will ruin their wife's and children's lives one day when they have to hear the truth. Isn't it better to just be able to accept a person for who they are not who they love?

There was a forum held at Yeshiva University that let hassidic students come out and disclose that they are gay. Can you image how hard that must have been for them?! At least YU let them have that opportunity. They weren't even asking them to accept their lifestyle- just let them be who they are and give them the strength to acknowledge who they really are instead of having to lie about why their relationships don't work out with woman. If the Hassidim can do that, why can't we?

I remembered reading a couple of weeks ago about this forum at Yeshiva University, the biggest and most prestigious institution of Orthodox education in North America. I was amazed that homosexuals were given a safe platform to have their concerns heard about growing up gay in an unaccepting environment. I looked up the link on Jerusalem Post, and added a section about this event in the "Orthodoxy and Judaism" page of the website.

Discussion Board

concerned citizen ~ January 20th, 2010

those of you that are making snide remarks, I know that you are trying to shut down this website with your slandering. so stop it and take in a dose of reality pleasessssssseeeee!

cum face ~ January 20th, 2010

hey this question is for the creator of the website. I know a guy Joshua Norwick who is gay but is scared to come out with it, any advice?

Big, loud, screeching Hollywood sound effect! *WHAT?* Did someone just out someone else on the Board? How low can some of these people get while trying to have a discussion? That kind of behavior was totally not acceptable. I didn't know Joshua Norwick, but it should not be up to others to out him under any circumstances.

As soon as I opened the email notification with the text of the entry, I was shocked. I dropped everything, and signed onto the website's administrator's page. Unfortunately, in the meantime, a few people had seen the original posting with the name, and already commented on the issue. I deleted Joshua's name, but kept the rest of the posting for a documentation of what just happened. I also inserted the following addendum to the note. I didn't want my addendum to come across as though I was protecting other gays from being outed. Rather, I wanted to emphasize manners and civility as a universal guideline for any discussion topic.

RESPONSE FROM ISAAC:

Since you are guests on this site, I implore all members to be respectful to each other. I really hate to use my ability to delete or censure anyone's free speech. That is totally counterproductive to the process.

And the discussion continued.

Discussion Board

betterperson ~ January 20th, 2010

there is a reason the person of the last remark chose the alias. what a perfect description for a sad, sad person.

concerned citizen ~ January 20th, 2010

2nd to last person to comment, you know who you are. the fact that you just named someone in the community is a prime example of what's wrong with the community- you are an example of what I hope our youth NEVER turns into and if you call yourself a pious "modern orthodox jew" you are making a mockery of our faith

gay is the way ~ January 20th, 2010

is there a class i can take to become gay, such as gay101?

Joshua Norwick ~ January 20th, 2010

Hi! My name is Joshua Norwick and I would like to use this message board to let everyone know publicly that I'm gay!

Again, someone was playing dirty tricks. As soon as I saw this message, I went back and deleted Joshua's name. I left the remainder of the message for others to see. Whomever was playing this cruel joke was completely out of line. Although this time it only took me a few minutes to act in a timely manner, I am sure that once again the name was visible to those monitoring the discussion before I got the chance to change it.

Discussion Board

gay marriage ~ January 20th, 2010

hey i am gay and i am adopting a son, any names that you suggest that are appropriate?

concerned citizen ~ January 20th, 2010

same comment to you last person to comment, i am will never lower myself to be as scummy as you...but you are EVERYTHING that is wrong with Kartaqis....i will not stop responding as long as people like you make rude comments such as the one above.

Kebab House ~ January 20th, 2010

cum face - you are so off limits. no wonder so many of us fear to live and one day raise kids in this community. i dont know the person you mention but that is sinful.

illegal immigrant ~ January 20th, 2010

so in other words, you'll continue to just linger around this board and not have a life?

The posting below is heavily laden with references to various Jewish holy books and periods in Jewish history. Although a bit long for the format, and often too condense for the novice reader, the entry was written eloquently and is worthy of a reading even if one might not fully appreciate all the nuances.

Discussion Board

shamed kartaqi/proud jew ~ January 20th, 2010

This is a response to Hailey Hoffman: I appreciate your point and I'd like to add further. I want this to stop being a religious debate before it even starts, so I'll make a few points and see if we can move on to the topic of "kartaqi crisis":

In order to have a temple to maintain ancient Judaism were impossible without having our own land, which we lost for 2000+ years until 1948. So obviously Judaism has evolved, but evolution and complete change are different things entirely. Obviously with the advent of technology, for example, our sages were faced with the issue of what should be considered allowed on Shabbat. So the ancient laws of Shabbat regarding not being allowed to ride a donkey are only left to rabbinic authority to decide that driving a car is the modern equivalent. The pharisaic Judaism we have today is the end result of its origin in the *anshei knesset hagedola* and *Sanhedrin* (ancient Israelite parliament), pre temple era.

The fact that Jews have one wife mainly stems from those same rabbinic authorities instituting the law of "dina bemalchuta dina" which requires you to follow the laws of the foreign land of which you live, and in most cases bigamy being illegal. However, some Jews today, in morocco for example can marry few wives, so it is not a worldwide phenomena.

I agree that Jewish interpretation of the torah has evolved to the point that nobody recognizes the original message. Ancient Hebrew is a codified language made up of an intricate mathematical system called 'gematria', which in turn can lead people to misunderstand what they are reading. Therefore in order to truly understand the torah one must not translate it to another language, yet understand it in its original form. For example most people read the literal translation that the world was created in 6 days implying that the world is only 5000+ years since Adam. Yet most people don't realize is that the torah never makes the claim that this is the age of the universe/multiverse. Since we know that the sun and moon, tools which we use to measure a day, were created on the 4th day of creation, so clearly the term "day" is being misunderstood. Especially when the word for "day 1" is *"yom echad"* when logic would tell you it should be *"yom rishon"* (first day). In any event, Rabbi Aryeh Kaplan, the late modern physicist/kabbalist pointed out in one of his works that Rabbi Isaac of Akko, among many kabbalists before him, learned out from this very same "rabbinic torah" you speak of, the true age of the universe. Here is an excerpt:

"In his work Otzar HaHayyim, Yizhak of Acco writes that, because the sabbatical cycles referred to in Shitat Sefer Temunah existed before Adam, they must be measured in Divine years, not human years. Therefore, Sefer Temunah is speaking of Divine years when it states that the world is 42,000 years old. According to midrashic sources, a Divine day is 1,000 earth-years long (said by King David). A Divine year would therefore equal 365,250 earth years. So, according to Yitzhak of Acco, the universe would be 42,000 x 365,250 earth-years old. That calculation comes out to 15.3 billion years, very close to current estimates for the Big Bang." This was written over 600 years ago. Also note that these so called "babylonian rabbis" claimed: "The Talmud (Chagigah, Page 13, Side B) says that there were 974 generations before the creation of Adam and Eve. This is derived from Psalm 105:8 ("He has remembered His covenant forever, the word which He commanded to a thousand generations"). If one follows through the genealogies from Adam down the line to Moses (the "begats"), one finds that Moses was the 26th generation from Adam, implying that there had previously been 974 generations. These pre-Adamic humans weren't people as we know them - Adam and Eve were the first creatures made in G-d's image, with the power to make moral choices - but they resembled us closely enough that the Talmud includes them in our species. And to top it off the Zohar discusses the 10 sefirot/dimensions that G-d used to create the world. 4 visible dimensions and 6 hidden dimensions folded into 1, known as "Zeir Anpin", which scientists only today have come to the same conclusion which is called "superstring theory" (google it). The point I'm making is there is an answer to all these claims, but be careful bashing the Torah; religion is never the problem, people are.

Let's get back on the topic at hand, a religious debate will take up too much space and people didn't come here to talk about this. But I had to slightly delve into this to show that the community is so devoid of spirituality that they don't realize the answers are right in front of them.

(Hailey, This is not a place to get into a religious debate, but if you want to take it somewhere else we can discuss the Sadducees, the epic of Gilgamash, Mesopotamian ruins, the document hypothesis and the 2 accounts of Adams creation...all arguments which have their own flaws and valid scientific and intelligent answers from rabbinic perspectives. The only reason we believe messiah is supposed to come is to clarify the Torah through understanding the Zohar, which few are capable of teaching over properly)

If you ask me, pharisaic Judaism single handedly saved Judaism, and most of us wouldn't exist today as Jews if it weren't for the rise of the Yeshiva of Yavneh and the uprisings against the Roman Empire. Yet, I agree evolution certainly has taken its course somewhat, and that's the point. Jews have been exiled to all corners of the world, influenced each civilization whether positively or negatively, and miraculously ended up back in our land after all these years with the same 1 Torah intact. The ancient Persians, Babylonians, Egyptians, Romans, Greeks, and all other empires at one point ruled the ancient world. Where are they now? As soon as they messed with us and they disappeared from the face of the earth. We have always stayed under 20 million people yet we are still here? Clearly these Pharisees had no idea what they were talking about with the survival guide they gave us, right? The only way the Jews could have become "the light unto the nations" is if the nations had the opportunity to be influenced i.e. jews living in other lands (predicted in the Torah: Parshat Haazinu). Now we have become a collection of worldly knowledge and experience and have created the most successful country per capita the world has ever seen, Israel. The Age has already arrived.

Kartaqis wake up! You are not Kartaqi anymore, you are presently American!!! But more importantly you will always be a JEW!!!!!

gay dad ~ January 20th, 2010

Hey, my name is gay dad and I am spending my entire night arguing with a bunch of guys who are clearly joking around because i have nothing better to do. If you guys dont stop making fun of me i am going to take this to the central board of the kartaqi community

very concerned dad ~ January 20th, 2010

I think that the problem with our community is not people like me. It's people that like to spread rumors about people and people and make racist comments- that is why I am furious. I have nothing against gay people. All I am saying is that kind of information should come from an individual himself. Even if it is a joke- this is not the place to make such a statement. It was made to perpetuate more bullying. I am not wasting my time- I am trying to teach you all about tolerance and the behavior shown on this page by people belittling one another is what is wrong with this community, not concerned

221

parents like me.

:-) ~ January 20th, 2010

AKA you're gay.

Joshua Norwick ~ January 20th, 2010

Isaac please dont delete this:

LADIES AND GENTLEMEN.

The post you saw a few hours ago was by a foolish friend trying to be funny. I am not gay, bisexual, transsexual, omnisexual or any other big word referring to me not loving only women. One more time for those of you who didn't catch what I just said..

I AM NOT GAY. (it sounds so pathetic to have to say that)

Isaac, until now this board hasn't hurt anyone. It has hurt me. People are asking about my sexuality because of this despicable fool. Please take this site down now....

Relax. ~ January 20th, 2010

you see, "very concerned dad". Look what you made the poor guy have to do. Be ashamed of yourself. Because you're so uptight, people really thought he was gay. Get a life.

very concerned dad ~ January 20th, 2010

Wow exhibit A! See he is upset...now do you understand what I am saying. Joshua Norwick thank you for posting this. This was not taken as a joke. So stop trying to kid yourself. This forum is the best thing that has happened to this community. I do not want to see this momentum stop. I would like to see the bullying stop, that would be wonderful.

Relax. ~ January 20th, 2010

He's upset because you blew it out of proportion! You're an uneducated dad, you fool.

Mockery ~ January 20th, 2010

How could you make a mockery of this purple website? How dare you?

gay dad ~ January 20th, 2010

hey guys, its me again. For those of you who dont know me, my name is gay dad. I think i am smart even though i didnt graduate college. i am in jewelry and i have no understanding of anything else in the world regardless of how clever i try to sound. i try to act really religious even though i went to a high school that taught us islam. I want to keep arguing with you guys because my wife is 10 years younger than me and we have nothing in common besides a love for money. If you guys dont stop joking around i am going to cry and report this to the kartaqi central board

wow ~ January 20th, 2010

the discussion board just became even more pointless.

very concerned dad ~ January 20th, 2010

Hi. I am very very alarmed by the comment made by one person mentioning a person's name and claiming that they are gay. Is this is the kind of behavior that stemmed from the speech this past Saturday and what my children are exposed to when they go to

Synagogue? I will surely be changing synagogues. I will not support the Kartaqi synagogue and community with large donations this year. We must teach our children to be real and g-d fearing, these are not words of g-d fearing youth! This is bullying at it's worst! I will be taking this up with the Central Board immediately.

shamed kartaqi/proud jew ~ January 20th, 2010

very concerned dad - i agree, thats exactly the point i was making in my first post regarding "lashon hara", when will people realize thats our biggest problem?!

Relax. ~ January 20th, 2010

If you guys look at the previous pages of this board, you'll see that the "victim" posted under his own name in a joking manner. The person who "victimized" him was obviously joking too. Each one of you have your panties all up in a bunch. Straighten yourselves out. (no pun intended) G-d! (pun intended :-)

very concerned dad ~ January 20th, 2010

shamed kartaqi/proud jew- Yes "lashon hara" is a major problem. I will not sit back and have my children exposed to this nonsense. For Relax, please don't tell me to relax, this is not a laughing matter, even if it is a joke. It's not a joke. This young man's reputation will be in the gutter tomorrow. This news should come from a person himself, if he chooses to share with family. I am furious.

old kartaqi man in mid 50's ~ January 20th, 2010

seriously...you guys need to relax. Go get yourself a girl or something, what are you gay?

Relax. ~ January 20th, 2010

gay dad, please dont worry about his reputation. Make sure you have a good night sleep tonight. Sheesh. Go take care of your family. Play catch with your son. What are you spending your time doing?

Kartaqi man ~ January 20th, 2010

this is to the "very concerned dad" who seems to be so concerned over this situation. If you don't have a problem with someone being gay then why are you making a big deal out of it if someone is publicly telling people that one of his friends are gay? It shouldn't be that big of a deal for people to know that he's gay. I think people like you are the reason that the kartaqi community sucks. Since you have nothing better to do you just talk about these stupid topics and make them bigger than they actually are. You fuel the fire by "taking it to the central board"

Relax. ~ January 20th, 2010

BURNED

jhbkbj ~ January 20th, 2010

fully agree with 26marriedguy

> RESPONSE FROM ISAAC:
>
> I am fully aware of the traditions of our community. I decided to take my life and lifestyle elsewhere when it was obvious this would contradict the community's values. I did not make a display for the community, and nobody from the community was invited. The posted pictures were for American friends only. The clash happened only when another member of the community, un-invited to the website, got in and disseminated the information. Analogy to the cheeseburger story: as long as anyone decides to eat a

cheeseburger in the privacy of their home - nobody's business; but if they bring the cheeseburger to synagogue, then it becomes public display. My marriage was kept far away from the community, and I never demanded any attention for it.

I'm sorry to say this issac but did you really expect to get married and the kartaqi community not to find out about it?

Email

From: Joshua Norwick

To: Isaac

Date: 1/20/2010 8:13:41 P.M.

Subject: Postings

Hi Dr. Namdar,

I'm sorry to have to bother you about this. But these joking posts about me have started serious problems. People are getting phone calls at a faster rate. If you dont mind I'd appreciate it if you could take down any posts have my name or are posted by anyone posing as me. Thank you so much. Sorry again

Email

From: Isaac

To: Joshua

Date: 1/20/2010 8:26:44 P.M.

Subject: Re: postings

I removed your name already, and I'm trying my best to keep it all civil. I'm sorry, the entries are coming in so fast it is hard for me to keep monitoring everything in the middle of a work day.

Email

From: Joshua

To: Isaac

Date: 1/20/2010 8:40:36 P.M.

Subject: Re: postings

Thank you so much. Also the one where I called someone an idiot. That seems a little out of place without the others. ;)

And if you'd like, I have some experience with web sites. We could talk about your options as to how to take this off of your hands.

Email

From: Isaac

To: Joshua

Date: 1/20/2010 8:43:37 P.M.

Subject: Re: postings

As long as it is a neutral site, not governed by any one person or entity, especially the CB

Email

From: Joshua

To: Isaac

Date: 1/20/2010 8:47:47 P.M.

Subject: Re: postings

The CB? Those Neanderthals won't even allow Scrolls to discuss whats going on, let alone run a forum.   But someone WILL have to monitor the site. Keep it from spiraling out of control.

I mean look at whats going on, its like lord of the flies in there...

Email

From: Isaac

To: Sarah

Date: 1/20/2010 9:56:01 P.M.

Subject: Board

Do you have any experience with yahoo groups or any such that we can transfer the Board to? It's becoming a full time job to babysit all these comments.

Email

From: Sarah

To: Isaac

Date: 1/20/2010 9:59:28 P.M.

Subject: Re: Board

Not really but if you can hold off until shabbat and move it over after shabbat that would be good. That way people will at least speak about it saturday and what an impact it has had.

I will help you babysit if you want and stick to your guidelines. As is I follow all entries from work.

So let me know and I will help

Discussion Board

Impartial ~ January 20th, 2010

WantingaBetterCommunity:

I am not a member of the CB and I am not a future candidate. It's a great responsibility to be on the CB. With the power and the position come a great deal of expectation from people. It's easy to blame the CB and the Rabbi's for our problems. Nevertheless, this a great community and you and I are lucky to be part of it. If there are flaws within us, it's only natural. With the flaws come of a great sense of belonging which in my opinion is basis of Judaism. So be proud to be Kartaqi and let's all take responsibility for our own problems rather than blaming them on the Rabbi's and the CB.

love2010 ~ January 20th, 2010

keep going ! this community has bad thing and good thing but in general they are nasty !

Worried about intolerance ~ January 20th, 2010

For a community that is so supportive of Israel, why are we beginning to sound more like Fundamentalist Kartaq, than Israel?

Concerned For Community ~ January 20th, 2010

To "WantingaBetterCommunity": We're not blaming our problems on the Rabbi and Central Board. We're blaming intolerance on them.

cool dad ~ January 20th, 2010

To the people on this board who support what the rabbi said in synagogue...We cannot start acting like other extremists. How do you like it when Farrakhan speaks out against Jews? That is the same type of intolerance as when our rabbi speaks out against gays. We cannot condone intolerance, no matter who it comes from.

pissed ~ January 20th, 2010

Did everyone hear the great news?

The Central Board is not allowing Scrolls to publish ANYTHING regarding this subject. They are totally banned from even touching it!

Iron Sheik ~ January 20th, 2010

[profanity]

OneWayTicket ~ January 20th, 2010

People who are prejudiced, intolerant, and believe in these backwards views, should go to a place where they also believe in those views...like Zameen. I'll buy you a one way ticket back.

fif ~ January 20th, 2010

I'll tell you what the main problem is:

FACEBOOK MOMS FLAUNTING THEIR SCANTILY CLAD (AND SOME HEAVY) BODIES ALL OVER THE INTERNET.

WHAT HAPPENED TO THE VALUE OF MODESTY AND ACTUALLY BEING A MOTHER???? MOTHERS SPEND MORE TIME ON FACEBOOK PLAYING ON FARM(HARM)VILLE AND COMMENTING ON "OH YOU LOOK SO GORGEOUS!" THAN SPENDING QUALITY TIME WITH THEIR OWN KIDS.

VERY VERY SAD..

moms are the main problem ~ January 20th, 2010

PARENTING in the community is the MAIN problem and the reason why our community has gone down this spiral.

another pissed off parent ~ January 20th, 2010

wow Scrolls is not going to write anything regarding this subject! what a shocker! more and more denial-- this will have to change. as for the kids playing jokes- i have a 16 year old son and if his friends put his name on this site saying anything negative about him i would be furious too! even if it meant to be a joke

fakebook ~ January 20th, 2010

fif brings up a great point! Mothers have poisoned Facebook. Get off! You're an embarrassment! We all see through your fake comments about how "cute" a baby is and how you want to "eat them up". Give me a break. For G-d sakes learn how to spell, also.

Concerned High School Junior ~ January 20th, 2010

I am a high school junior and this is the first time I post to this board. Together with my friends we have been reading everything and are so happy we finally can hear the truth about how many kartaqis feel like us about what is going on in the community.

Please do not take this board down. It is so important for us to have this place to share our feelings.

My uncle is friends with a Central Board member and was just told they will do whatever it takes to take this board down. Including having Kartaqis post bad rumors so people get hurt and lead to it being taken down. The Rabbi also has started a Facebook page (strangely on the same day this board heated up) to take attention from this board.

They are using their radical tactics to scare us and shut down this healthy place for us young people who never get to speak without being scared of our parents and relatives.

The Central Board is making our life hell as young Kartaqis. This is what we young people have to live with as kartaqis. Me and my friends are so scared of the radical behavior. We don't want to live anymore under this regime. Please, please let us continue to speak out here. Our parents don't understand us, the people on this discussion board do. I wish some of the people that posted so many true and great things could work with the youth group to help us, we need your help. Please.

another pissed off parent ~ January 20th, 2010

Wow the central board is not controlling our right to freedom of speech! How wonderful! What a great reaction to all these posts. What a sign of progression- shut up the majority of the pissed of community!! Got to love being ruled by a tyranny! One way ticket back to Kartaq for all people who can't accept change!

Kartaqi High School Juniors ~ January 20th, 2010

My friends and I are terrified. We read your board after school and now are posting as group. Please dont take down this board. The Central Board is trying to rule our lives. This board is the only place we have. My uncle just told me that his friend on the Central Board said they will do everything to bring down this board and also have people play bad jokes so it is forced to come down. We are terrified of living under this regime. We need someone to understand us like so many people that post your support on this board. Please.

concerned citizen ~ January 20th, 2010

Wow Wow Wow. If this is not a plea for help then I don't know what is! This is the voice of our future speaking. The Central Board should be very very ashamed...but of course they are not. I have written countless entries. To the youth- it is your right to have your voice heard and it is so sad that it has taken a tactically planned speech to open the doors to Noah's Ark. Don't worry, I will personally do all I can to not let this momentum stop. I was once a teen sitting where you are, pissed off with no one to talk to. No person that understood, I understand you completely. The voices on these pages are too loud to go ignored. If I have to go speak to every member of the CB myself I will do it. For the sake of the future of a community I actually do hold very close to my heart.

kid ~ January 20th, 2010

so let me see, the CB is going to post rubbish, *lashon hara*, and employ otherwise childish tactics to take this forum down? Why can't they call Isaac and ask him professionally and politely?? Oh, I forgot, they excommunicated him and are not allowed to talk to him!

Concerned For Community ~ January 20th, 2010

Woops. My comment was meant for "Impartial".

Young not married yet kartaqi guy ~ January 20th, 2010

To fakebook, I TOTALLY agree with you. All babies look the same when they are born , whats so 'cute' about them and why do these woman have to say it 100x. Once is enough. Babies have become like cadillacs in our community. Most of these woman cant even stand parenting (my older sister who is married and has kids told me) but every year have a baby to keep up with the Kartaqi quotas. If something isn't done soon all these babies born will grow up in a radical kartaqi community. Good Luck to them and by then I will have found myself a nice and non-radical American wife (Jewish of course) like many of my friends plan to do when we are at marrying age. For us thats in our late twenties NOT when we are still wearing diapers at 21.

Leave the moms alone ~ January 20th, 2010

"FIF" is a [profanity]. Now moms are to blame??? First, the gays, and now the moms? What about the Ahmadinejad-style dictators in our community. The only reason our community has a problem is because of the Central Board and the rabbi! NOT the moms, and not the gays! The moms in this community are some of the best examples for motherhood in the world.

kartaqi girl ~ January 20th, 2010

haha young not married yet kartaqi guy! you read my mind--- i am totally marrying an american too! since the community has pissed me off so much- why would i want to expose my unborn children to this garbage?

Leave the youth alone! ~ January 20th, 2010

the moms are the root of all the problems. They gossip to no end. Whether it's true or not, they rip through relationships with their tongues. Shut your mouths if you knew what was good for your children and the children of this community! Stop spreading everything!! Leave us alone and we won't hide things from you.

Young Kartaqi Movie Buffs ~ January 20th, 2010

There is a movie with Adam Sandler called: You don't mess with the Zohan. My friends and I think its a funny movie and we watch it all the time. Isaac, you are our Zohan. Like Zohan does with his clients at the hairdresser you bring out our true feelings. It might sound funny but it is true. My friends and I just thought of it and wanted to tell you. You are the Kartaqi Zohan.

RESPONSE FROM ISAAC:

I'll take that as a ...compliment?!

kartaqi synagogue ~ January 20th, 2010

i have gone to Ashkenazi synagogues and mostly old people and boring. there is no reform service on shabbat nobody shows up . temple israel is meaningless and empty unless there is bar mitzva. kartaqi synagogues are vibrant friendly and no membership. i love it with all its flaws

honest kartaq ~ January 20th, 2010

Can some one tell me whats so great about our community???? We have leaders that are on drugs , *lashon hara* at every turn (the minute the person turns around) married women partying at nights , married men in topless clubs, miserable newlyweds, jealousy , envy , flaunting, putting down the weaker, child molesting , hating (we hate the people in our own clique or group) we are uneducated , we are closed minded, we are rude(ask any other person living in GH) SO WHAT IS IT THAT MAKES US GREAT????? we are not even religious ....we drive to the synagogue for gods sake !!!!!!!!

Sad Kartaqi son ~ January 20th, 2010

I just realized when I'm my grandfather's age (I'm in my early twenties), there will not be a Kartaqi community. That is terrible and so sad. The community they cherished, loved and SAVED from the atrocities in kartaq will be dismantled because the misguided youth think marrying a cute French girl will give them a better life. They don't realize all they have that they take for granted, the thousands of friends and relatives they're BORN with. The fact that they have a group of friends with no effort whatsoever because their parents set a group up for them. Think about all the activities and parties the CB and KYC put together for our sake to bring us closer together. Now think about living alone in the outside world. Think about getting in a car accident and having NO ONE come to the hospital to comfort you.

Think about marrying someone you have no idea what they're about, their financial situation, their religious beliefs, and their medical history. There's a reason the divorce rate outside our community is so high. I agree there are unnecessary pressures from our parents and grandparents to marry for certain characteristics and at the wrong time in your life, but think about what life they HOPE you have that they didnt have! They got set up by their parents and that was it. Next thing they knew they were married. It's not like that this day and age and don't cry and say it was for you. You could have prevented it. There are no arranged marriages as far as I know. Be proud of being Kartaqi and know that there are many, many Zameenis and Americans looking in, desperate to have what we have.

Everyone needs to CHILL ~ January 20th, 2010

Personally, I do not understand what the big issue is here. Gay people exist, and there's nothing you can do about it. You can't prevent them from being gay. Most of them do not CHOOSE to be gay, but it is the way it is.

Unless the person did nothing to hurt you, then there's no reason why you should hurt him or her, either through words or any other way.

And even if a person does hurt you, you still shouldn't hurt them and just leave it to G-d to take care of it.

For those of you who are worried about what might come of your children and your values, you have every right to be. However, your children will be exposed to all kinds of things that you would not want them to be exposed to. Whether it is in America (sex, drugs, and rock and roll), or whether it is in Saudia Arabia-where people are hanged or lashed. For this reason, 1. u should be happy you live in the U.S. with shelter, food on your table, and a community that supports each other. 2. As a result, you should be thankful enough to have mutual respect amongst one another.

It is the values and teachings that you instill in your children that will determine their actions. Them being exposed to a harmless Gay person in the community is not going to change their motives. It is

YOU, and as a whole, the community's values that are embedded within your children that will mold their lives.

They go to school. They are exposed to pot, crack, cocaine, sex, and things that are much WORSE than being gay.

Most importantly, the gay people in the community are your OWN blood. Love each other, and only bring each other to better light, instead of shaming each other.

There are people that also cheat, and do a great deal of things that go against the Torah. We must, as jews, and as a community, bring each other closer and enlighten each other. The future relies on us.

Frustrated Young Mom ~ January 20th, 2010

It's become almost painful going to synagogue these days. If I hear another radical speech from Rabbi Levy, I'm really going to make an effort to mobilize people and have him removed. He is not Kartaqi, he is not one of us, and yet he is spreading his radical ideas upon us. We are not radical.

First, the thing in synagogue about married women not having male personal trainers, now the speech about gays. What's next? Women in burkas? Stoning the gays? This is not fundamentalist Islam. This is Judaism. We are not intolerant and we do not spew hatred.

Btw, considering many of the gay men in the community are married, you all need to be careful of these speeches. You all have gay in-laws, relatives, cousins, brothers, friends in your groups, etc. Should these people be excommunicated too? Be careful what you wish for. It may be your husband or in-law who gets ex-communicated.

As a matter of fact, 3 of the young gay people I know (one is married with a kid), are all from very wealthy, respected, influential families. The kind of families that you do not want to piss off. And the kind that give big donations to the synagogue on holidays.

Better be careful speaking out against the "gays". Your donations might dry up.

Mark Cohen ~ January 20th, 2010

Isaac. I don't know you and had never heard of you before this whole supposed scandal started. First of all, I want to congratulate you and Andrew on your wedding and wish you both a happy and healthy future. I am proud that a member of our community has finally ushered into the 21st century. You are paving the way for many Kartaqi youths who are and have been suffering thru a life filled with lies and self denial. I am in complete support of what you have done. I am also in complete support of this discussion board. Please protect everyone's anonymity. Unfortunately, that is the only way we can have an open and honest forum.

Young Kartaqi and brothers ~ January 20th, 2010

Sad Kartaqi Son: It is nice you feel this way. Many of us don't and that is why we are on this board. None of my American friends or Zameeni friends envy me for being Kartaqi. In fact they think its all queer that we marry each other and are all related in some way and that our weddings have 800 people and that we are not encouraged to becomes drs, lawyers and teachers like they are.

older kartaqi dad ~ January 20th, 2010

Dear sad kartaqi son : There are no zameenis or americans that want to be us ,they been making fun of us for a long time. As a matter of fact all the stink that the older generation created about gays. Did you know that it was common practice amongst our older kartaqi men to have sex with each other?? they called it (avis degas) they even kept a diary, if you dont believe me go and ask the older people . So lets get off our high horse

Great point ~ January 20th, 2010

To Everyone Needs to Chill, fantastic point!

Email

From: Sarah

To: Isaac

Date: 1/20/2010 10:00:28 P.M.

Subject: Re: Board

Cute! Some kartaqi kids comparing you to the Zohan. Very sweet. Zohan let his clients open up to them. Clever analogy!

Email

From: Sarah

To: Isaac

Date: 1/20/2010 10:05:47 P.M.

Subject: Re: Board

I am still looking for the speech for you. They are not releasing it. They usually release speeches every week

Email

From: Isaac

To: Sarah

Date: 1/20/2010 11:42:04 P.M.

Subject: Funny

Leave it to the gays to bring some openness to the community. The discussion board is on fire. LOL

Discussion Board

anonymous ~ January 20th, 2010

Seriously shame on all of you. Who are you to throw around such insulting words about our rabbi and our community leaders. Did your parents not teach you about respect? You guys have no values. Imagine if any one of our ancestors rebelled, decided to insult all their elders and throw out all that was already established before them, do you think we'd be the strong, successful, growing community that we are today? TRUST, they have gone through much more difficult and life threatening moments in life, and do you think they decided its their right to leave the situation/their families/their friends/their unity? Its very sad to see that you really must not understand the beauty of our community. Of course there are some down sides to the kartaqis, but its really amazing that we are growing to this day, several hundred years later!

And if you're gay, do it in the privacy of your own life, don't make a public statement to shake up the roots of our blessed and growing community.

Humble Cynical Man of 2 ~ January 20th, 2010

fif... youre TOTALLY right.

the PROBLEM is: A. slutty mothers - who walk around with their (saggy) tits flying out... who flirt with (younger) men who are NOT their husbands. (HAVE SOME CLASS. BE A MOTHER. GET A JOB. READ A BOOK.) I sit on the train with some young men.. and all i hear is them talk about MOTHERS. they say things like "oh shes a MILF, oh she has a great rack" I dont blame them, these mothers ask for it... and they enjoy it.

Now the next problem..

b. idiot husbands: hah! thats a whole other story. the husbands who married these sluts are a bunch of MORONS. (Not saying all, so i dont want to generalize all kartaqi husbands..) but really, WHY WOULD YOU EVER MARRY SUCH SUPERFICIAL/DUMB/IMMATURE/ NAIIVE "women?" And then you cry and say youre unhappy and your wife sucks. go figure. The men are such pigs... my friends + cousins included...(no wonder so many of you cheat. none of you even love your wives-- YOU USE THEM AS DOLLS TO SHOW OFF TO EACH OTHER!!) Wake up: youre wife is not a doll that you play dress up with so you can show her off, so your idiot kartaqi friends can talk about. I Thannnnnnnnk G-D EVERY DAY!!!!!!!.... i have the best wife that i could have ever asked for... BECAUSE.. I.. CHOSE HER MYSELF. (and they call me humble) No one picked her for me. Not my mother, not my grandmother, not my brothers trying to convince me to pick a "young pretty girl." She is classy, sweet, sincere, loving, modest and she is the worlds best mother! (i love you suggerlip) My friends are such fools. They all complain to me about how their wives are so spoiled, bratty, DUMB...

but i dont sympathize with them AT ALL. YOU IDIOTS CHOSE YOUR IDIOT WIVES. Its one thing if you were FORCED to marry someone, maybe if someone put a knife to your throat. BUT TO CHASE AFTER A GIRL... because shes hot and part of a "cool clique" is probably the most pathetic thing .

MARRAIGE IS A BIG DEAL--

Everyone should grow up, and think on their OWN. now.. whos next.

c. disgusting kartaqi teens (16-26 range):

respect? values? Class? nothing. such filth, such garbage.

...*lashon hara*, jealousy over friends being skinnier or prettier, greed..like which friends are richer, anger... and so much pride, for NO REASON!!! like i said before, this is not all of you. The kartaqi slutty mothers, the idiot kartaqi husbands, the kartaqi teens who have ABSOLUTELY no values or respect.... all of you are a problem.

Lastly:

d. kartaqi grandparents....(didnt let you guys slide..) --they praise their grandchildren as if they are made out of gold.

I actually heard a grandmother once tell her grandson.. "YOU ARE THE BEST LOOKING MAN IN THIS COMMUNITY!!! DONT YOU DARE SETTLE

FOR ANYTHING LESS THAN YOUR LOOKS!! YOU ARE THE WOLRDS MOST HANDSOME MAN!! You deserve the best and only the best!!!"

Wow, what values you teach your grandchildren- that marriage is based on looks, and looks only. Pathetic. and what the hell is "the best??" the best what?? (Meanwhile, this man is UGLY, RUDE, and FAT-- no wonder the men have such egos. They really think they are something. Grow up, youre not.)

Please note: I may be cynical, but still very humble. thats why i chose not to say my name.

Sad Kartaqi son ~ January 20th, 2010

Young Kartaqi and brothers, dont give excuses as to why you didnt become a doctor, lawyer or teacher. There are many people who I know who have become one of those professions or who are going to become one of those professions. Don't blame your inadequacies on the community or your parents. Most Kartaqis are thank Gd more well-off financially than "an American". We have opportunities in the professional field that many others do not. If you're going to be weak and let your American friends insult you because theyre ignorant, that's your INDIVIDUAL problem, not the community's. I dont know about you but I'd want hundreds and hundreds of people to celebrate my marriage. I don't see anything wrong with having a big wedding. The more happiness I spread the better. You're living in a sad, sad world my friend. Open your eyes.

kartaqi teenage boy ~ January 20th, 2010

First of all, you marry somebody because you love them. Kartaqi or not. Second, I am a teenage boy and my mom is 50 she is an example of why kartaqi moms are the best moms in the world....BUT, the young moms right now are not in her generation and they are a completely different story. They are more concerned with what they wear and how expensive their ring is than their own kids. This is coming from a teenager guys not an older mom out of her prime. Also, who gives a fuck if somebody is gay or not? What if that was your cousin? Would you excommunicate him? Overall, the kartaqi community is the greatest thing that ever happened to any of us and people that think it is a bad community are honestly stupid people. Nobody is forcing you to be an active member in this community. It is easy to isolate yourself. These problems that we are dealing with are very minor and the benefits we receive from this community are far greater. And to all the young guys...please stop going into jewelry its a dying business

kartaqi newly wed girl ~ January 20th, 2010

Humble Cynical Man - you got it right on. Thank you for such honesty. Anyone who reads the posts on this board (and i just saw there have been 2220 hits so far) realizes we have a crisis. Kartaqis in Crisis. If people chose to ignore all these voices the crisis will deepen and Kartaqi community is gone and whats left is a religious fanatical left-over of what once was a great community.

RITZ ~ January 20th, 2010

WELL SAID SAD KARTAQI SON

typical dad ~ January 20th, 2010

thanks sad kartaqi son for your thoughtful comments. I thought i am the only one who considers himself very lucky to live in this community with all its flaws.

To frustrated young mom ,rabbi did not give a radical speech . there was no gay bashing . I find him to be very respectful and doing his job .

ZameeniGuy ~ January 20th, 2010

Most of you are probably going to read this simply because of my name. Surprisingly, you're curious as to what a Zameeni has to say.

A. For those of you who believe that Zameenis or other non-Kartaqis are desperate to be a part of your community, it is not true. Your community has wonderful benefits, such as the immense amount of support and closeness between each other. However, we are used to a life where rumors do not run rampant, where cheating doesn't occur with your best friend's wife, and where gossip and jealous girls do not ruin our opportunity for marriage. Again, this is our perspective, this is what we see on the outside. If there isn't any truth to what I said, please please correct me.

B. I grew up in a household with parents that stressed education. I am not going to be relying heavily on my parents, but on myself. My parents aimed to build in me a sense of strong character so that I will be able to face challenges ahead of me. Education, I believe, has a big impact on lifestyle and choices made. Education is something you can always fall back on. I am proud to have had parents that stressed education, so that one day I can have a backbone to support a family not in just mere financial ways.

You guys do have a great community, but its too bad that education is not valued so much.

C. Yes the amount of divorce outside of the Kartaqi community is greater. But compared to what? Kartaqis let's say have a population of about 5,000 give or take a few thousand, where non-Kartaqis (Zameenis) have a population of about 20,000 (give or take a few thousand.)

So obviously, there are bound to be more divorces. And, in the Zameeni community, divorce is HEAVILY looked down upon. I know many many couples that are in great marital stress, and due to the pressures of our community still hold on to each other.

D. Your sense of togetherness is wonderful. The support you give each other is wonderful as well. The only way a Zameeni would ever be "Desperate" to be a part of your community is if you improved the above mentioned things.

(i.e. *lashon hara*, lack of education).

I do not speak for All Zameenis, but most Zameenis.

At the end of the day, we are all Jews. We are not that different in our values. We both value our religion and sense of family.

In order to save your own community, stop thinking you are perfect and work on your flaws. Your kind of community is rare, and has GREAT potentials. Please do not take anything I said offensively, but use it as constructive criticism.

Take care

El Al Traveler ~ January 20th, 2010

I am a latecomer to this board. Probably because I spent the last day on a long El Al flight (greatest airline on earth). I heard about it from my Kartaqi family who lives in Israel. That is how international this board has become. I read every entry and am inspired by many of them. Where have all you unbelievably passionate and articulate Kartaqis been hiding. This board beats any Scrolls article or speech I have ever read or heard in the Community. We have such talented writers in our Community and don't acknowledge them. I am so impressed. I need to digest this. It has given me a new pride for being Kartaqi. Pride that had gone away over the years and now I am so proud to see this incredible talent. I feel like a miracle is happening for me and for the future of my young children.

Local University Kartaqi students ~ January 20th, 2010

Zameeni Guy, you hit the nail on the head. Nobody rewards us for getting an Education in our Community. It is not a focus. We are raised to get married and if we go to college we need to get married right when we graduate. Then we need to have many kids (at least 4 or 5) to get respect from our family and the community. Nobody takes us seriously for going to college. Some kartaqi parents do and i wish those were my parents. I go to local university and want to get a masters degree at brown university to study political science, its my dream. It will never happen because i cant do it without the support of my parents. they tell me 'enough is enough, we let you go to college, now you must get married'.

You Zameenis got it so right when it comes to EDUCATION.

Please teach our community how we can make education a priority.

The Right Decision ~ January 20th, 2010

SPEAKING AS A FAIRLY YOUNG, single, kartaqi male member of this community, I am saddened as I read each and every post on this discussion board. This message board has unfortunately transformed this community into the laughing stock of Green Hills overnight. And for all of you who will immediately respond with a comeback about our "disaster of a community" I kindly suggest you step back for a moment and think before you continue your thought process.

You all cry of being held captive under a dictatorship no different than the regime our ancestors lived through in Kartaq. You scream and beg for our leaders to allow you to be free and to remove the shackles from our hands and feet. Oh, the humanity! I understand the majority of these posts are being submitted by our youth in high school. Let me present to you a few questions and hopefully this post will not be removed like many other posts in the past few days. Were the women in this community allowed to go out of state for college 20 years ago? How about 10 years ago? How about today? Were our grandfathers allowed to choose their wives in Kartaq or were they given to them as gifts with no return policy? Granted, maybe kartaqi guys today dont have 100 million girls to choose from but do they at least get to choose from a pool of say 200? Did our grandmothers show off their cleavage at weddings in Kartaq? Were they even able to show their elbows? Most of us have an uncle that eats at Gino's and an aunt that sends her children to Yeshiva, and yet we all still have Shabbat dinner together and remain one big happy family. That is the beauty of this community, not the downfall. I believe we would all agree to call these things PROGRESS and they are indeed steps forward as the society around us transforms and we become more and more modernized.

This discussion board is being attacked by some very dramatic community members, who for whatever reason, feel the need to slam every inch of culture and heritage down that has been passed down to them from generations past. They are, for all intents and purposes, spitting in the faces of their parents, grandparents, and great grandparents, who have paved the way to America. They had to live through the tortures of Kartaq, not us. This community is making moves forward, and is the envy of many, and let me repeat many, Jewish communities throughout the world. All we can ask for is progress as times change. All I am asking for is that this to be the last post. For the sake of our grandparents and our grandchildren, these posts need to stop. You are all ruining a great thing. Our elders don't know how to use the internet to read this, but they cry when they hear about all this that is being said and done on this website. I have seen it with my own eyes.

To the recent newlyweds, all the best in your future endeavors. No matter what your objectives were with this message board, I hope you were successful. Take a long look at what has been going on here the past couple of days. I know you are both highly educated, compassionate people, so I am hoping you do what you think is best.

Good Night

Zameeni ~ January 20th, 2010

Local University Kartaqi students--

No one said you can't get married while in school. Marriage is a great thing.

Education is also a wonderful thing. It opens you up to a different world and a different way of thinking. Good for you.

Your parents want the best for you, so don't ever take what they say for granted.

Education is important for many reasons. What if G-d forbid your father's business doesn't work out? or what if G-d forbid something happens to your husband and you need to support children?

Besides the fact that it educates you and makes you stand out from others, it's also something to fall back on.

To mothers and fathers. Marriage is a wonderful thing. Having children is a blessing from G-d. You can do all of it, but why not let your child pursue education as well? Once they graduate from college they will end just working until the right person comes along. In the meantime, isn't it better to receive an education than to sit in an office and answer phones, or to sit in an office and just sort jewelry? One day G-d willing when their children are old enough, they can spend their time applying their education in the workfield instead of sitting around and having tea-parties and gossiping.

Think about it...

Local University Kartaqi Student--I don't know you, but I am proud of u.

Throughout our relationship, Andrew had remained shielded from the Kartaqi community at large since I kept my sexuality private. He had no knowledge of the norms of my community, nor had he had a chance to form any subjective opinion about their behavior. His first introduction to the Kartaqis was reading through the pages of the Discussion Board, and asking me for an occasional clarification. He had personally never experienced this level of homophobia or hatred in all of the twenty years since had come out of the closet. Ever since the events of this book started, he had let me handle the situation as I saw fit. Now he felt compelled to leave his own remarks. Following my lead, he made his input eloquent and respectful.

Discussion Board

Andrew Mitchell-Namdar ~ January 20th, 2010

As the newest Namdar I feel compelled to thank so many people on this discussion board for their love and support. It has truly touched both of us in so many ways.

Andrew

meatballs ~ January 20th, 2010

The Right Decision: our Shabbat dinners have become painful since the leaders of the Community became religious fanatics as half of us are very religious and half of us are not. It has split our family so sadly your comments may apply to you but to many of us the religious edicts and doctrines have created a lot of tension in families. The days of Brady Bunch Shabbat dinners are over in many homes. Lets be realistic, its not happening like it used to.

misc... ~ January 20th, 2010

Thank you The right decision. you said it perfect.

Namdar ~ January 20th, 2010

Hi Andrew Mitchell Namdar nice to finally hear from you !!!!
Welcome to our community

other stew~ January 20th, 2010

hey meatballs.

that is asset of our community that we have tolerance at our shabbat dinners . religious and not and plenty in the middle

stop looking negative at everything .

panties in a bunch ~ January 20th, 2010

Why are you people talking about education? The topic we should be discussing is the gay marriage. If you want to vent about something else, write a book or google a specific blog. My goodness, you're taking the spotlight off the Mitchell-Namdar situation. If you want to talk about relevant things, that actually have purpose or a point, then by all means, go ahead. If you want to talk about how your parents don't let you get educated because they want you to get married, I don't see a link to that and being gay, so no one cares.

Thanks

anonymous ~ January 20th, 2010

RELAX PEOPLE, there is no crisis, you guys are all drama queens.

Zameeni - Its honestly RARE to see a couple if any of the kartaqi high school graduates these days not go to college, THE MAJORITY OF US GO TO COLLEGE AND ARE EDUCATED, and our parents are proud of us for it.

Meatballs- I will agree with 'The Right Decision' on this one, I don't know what type of internal issues your family is currently going through, it definitely does not represent the rest of the community, and absolutely does not reflect what happens during my shabbat dinners with my religious and nonreligious aunts/uncles/cousins. We still stress unity, and we love each other's company.

el oh el ~ January 20th, 2010

yo andrew why did you delete the iron shieks comment is was hilarious

RESPONSE: Profanity will not be allowed. Anything else is freedom of speech.

anonymous ~ January 20th, 2010

everyone should read 'the right decision' post twice

Evita ~ January 20th, 2010

dont cry for me argentinaaaaaaaaaaaaaaaa....the truth is I never loved you.....na na na na na.....na na na na na......na na na na naaaaaaaaa....na na na naaaaa naaaaaa

gucci girl 101 ~ January 20th, 2010

my husband stopped buying me gucci bags

does he still love me

homosexual ~ January 20th, 2010

gucci girl....wanna cry on my shoulder?

69.....lol

Rice ball ~ January 20th, 2010

To Zameeni: Don't you love these Kartaqi food names. If you think that Kartaqis lack education, keep in mind that Isaac himself I believe is an ENT doctor. We Kartaqis are allowed to bad mouth ourselves, but we don't tolerate others putting us down. That's called unity.

confused ~ January 20th, 2010

hey homosexual and stud muffin......tag me in when your ready. gucci girl, i travel with louie VVVVV

dave- the american guy ~ January 20th, 2010

hi, my name is dave. i am not kartaqi, nor zameeni. just an american guy who knows lots of kartaqis--

i think you should all stop-- i wish i was in a community like yours..

you all obviously need a solution to the "crisis"-- so solve it! fix it! instead of discussing the problems- find a solution! be grateful for having such a closeknit community.

i am sure it has problems, but everywhere you go has problems.

gucci girl 101 ~ January 20th, 2010

stud muffin... im only mocking. i dont commit adultery

Stud muffin ~ January 20th, 2010

gucci girl...I'll put it in your coochie giiiiiiiiirllllll

the better Andrew.... ~ January 20th, 2010

hey dr. Namdar, if it doesnt work out with this andrew, there is another andrew waiting for you......younger and energetic

concerned citizen ~ January 20th, 2010

dave- well thank you for that positive comment..i would love to hear your thoughts as you can see with a clear vision as how to approach this dilemma? being serious. thank you in advance

biatch ~ January 20th, 2010

[profanity]

song singer ~ January 20th, 2010

i sang "Love is Blind"

E.H. ~ January 20th, 2010

So now that we know worldwide anyone could be looking at this discussion board, let's be careful in using any opposing language. All of us should unite and not discriminate or be racist, nor excommunicate anyone from our community so we can be viewed as a proud group of Jews in this modern society!!!

Stud muffin ~ January 20th, 2010

confused, a minute ago you were ready to tag in...what happened? Oh. I know. Your sexual orientation suddenly changed. That happens! Ok. You're free to go.

ultimate varrior ~ January 20th, 2010

i can break your back make u humble and then, you know what

Randy Savage ~ January 20th, 2010

Elizabeth was a good woman!

That evening I met Zach for the first time. He was a very nice and level-headed guy, in peace with himself and his sexuality. Like me, he had tried to maintain his interpersonal relationship with his family, but had decided it was best for him to live his life outside of the borders of the community. We shared some stories, and had a few good laughs. To this day, I am really appreciative of how he courageously reached out to me and provided a level of personal support as I was handling the most difficult time of my life.

At this point late Wednesday night, into the wee hours of Thursday morning, an excessive number of irrelevant entries were posted. My belief is that some people who were threatened or otherwise were bothered by the freedom of speech on the Discussion Board tried to make it less relevant by clogging the pages with spam or downright rude remarks. I eventually recognized this phenomenon, posted my own response to this kind of behavior. I also went to the administrator's page and hid all the spam entries in order to maintain the flow of discussion. However, I am enclosing all those entries here so that the reader of this book can truly appreciate the real dynamics that ensued. I trust you will find reading the next few pages here boring, as was the intent of those trying to sabotage the discussion.

Discussion Board

anonymous ~ January 21st, 2010

E.H. - except the gays

Clown ~ January 21st, 2010

wooooowooooooowooooooowooooooowoooooooo

this is a circus now.....moms, you could 'x' the window now...you wont be getting anymore gossip from us

wooooooowooooooooooowooooooooooowoooooooooowooo

Namdar ~ January 21st, 2010

lets all marry the same sex so we can live on for generations - who is with me?

the King of Vodka ~ January 21st, 2010

i love vodka it tastes so good

British Bulldog ~ January 21st, 2010

it came to an end so quickly

a fan ~ January 21st, 2010

L.B. got mad skinny!! good for her!

Sleepy ~ January 21st, 2010

Let's watch our language. Our host is a busy doctor and won't have time to read all posts and censoring them.

Damien Rice ~ January 21st, 2010

and so it is

just like you said it would be

life goes easy on me

most of the time

......

host ~ January 21st, 2010

[profanity]!

dave- the american guy ~ January 21st, 2010

concerned citizen.. of course! glad you are the only mature one here. obviously there are perks and downfalls with every community

i am an Ashkenazi man. all i can say is- did you see mean girls???? my daughters watch it at home. youre community needs a THERAPY MAKEOVER. EVERY NIGHT- FOR THE NEXT YEAR.

Thank G-d for blessing you with such a strong and close knit community-- but now use it to your advantage!! Clean up your acts, stop the hatred, pick up some new values, love each other, end the jealousy, end the greed... and be thankful for WHAT YOU OWN.

also- what happened to spiritual values??? modesty is gone, respect for one another is gone... problems can be fixed.

-dave, the american guy

Ricky Bobby ~ January 21st, 2010

if you aint first ur last

Dave you liar ~ January 21st, 2010

Dave we all know you arent american, you are a liar.

Flava flav ~ January 21st, 2010

you think im gay?

concerned citizen ~ January 21st, 2010

Obama is black :-(

sexay ~ January 21st, 2010

put up demm honeymoon picss asap, mr and mr Namdar

Another Kartaqi ~ January 21st, 2010

TO shamed kartaqi/proud jew ~ January 20th, 2010.

BRAVO!!

i like dave ~ January 21st, 2010

your a cutie dave. i would ask how old your daughters are, but i think im more interested in you....

important question ~ January 21st, 2010

can christmas tree ornaments be gay?

Blahhhhhh ~ January 21st, 2010

Moms, get off the phone. Your husbands are cheating on you as you read this. You're too concerned with this message board...tend to them!

never fun to play the blame game ~ January 21st, 2010

stop blaming one another.

dave is right, this sounds like mean girls. (love that movie)

kartaqi dad ~ January 21st, 2010

anyone who is upset about their marriage.. i do not pity you or feel bad for you..you chose your life. fix your marriage.

anyone who is not married yet... word of advice... marry someone with your values. looks fade, money brings nothing, and a body can get fat. find someone who is good for you and is good for others.

as you can see by our married friends on the blog... it is better to be single and alone, then be miserable and married (to a cheater, a pedophile, an abusive spouse)

ISAAC NAMDAR ~ January 21st, 2010

For the large part, I have been trying to stay out of the Discussion Board and express my opinions only on the homepage.

I applaud that many of you are able to exercise your freedom of speech and express your opinions. Again, I am humbled that you use my web resources to connect to one another.

However, some of you may be misusing or even abusing this freedom to inflict pain and insult on others.

To start with, I am personally extremely proud of my heritage as a Kartaqi Jew, and a product of our great community. I would never exchange it for anything else, and would never abandon the good values it has instilled in me. Although my personal lifestyle may not be in accordance to our community's norms, there are still a lot of good values I will always carry with me.

I am personally saddened to see some of the frivolous negative comments left by some. My intention with this Discussion Board was to build bridges, not to destroy them.

I would also like to take this opportunity to apologize to our Rabbi, Central Board, and all the people who have plenty of good intentions when leading the community if some of the posts on these pages have been anything less than complimentary to you. Although I may not agree with you on your handling the events surrounding my outing, I still have great deal of respect for the effort you put in to maintain the cohesiveness and Jewish nature of our community. Please accept this olive branch from me as a sign of good will.

For the record, an enthusiastic Scrolls staffer approached me earlier today and asked me to write a column about this whole experience for the upcoming issue. It was ME who reminded them that Scrolls is supported by the Central Board, and that any input from me would be a violation of the edicts issued against me this past Shabbat. After they checked the facts, they agreed that neither party wants to be in violation of Central Board's decision.

This Discussion Board, hosted by me, has gone beyond its original mission. I would like to see if any community members have any suggestions about transferring it to a neutral location, so that I no longer have to be the responsible party for maintaining its purpose.

Additionally, I am temporarily disabling NEW comments while the good doctor goes to sleep. You can enter new posts first thing in the morning (which is early for the doctors). And you can still read all the previous comments.

After I hid all the spam entries and changed the setting to require my approval before any new posting is published, I went to sleep, exhausted and consumed.

Thursday, January 21, 2010

That morning I hoped that the spam activity had stopped, and people can resume intelligent conversation. I revised the settings on the Discussion Board so that new comments will be posted immediately, hoping to restore productive conversation. Alas, they were still at it.

Discussion Board

important question ~ January 21st, 2010

are christmas ornaments gay?

impressed ~ January 21st, 2010

Wow! Dr. Namdar, you have once again shown yourself to be a true gentleman. If everyone was as selfless and thoughtful as you, the world would be a much nicer place.

You gave us freedom of speech, and many here decided to abuse it. Then you apologize to your 'nemesis' for the action of others, even though that nemesis has been scheming to take down this discussion board. I truly applaud you.

And hackers: we all know you have been trying to post junk here to devalue the discussion. Stop it! The doctor has better things to do than to filter your spam, and frankly your childish behavior is hurting everyone's freedom of speech.

May I also ask everyone posting from now on to please please please stay on focus, and try to be constructive rather just complain? Please!

impressed ~ January 21st, 2010

Once again addressing the hackers: I don't know if you are acting independently, or are agents of the CB. Your actions show that this community cannot have an intelligent conversation even if given the chance through a true democratic channel of free speech. And THAT reflects on us more negatively than all the complaining and the whining that has been written here by others. So please let others express themselves, and stop trying to destroy freedom of speech.

question ~ January 21st, 2010

what time does the donut shop open?

Guss ~ January 21st, 2010

While we are aware Wall street is a target right now, we understand that main street will continue to get hurt with these small transaction taxes.

tax attorney ~ January 21st, 2010

It is pretty evident that if you tax one entity, you must worry that it will be passed along to people that dont deserve it...

important ~ January 21st, 2010

How would the tax payers get compensated? Does it just pass through the OTC derivative areas along with the rest of the products?

no ~ January 21st, 2010

it is all about sustainable recovery. main street and wall street run parallel! we need to remind our leadership of that!

donut answer ~ January 21st, 2010

i think it opens at 7, but i could be wrong...

Bob ~ January 21st, 2010

why are all the liberal posts left on and the conservative posts removed immediately?

this does not seem fair

everyone should be able to speak their mind

It seemed that the hackers were back at it again, so early in the morning. Once again, I had to change settings so that new entries would be published only after manual approval. This way I could prevent the spam from clogging the pages, and dissuade them from this activity once they realized that they could be edited out so easily. But by this time I had left home and was just about to get into the car and drive to work. I had to make all the changes from the small screen of my smartphone (not an easy task).

Email

From: Sarah

To: Isaac

Date: Jan 21, 2010, at 7:33 AM

Subject: Re: Board

Isaac, your post is wonderful. I am looking for a neutral place for blog. But will you still have the login for that so nobody can hack it even though you no longer supervise it? Don't want central board to get its hands on it and they already sent their young supporters I hear to post so much spam to destroy the integrity of it. I hope you can keep this up until friday and then move it over the weekend after the synagogue has responded (which I assume they will). I suggest you review the postings as they come in (and not let people post it as they write it) like you did yesterday for next 2 days to maintain integrity of the site. I know its a lot of work but this is so critical for these young and desperate minds. Again these are merely suggestions and I can help monitor if you like

Email

From: Isaac

To: Sarah

Date: Thu Jan 21 07:48:33 2010

Subject: Re: Board

Will try to do. Meanwhile can u please cut and paste this letter u just sent me into a new posting and I will release it for publication. Can't do that kind of cut and paste from the iPhone.

Email

From: Sarah

To: Isaac

Date: 1/21/2010 7:57:29 A.M.

Subject: Re: Board

I can't post as me because my dad's best friend is on central board and I don't want my dad to freak out even though he is totally on my side and beats up his friend all the time

Email

From: Isaac

To: Sarah

Date: 1/21/2010 8:00:21 A.M.

Subject: Re: Board

Post with fake name

Discussion Board

Kartaqi Friends of Isaac ~ January 21st, 2010

Dear Isaac. Your post below is wonderful. My friends and I are looking for a neutral place for you to post but we still want you to have the login so nobody can hack it. One of our friends is a computer whiz so we will have some answers for you soon.

We want to support you as much as we can. We do not want the Central Board to get its hands on this discussion board.

They already sent their young supporters to post so much spam to destroy the integrity of the site. My dad's closest friend is on the Central Board and I was told that this is their strategy to stop the reactions people have had since Saturday. This site is too important for those of us that do not agree with the radical moves of the Central Board. I guess there will be a written edict about you in the mail soon. Therefore, this board must continue so they hear our voices and know that we will not let down. Thank you Isaac. Your are one of the most upstanding individuals we have ever met.

Hailey Hoffman ~ January 21st, 2010

I'd like to add, as a Mental Health Counselor, I also support any homosexual Kartaqi man or women who chooses not to come out of the closet. There is no right or wrong, while it is a complicated yet personal decision for each individual.

B.Z. ~ January 21st, 2010

How did this discussion board transform from an issue involving same sex marriage to an onslaught on the community and its rabbi?

In order for a message board like this to work, no posts should be deleted, whether conservative or liberal. If the administrators continue to remove the conservative posts then we are only left with one view.

barbara streisand ~ January 21st, 2010

You think that the central board hired hackers to take down this board? How does your mind work? You dont think it is just a group of people who think this board is a joke and is making a mockery of things? I am pretty certain that the people posting on this board as Kartaqi Mom or Kartaqi Dad or whatever are the same 5-6 people who keep changing their names and making up stupid stories just to stir the pot. Isaac, this board will get you absolutely no where, and it was foolish to start it, we arent central board members, we are community youth who think you are wrong. Live with it.

Grandmother of 9 children ~ January 21st, 2010

Human dignity must come first. I brought up three children in the community and now have nine grandchildren living in the community. The community always had its pluses and minuses and unfortunately education was never a virtue, but overall the children turned out well. However, over the last few years I've watched the community radicalize around some terrible leaders. The level headed thinkers have been pushed to the back and the propaganda and sermons have become so distasteful that I tell my children that they shouldn't bring up the children in such an environment. Many of my friends have written letters to the board (our understanding is that hundreds have been written with names attached) on various topics to no avail. These individuals have hijacked the community and they have taken away the ideals the community was built on and have focused on fear, edicts, rules, and harassment. We no longer donate to the synagogue and my children have been taking steps to have their children spend less time in this environment. Even the Hebrew school has become infected with propaganda. They should be getting a Jewish education not exposure to political propaganda filled with fears, lies, and hatred. Many of us have been sending their grandchildren to Ashkenazi Hebrew schools most recently. It's such a shame. We were so such a beautiful community, its a real tragedy as I watch us spiral into the depths of radicalism. It's a shame we can't turn it around. Human dignity must come above all other ideas, but this administration just doesn't get it.

p.s. ~ January 21st, 2010

Is it still working?

From an islamic country into a modern society ~ January 21st, 2010

Going back to the issue of being GAY! Being gay could happen to anyone regardless of their heritage. If it happens to the children of anyone in the central board or the rabbi, then they would understand that they can't criticize or judge or disband anyone from this community. If you do transfer the site to a different location it better be hosted by someone as gentleman as you are.

Moving on to the Future ~ January 21st, 2010

Wow that last few days, reading this blog have really opened my eyes to this community and it's many problems. The last few posts have made some positive progression.

Here is my stance, the Rabbi and Central Board are almost like our parents if you will. They represent the old school mentality that represents our heritage, grandparents and the foundation upon which our community is built...lessons like having respect for fellow community members, showing love and acceptance, tolerance, being a good JEW first and foremost. There is HUGE disconnect between the youth, their parents and our elderly. Our grandparents that have passed would look down on this blog in shame. There are some very positive entries and some very rude and defensive- causing more damage than good.

For a real change to come about there needs to be a healthy dialogue between the CB and the KYC (the voice of our youth). It is apparent that our community in general (not pointing any fingers) has become a whole lot more close minded and totalitarian than in the past. The only thing I can advise is to think about this rift as a parent/teenager relationship. The more demands and constricting a lifestyle a parent gives to their child, their child will rebel. This is what's happened. Instead of having our dirty laundry aired out for all to read- perhaps there should be room for acceptance and change on both ends of our community.

We come from a beautiful lineage- one that instilled respect, acceptance and tolerance, love for family, something that we have lost. We have to move away from this radical mindset- no person has to right to shun out a fellow Jew for who he chooses to love, doing so will only breed more intolerance and will not stop anyone that believes in this lifestyle from choosing that path. We have to have respect and trust for the woman of our community- the mothers of our community- trying to control who they work out with is an insult to the woman- families need to rebuild trust and raise children in a secure and healthy environment. We do not need to be ruled by fear in order to keep our beloved and cherished values. We need to work as a cohesive unit and move with the times- never insult anyone and their life choices- this is the only way to solve this conflict.

jboy ~ January 21st, 2010

Hello everyone,

I am a single kartaqi young man. I have a great job, a wonderful group of friends, and respectable family. I have been told that I am considered to be a "good" catch by kartaqi women. However, there is only one problem... i'm gay. Yes, you read it right. I am a gay kartaqi man who has been suffocating in the closet for 20+ years. I have been miserable for all my life because I thought that I will never be able to marry the man of my dreams. I never wanted to hurt my parents or family, and that is the primary reason for living the life I am expected to live. I always assumed that despite my attraction towards men and lack thereof towards women, I would marry a nice kartaqi girl and have a family with her. I realize now that it would be wrong of me on so many levels to live the life I am expected to live. First of all, I now know that I deserve to be happy and it would be wrong to deny myself happiness for others. I have faith that when I find my soulmate, he and I can be together. Second of all, how unfair would it be not just to me but to the woman I would marry if I chose that path? To all you single kartaqi women out there: how would you feel if you ever found out that your husband and children's father is gay?

how would you feel if you realized that he had been lying to you for all those years. To all the kartaqi parents: how would you feel if this happened to your child? Please take a moment to think about it. The actions of the central board can result in two things: gay people will either come out and be excommunicated from the community or they will be pressured to live a lie that will not only hurt them, but their future spouses.

To Isaac: you have inspired me to live my life for myself. You have offered hope to me and many other gay and lesbian kartaqis whether closeted or out. Thank you. You have changed my life.

RESPONSE FROM ISAAC:

I support you and others to live your life according to your inner self. And I am again humbled that you are using my website to express yourself.

However, MY decision to live my life the way I see fit was a purely personal one. I don't see myself as a role model, good or bad. I didn't try to start any movement or start any commotion. I am not trying to set an example for anyone. And I'll be the first to admit that I am not perfect. I'm just baffled how some people see me as a 'pioneer'.

As an aside, I am also the YOUNGEST partner in a group of 12 doctors with three offices. Yet all my senior partners nominated and elected me to be the managing partner, and now they all report to me. How come I keep walking into these situations???

I felt it was important to add the above response right away. Although I thought is is important for all people to live honestly and openly, I did not want to be the focus of an immediate avalanche of other Kartaqis coming out.

Discussion Board

noeddict ~ January 21st, 2010

dear issac

i just want you to know there was no edict or proclamation from rabbi or CB that i saw last week . just a message of please stay away which you gracefully have. you are fair person i clearly see that. so please make sure your plight does not translate into slander against just volunteers on CB and our rabbi.

sincerely yours

Isaac Namdar ~ January 21st, 2010

It seems that some individuals have been trying to devalue the discussion by posting multiple spam messages or plain profanity. I had to turn on the spam filter a few times to maintain the integrity of our discussion. If you don't see your non-spam postings published right away, it is because they need to be manually taken out of the spam folder. I apologize if this may hinder the flow of discussion.

kartaqimotherof5 ~ January 21st, 2010

after many many hours reading the board last night and in this morning, i completely agree with 26marriedguy and shamedjew...i couldnt put it better myself

Truth Hurts ~ January 21st, 2010

so according to the majority of the bloggers here, who needs religion or a community? G-d who? fear is officially out the window. imagine we lived in a world with no laws where everybody acted on pure instinct and desire.

murderers would run rampant, rapists would scar women for generations, people would walk around the streets naked, theft would become common place. it would become survival of the fittest, and the way i see it, the majority of these bloggers would not survive in that environment.

We, as a society, would move in reverse thousands of years. And all this for what? Because a few people weren't able to control their emotions. There are many things wrong in this world, but you cant go comparing evils. Whether it is murder, showing cleavage at a wedding, or acting on homosexual desires, they are all wrong in their own ways.

I hope there is room on the next ark for me, because I dont want to drown...

solution ~ January 21st, 2010

to jboy - you have one other option that you didnt mention, and its an option i believe to be the best in ur situation...be gay, have gay relationships, and be happy, just DON'T GET MARRIED!!

Helper ~ January 21st, 2010

jboy -why dont you say who you are? that's the first step. Then maybe you'll have others coming out of the closet and you wont be alone

soap bar ~ January 21st, 2010

To Truth Hurts.

I think it is shameful for you to equate homosexuality with murderers and rapists and theft. Homosexuals do not hurt other, innocent people. When they find their partners, it is by consent and by a love for one another. They deserve happiness and acceptance, just like all Jews and all good humans do.

Rapists, murderers and thieves, however, don't ask for consent, and often resort to violence that can adversely impact the lives of others. Coming to think of it, they are not so different from our Central Board.

To your other point, we need religion, we need community, we need G-d, we need unity. But we cannot have unity without acceptance.

We NEED to open our hearts and minds in order to flourish as a community for generations to come. This is an opportunity for us to set an example of a strong Jewish community of the future.

Btw, here's what I would have liked Rabbi Levy to have said: "We know homosexuality is not something condoned by the Torah. However, said individual is a son of our community and we must stand together and show our sons and daughters that we are there for them, and that we want them to feel that they can come to us and feel at home in our synagogues. We have survived generations and will continue to survive by standing together and supporting each other. We are brothers and sisters, and we don't want to upset anyone or turn anyone away from our beautiful religion."

Instead, I was even more turned off by an already uninspiring leadership.

Email

From: Sarah

To: Isaac

Date: 1/21/2010 8:05:37 A.M.

Subject: Re: Board

Done

Its first time I use fake name. Its 'kartaqi friends of isaac'

Email

From: Sarah

To: Isaac

Date: 1/21/2010 8:06:16 A.M.

Subject: Re: Board

And wouldn't post the junk like the gucci girl. That's all spam to use space on the board so people don't bother to read further. That's what my dad said

Email

From: Jerome

To: Isaac

Date: 1/21/2010 10:39:13 A.M.

Subject: The Site

I just did some morning reading and the site really is on fire, much of it heartening and plenty disheartening too. Even if it wasn't your intention, you could become a real agent of change — and someone we should all be proud of. Your comments/reactions on the site are so eloquent that they completely put some of the more profane, radical voices to shame, and rightly so. Thank you!

Email

From: Isaac

To: Jerome

Date: 1/21/2010 10:47:45 A.M.

Subject: Re: The Site

Thanks. One of the things I learned from Andrew is to always "keep your side of the street clean". One should always present themselves as the model of good behavior and let the other one self destruct. And that's what's happening there.

Email

From: Naomi

To: Isaac

Date: 1/21/2010 10:48:42 A.M.

Subject: Thank you

Dear Isaac,

My name is Naomi. I am a 22 year old kartaqi gay woman. I felt compelled to email you in light of everything that is taking place in response to your marriage. First of all, I would like to congratulate you and Andrew. Although I do not know either of you, I am genuinely happy for you, and the joy you have created is indescribable through words. My journey thus far as a lesbian who came out at the age of 18 who has attempted to maintain involvement in the community has been excruciating. You, however, have eased my burden tremendously. I met with Rabbi Levy several weeks ago regarding my recent threats against me. For example, many mothers of the children to whom I teach arts & crafts in synagogue have threatened to remove me from my teaching position because I am a lesbian. Unfortunately, I was pressured to agree to deny my sexuality to community members. As a gay rights activist, I felt hypocritical and ashamed about what I had agreed to. Nevertheless, I know that it is necessary for me to abide by the community's rules and continue being an involved member of the community until I am no longer dependent on my parents and family. Despite being in a relationship with another kartaqi woman for two years, I have not known of any other gay kartaqi who are out. Hearing about your story inspired me and has given me strength to remain true to myself. It is draining to fight this battle every day, and I was beginning to dry out. You have replenished my motivation. The main purpose of this email is to express my gratitude and that of all the lesbian and gay kartaqis who have confided in me because they felt they had no one else to talk to (many of whom I have encouraged to post on your discussion board). Thank you for coming out and raising so much awareness. Thank you for being such a clearly wonderful man and breaking stereotypes. Thank you for enduring the pain that such rejection inflicts - I know first hand how that feels. Thank you for offering so much hope to kartaqi members of the LGBTQ community. Please remember what a difference you have made in our community and world. I've been called selfish many times for coming out. I've been told that I only care about myself and not about the ways in which being out affects my family and friends. However, I know in my heart that it truly takes a selfless person to come out and sacrifice so much not only to liberate him or herself but to do what's in the best interest of the entire gay community. You have liberated many people in our community, and our world. THANK YOU.

Sincerely,

Naomi

P.S. Please feel free to contact me via email or phone at any time for any reason. My number is (987) 555-1212.

Email

From: Isaac

To: Naomi

Date: 1/21/2010 10:54:07 A.M.

Subject: Re" thanks you

Thank YOU so much for your wonderful words. Truth is, I never intended to be a role model or a trailblazer. All I wanted was to live my life in peace. But I guess this new leadership post thrust on me has been encouraging and controversial to many.

I am glad to see that you are happily partnered. Is this the first Kartaqi gay or lesbian couple or do we have more couples?

Email

From: Naomi

To: Isaac

Date: 1/21/2010 11:09:48 A.M.

Subject: Re: thank you

Hi Isaac,

Great to hear from you!

I used to believe that I would someday distance myself enough from the community to simply live my life in peace, as well. I never thought I would be the activist that I am today. I have since realized that revolutionary action is necessary in order be able to live in peace. What you have done has caused a HUGE progression in that direction. You are revolutionary.

There are many gay and lesbian kartaqis that have confided in me. Unfortunately, they are all closeted and as far as I know, none of them are in relationships with each other. However, some are in relationships with people outside of the community.

Email

From: Isaac

To: Naomi

Date: 1/21/2010 11:23:06 A.M.

Subject: Re; thank you

I think that many see me as a troublemaker. And yes, some see me as a revolutionary

Email

From: Andrew

To: Isaac

Date: 1/21/2010 11:28:09 A.M.

This web-site has truly taken off into unknown circles....I just want to be careful that you don't isolate yourself from the community too much...but it might be too late for that.

Email

From: Isaac

To: Andrew

Date: 1/21/2010 11:31:17 A.M.

Subject: Re: Scandal

I keep offering to transfer it to a neutral location. I couldn't be possibly more isolated than what the rabbi had ordered already. Except maybe people now can see that made a change, rather than being seen as 'that faggot' forever.

Discussion Board

Salazaar Slytherin ~ January 21st, 2010

Barbara Streisand, great post, just to make sure everyone read it:

> You think that the central board hired hackers to take down this board? How does your mind work? You dont think it is just a group of people who think this board is a joke and is making a mockery of things? I am pretty certain that the people posting on this board as Kartaqi Mom or Kartaqi Dad or whatever are the same 5-6 people who keep changing their names and making up stupid stories just to stir the pot. Isaac, this board will get you absolutely no where, and it was foolish to start it, we arent central board members, we are community youth who think you are wrong. Live with it.

Anyways, Isaac again you are not achieving anything. The Rabbi simply stated that you have already gone too far over the border and there is nothing to be done to bring you back, so just to let you be and let you live your life, but also to let you know that your choice is not welcome in our sanctuary, and I am sure thats something you knew when you made your choice. He never ordered anyone to attack you or harm you, those people act on their own and Rabbi Levy can not stop that. That comes with the territory, as I'm sure you know. If you are a homosexual living in this state you will hear hate remarks, same if you are an african-american, Latino, Asian, or whatever. Do not start a forum here to promote your ways, you made a decision live with it and leave us be.

jboy ~ January 21st, 2010

To "Solution": Thank you for your response and encouragement. Your suggestion is definitely a possibility. However, I cant help but wonder why I should deny myself the benefits of a marriage? A marriage provides both symbolic and literal benefits which I would like to enjoy someday.

Bravo ~ January 21st, 2010

The post that most resonated with me was:

Grandmother of 9 children ~ January 21st, 2010

Human dignity must come first. I brought up three children in the community and now have nine grandchildren living in the community. The community always had its pluses and minuses and unfortunately education was never a virtue, but overall the children turned out well. However, over the last few years I've watched the community radicalize around some terrible leaders. The level headed thinkers have been pushed to the back and the propaganda and sermons have become so distasteful that I tell my children that they shouldn't bring up the children in such an environment. Many of my friends have written letters to the board (our understanding is that hundreds have been written with names attached) on various topics to no avail. These individuals have hijacked the community and they have taken away the ideals the community was built on and have focused on fear, edicts, rules, and harassment. We no longer donate to the synagogue and my children have been taking steps to have their children spend less time in this environment. Even the Hebrew school has become infected with propaganda. They should be getting a Jewish education not exposure to political propaganda filled with fears, lies, and hatred. Many of us have been sending their grandchildren to Ashkenazi Hebrew schools most recently. It's such a shame. We were so such a beautiful community, its a real tragedy as I watch us spiral into the depths of radicalism. It's a shame we can't turn it around. Human dignity must come above all other ideas, but this administration just doesn't get it.

jboy ~ January 21st, 2010

To "helper": Thank you for your response. I believe you are right about the fact that coming out and revealing my identity could result in helping other people and encouraging others to come out. However, I believe every gay or lesbian should come out when he or she is ready to do so. Many of my friends have been outed involuntarily or have been pressured to come out by their fellow gay friends and it was destructive. I will come out someday. But for now, I am not ready.

admirer of 26married guy ~ January 21st, 2010

WOW. i am truly impressed by all the different writing skills and diversity of thoughts. its actually very inspiring. i must say 26married guy expresses me and many people i know very well and to the point.

Linda Stern ~ January 21st, 2010

To Isaac and Andrew,

A sincere congratulations to you!

Former Kartaqi KYC ~ January 21st, 2010

The Central Boards fingerprints are now on everything. They are even monitoring the KYC - the Kartaqi Youth Group. I used to be very involved in the KYC. But I stepped down and slowly even our youth group is being run by liked minded people like the Central Board from the younger generation. And the Scrolls is now also about to be censored by the Central Board and maybe already is. There is no freedom of speech in our Community. There are so many forces in place to scare our youth that nobody dares to speak up anymore. The KYC used to be a wonderful place to hang out, now its a disconnected group of young people of which half cant stand each other. The Scrolls used to be a great magazine, now its a controlled substance. Thank goodness we have this board now. We needed this so badly. Thank you Isaac.

;-) ~ January 21st, 2010

you're welcome Cindy

Gaydog ~ January 21st, 2010

Children adopted by a gay couple CANNOT (by jewish law) be Jewish. Isaac destroyed his own future within the community by making the decisions he has made. Excommunication is just a technicality which is a consequence of his own unfortunate action.

Enjoy your lives together; cause G-d knows you're going to hell in the next world.

Commuter ~ January 21st, 2010

Salazar Slytherin: you forget that your forefathers were persecuted in kartaq. You were not welcome as a jew in kartaq for many years. And jews were and still are persecuted. SO take a step back and dont do unto others what they did to your forefathers and bring in blacks and puerto ricans and compare that to what the rabbi said about isaacs lifestyle on saturday. We know that many kartaqis are racist, they even admit it. I cannot even tell you how many times I have heard that awful word **** in a derogatory way which translated means nigger. Or the word 'Spanish' in a derogatory way. It is so sickening.

America let the Kartaqis in with open arms and now we have turned into the most racist minority in Green Hills, the African Americans and Hispanics were here before we landed in this great country so please show some respect.

Just remember what happened to the Jews and the Kartaqi Jews many years ago before you go on your high horse putting down other races and lifestyles. Racism breeds racism and Kartaqis are on their way to being the most unpopular minority in Green Hills. I am sure you dont care but some of us on this board do care and live in Green Hills and would like to live in peace with our neighbors in Green Hills, regardless of their color or religion.

golfie ~ January 21st, 2010

To Gaydog,

Do you really think that it's about the desire to be a part of this community? Do you think Isaac is sitting at home, crying over the fact that he has no future in the community? He is more accomplished and more respectable than the entire community put together.

The more this community radicalizes, the more people will choose to leave. And as we have witnessed this past weekend, some of them will not be given a choice, which is a shame, really.

In the end, the wonderful community we once had will be sliver of religious extremism, with no room left for moderate voices.

It's a shame, really.

moving on to the Future ~ January 21st, 2010

To Truth hurts. The truth hurts it really does and so does reality! A healthy dialogue involves both sides. Meaning the CB be open to peoples views!! We are not trying to abandon our faith or denounce the values of this beloved community.

The angry people just want their voices heard and unfortunately this is the only outlet they have. The problem here is the radical control certain people want to have over this community.

A) Sending out letters signed by the CB and our Rabbi without consent of the community at large is insulting and shows that there is no room for compromise. *ex. I was revolted when I received a decree telling me I can't bring a converted person into the synagogue I go to every week. It should be realized that there are converts out there who genuinely want to be Jewish, the conversion process being very difficult to pass and most people upon successfully crossing over become more religious then our own congregation!

We are being led into a deep abyss with this leadership. Another example: a young woman coming to Synagogue to hear an enlightening sermon, instead she hears how it is inappropriate for woman to work out with male trainers!! What message does that send to the youth of our community? Next week will I have to hear that Kartaqi woman should not have male doctors or go to the gyno b/c of the temptation of sleeping with our doctor!!

This is the exact behavior that is crossing the line between sound leadership and tyranny.

Cindy ~ January 21st, 2010

All,

I dont know who this "Former Kartaqi KYC" character is and I dont know who just thanked me....but please leave me out of this.

I no longer have any affiliation or authority with the KYC or any other boards within the community.

Please do not use my name to state your own, personal opinions. No matter what the situation, please keep it respectful.

Thank You!

moving on to the Future ~ January 21st, 2010

Frustrated ex member of KYC! Nice to know there is absolutely no place to have our voices heard...now Scrolls is also being tarnished. Thanks to those lovely few people adding to the demise of this community- thanks a lot!

Another idea ~ January 21st, 2010

If we allow an edict against gays, why not have one against married couples who are also first cousins, or, from the largely older generation, the few cases where women married their uncles?

Our synagogue would soon resemble a ghost town.

Doesn't anyone realize how inappropriate edicts are?

moving on to the Future ~ January 21st, 2010

Edicts will just be the end of this community- who will the CB have left to preach to? I for one will leave the community if nothing changes...I refuse to raise my children under a dictatorship...end of discussion!

j-woww ~ January 21st, 2010

Another idea,

Gays must be banned from all Jewish circles, particularly ours, b/c they destroy something key to a Jewish home:

The Nuclear Family.

A family has always been, and should always be, based on the union of a Man and Woman. If you want to change this core value of our lives, you might as well other essential ideologies, like our 10 commandments.

anonymous ~ January 21st, 2010

To the people who say that a gay man should not force himself to fake and marry a woman because he won't love her:

I disagree. I am married and I do not believe sexual attraction has anything to do with feeling love and respect for your spouse. I may not have the most attractive wife, but I don't look at her as ugly. I love who she is as a person, and thats what gets me hot. In a marriage, love and respect for one another have nothing to do with physical attraction. If a gay man can manage to get it up for his female wife, then the emotional love should come as well, since the physical and emotional are 2 separate responsibilities.

real problems ~ January 21st, 2010

can we talk about the real issues here?

i refuse to pay $319 + tax per night at the W hotel in miami for Passover! I mean seriously people! Business is slow!!!

10commandments ~ January 21st, 2010

to i-woww---i am deeply disappointed by your suggestion to ban gays from all jewish circles. You reasoning has no merit--the nuclear family can still exist with acceptance of gays. Furthermore, you discredited yourself completely by mentioning the 10 commandments, because most Kartaqis I know, even the so-called pious ones, break them on a regular basis.

Pathetic ~ January 21st, 2010

So stop being a pathetic follower

Helena Hufflepuff ~ January 21st, 2010

Gaydog

Ingenious remarks!! You truly brilliant. Isaac, take down this forum
you are making a mockery of yourself (if you havent done so already)

guilty and honest ~ January 21st, 2010

I work on jewelry district and am a married man with children. I have
been reading every entry. I read what was written on other sins in the
community. I am sorry to say I am one of those men on jewelry
district that goes with other woman. And even if the truth hurts, it is
well known that many men that work on jewelry district (even
religious ones like myself) have relations during lunch or when we
travel. Many of us go to the hotel where we rent rooms for few hours
or the massage parlor around the corner. Some of us have mistress
and we tell each other. Maybe we are sex addicts and that is a big
problem with some men in the community but we have no help line.
Nobody to talk to so we do it because our friends do it.

I know this post will come as a shock to many of you but after what I
heard in synagogue on Saturday and on the board I feel very guilty
that Isaac is being punished and we can go with other woman behind
our wives and nobody says nothing.

I heard there is a brothel in Brooklyn just for Hassidic men so maybe it
is ok for a religious Jewish man to go with woman. I know this is a big
problem in our community and we need to take care of it and gay
men is not a big problem like adultery.

I want to say sorry to Isaac. We should be the ones punished not you.

284

Desperate Kartaqi Dad ~ January 21st, 2010

I got married at 24 to a girl who was 18. I am now a 34 year old and a father to 4 children, all being raised in this community. I have run a very successful jewelry business for most of my life, but now business has nosedived and I am still responsible for providing for my family! Providing what apparently? Diapers, food, clothing and shelter right? Not exactly, designer clad clothing, a new freaking designer bag every month, Passovers in Miami with a group or people I particularly consider backstabbers, not friends. All to keep up with what? A community has become dishonorable and disrespectful- there is nothing characteristic of Kartaq in our lives today. A clique in Kartaq meant an extension of our families- all it is now is a means to shun people and make certain groups more popular. Honestly the mothers and fathers in this community are not any better than teenagers, in fact my enlightened children are reminders of what's still pure and good in this world. The pressure to keep has caused me to drink as that has become a release for me and my tension. Did I mention that my wife only gets intimate with me if I buy her stuff! I have to borrow money from my father just to keep up with the demands decreed by the social system our community is based on!

Logical ~ January 21st, 2010

With all due respect to Isaac and Andrew, I must say I agree with the Central Board's resolution.

Our community, with as many negative characteristics as it may have, has the core fundamental purpose of preserving our values and protecting us from the non-jewish ideas of the non-kartaqi world. Since we all have the freedom to do whatever we want with our lives, any rules the Board makes can only be enforced in the public forum, but people still have the right to do whatever they want in their own private lives. It is not only gay-marriage that is being picked on. Anything contradicting our Torah is being ruled against. That includes keeping kosher. Since our religion requires the observance of Kosher laws, we are not allowed to serve unkosher food at kartaqi parties. But kartaqis are more than allowed to go eat at unkosher restaurants and keep unkosher food in their house. But once you expose to the public, the community forbids it. The same with gay or inter-marriage. You will not be thrown in jail or killed, but your marriage will not be allowed into our community events. Isaac and Andrew still deserve our respect and we should not badmouth anybody else that comes out in the future. But their un-jewish act will not be allowing in the synagogues or parties.

I wish Isaac and Andrew the best with everything.

-Logical

israeli women ~ January 21st, 2010

isaac. i don't knew you and you don't know me but i want to wish you and Andrew a happines good life and MAZAL TOV.

froom israel.

kartaqi supporter ~ January 21st, 2010

What is the point of our community if we don't uphold our core values. If we don't set these rules for ourselves, what are we here for? Just for the parties?

really mad ~ January 21st, 2010

guilty and honest- what you just described is the reason why i never ever ever ever want to be exposed to marry a kartaqi man! how can you trust a life with someone after hearing that statement!- oh my god. you are treating cheating like peer pressure- are you a 5th grader- you should be ashamed! beyond ashamed.

Truth Hurts ~ January 21st, 2010

Ok, so you dont want to equate homosexuality with murder.....my apologies.

What about men who are born with the urge to have sex with animals? Why is that different? Why is that wrong?

This is not a joke - I would like some serious responses...

Truth Hurts Response ~ January 21st, 2010

Halachically (according to rules of Judaism), no difference...

shwarma on a baguette ~ January 21st, 2010

Anybody hungry? I'm in the mood for some falafel

Ashamed ~ January 21st, 2010

I never knew our community was this despicable. All of these personal stories I've been reading these past couple of days have been disgusting and I'm terrified of growing up among you people. Going to synagogue this week will be so awkward for me. I'm going to look at everyone in a new light after this. I'm sick to my stomach!

Truth Hurts Response Response ~ January 21st, 2010

@Truth Hurts,

It depends...how sexy is the animal?

Isaac Namdar ~ January 21st, 2010

REMINDER:

The purpose of having an open and honest discussion is not to belittle each other, our community, our leaders, or our religion.

On this note, I will have to side with the more conservative voices here that gratuitous condescension will not achieve anything but chaos. Rather, we need to make an effort to express our opinions in a more positive and constructive manner.

Although many of you no longer see me as part of the community, I take personal offense every time someone puts down our community. We should all be proud of whom we are, although we can always better ourselves every day.

ISAAC

Truth Hurts ~ January 21st, 2010

Ok Dr. Namdar, maybe you can answer my question?

Truth Hurts ~ January 21st, 2010

Very simple question has been placed on the table here:

Explain why there should be any difference among the following 3 actions:

1) Man has sex with man

2) Man has sex with sister

3) Man has sex with animal

All 3 condemned by Torah - all 3 frowned upon in the majority of human eyes.

Reponses?

kartaqi supporter ~ January 21st, 2010

Ok, we need to stop bashing on Isaac and Andrew. I do not believe we should allow homosexuality in our synagogues, but I do believe they have the right to be homosexual in their own homes

James Kamins ~ January 21st, 2010

When gay people have bachelor parties, do they have separate ones, or do they have one together? Also, I assume the stripper is male. Can somebody please confirm?

Response to Truth Hurts ~ January 21st, 2010

I agree that none of these are good acts, but whatever a person does with their life is their own choice.

Some people might not agree with you and me that all 3 are wrong, so let them go do what they want. Just keep our community out of it.

apples ~ January 21st, 2010

I am very disheartened to hear that the CB has now decided to control both the KYC and Scrolls!! The only outlets out youth has to have their voices heard. I know the great minds and voices that you have shut with your sense of control and have forced them to silence themselves and step down from positions of authority all so you could yes..my friend who had such a great vision and was once so involved stepped down....they are driving out all the open minded youth and putting in little mini me's of the CB to run KYC they really remind me of Hammas like tactics.. it's very scary

Ravena Ravenclaw ~ January 21st, 2010

First commandment in the torah, *pru urvu* - be fruitful and multiple. Unfortunately that is impossible with 2 men, and I am pretty sure G-d, being the almighty superior being that he is, made it that way for a REASON. There is a reason a man has a penis and a woman has a vagina, and a reason why when they get together they bring LIFE. That is the foundation our torah is built on, and our community is built on the idea of orthodox Judaism, and if you want to bring up that the majority aren't orthodox, fine, but we still have orthodox jewish values that we will never get rid of. These are the rules and these are the laws. Isaac, have a great life, if you want to be left alone I suggest you stop trying to look for assurance through this ridiculous forum

KartaqiBisexual ~ January 21st, 2010

Dr. Namdar,

Please do not take this forum down. I know your mission was not to become a pioneer or an idol to others, but whether you like it or not YOU HAVE. I am Kartaqi and I have a lot of closeted Kartaqi friends. Your forum has become an outlet for many of them. Although, I have the most respect for our community rabbi, central board, KYC, Scrolls..etc. they need to realize that they are doing much more damage than good for my closeted friends.

First of all, bad mouthing others is one of the deadliest sins in Judaism and it seems like our leaders and rabbi have pretty much covered that already. Second of all, does no one realize what they are doing to those who are stuck in the toughest of areas? Between the life their parents have chosen for them and that which they desire to live.

I see the pain and anguish that my closeted friends, like "Jboy" have to live and my heart goes out to them. Instead of our Rabbi stepping up on Shabbat to discuss the "sins of being gay" and then walk away patting themselves on the back. Perhaps, they should look a little closer and see of the mental unhealth and severe levels of depression who have stricken my closeted friends.

Again, I have lots of respect for the central board, but if they really wanted to make a difference and do something that matters (instead of acting like communists), they should figure out a way to outreach to my closeted friends and maybe not necessarily support them, but to help them emotionally and mentally.

For god's sake we have cheating men in Jewelry district along with Kartaqi moms sleeping with personal trainers and the community's concerns have become the happiness of this couple??? Chances are Dr. Namdar and Mr. Mitchell are going to have a much happier marriage than a ton of other heterosexual Kartaqi marriages. They chose to live a life of happiness and truth and I wish them all of the best in life!

freedom of choice ~ January 21st, 2010

why are so many people anti-religion in the kartaqi community? if you don't want to observe any particular religious rule, you don't have to, but please don't ruin it for the rest of us. if you want to do things against the religious values, go ahead nobody is stopping you, just don't force us to watch and clap for you.

Good luck Isaac and Andrew, with much respect.

Answer to truth hunts ~ January 21st, 2010

Maybe you should go out there and experience life and see how many gays are out there, Jewish or not, who are living a normal life. If having sex with your sister or an animal is what's on your mind, then you're the only one here who's standing out!

why? ~ January 21st, 2010

guilty and honest---why do u cheat? what's the reason? Although there shouldn't be any excuses, are you unhappy with ur marriage? are you unhappy with life? are you looking for greater satisfaction due to some void in ur life?

I'm very curious, let me know if you can. Thanks

Respect Others ~ January 21st, 2010

With respect to Isaac and Andrew, I also want to respect our Rabbi. I heard the speech this week, and the Rabbi didn't say anything derogatory about Isaac and Andrew. To the contrary, he said that he respects their decision and they can do whatever they like with their personal life. But the Rabbi has a responsibility to address the issue of gay-marriage and he did so with much class. So please get off his back

Guilty and Honest ~ January 21st, 2010

I cannot control that I cheat. I feel guilty about it. My friends do it too so I am not only one. It has become like with many things in our Community. If nobody knows then its ok. Nobody knew about Isaac but they now know and its not ok. There are many more men cheating than gays in our Community and nobody says anything to us. In old Kartaq men were allowed to cheat so maybe that is reason we are doing it without feeling its not right. But in my note I said I now feel guilty. After Saturday I feel very guilty and that is why I made the post. There are many worse problems in Kartaqi Community than gay men. And I wanted to say that adultery is a big problem. We need to take this problem very seriously because even newly wed men start it when they hear the other men are doing it.

Agreed ~ January 21st, 2010

YES!!!!!!! I agree with Respect Others! The Rabbi has a duty to address issues in this community, he had nothing WRONG to say about Issac and Andrew, he actually wished them much luck with their life. But addressing the fact that GAY MARRIAGE is wrong, HE HAS EVERY RIGHT, because it wrong, it is against Judaism and torah law. Whether you agree with it or not, ITS WRONG. You cant help being a homosexual or having homosexual feelings and you have been living with it for a long time, thats fine, some of you may say its not something you control, still fine, but to act on those homosexual acts and get married when you knew it was wrong against your religion, a rabbi doesnt need to tell you its wrong, ITS WRONG!

Rabbi Levy is one of the best things that happened to this community, he has brought more youth together than any previous "rabbi" or authority figure, he does not preach, he does not brainwash, he teaches the way of the Torah and its up to you to choose to follow it or not. Have you seen him not speak to someone who drives to synagogue on Shabbat? NO he treats everyone equally with the respect they deserve. He is one of the most sincere men I have ever met in my life, so much respect for his family and wife (something most men and women in this community should learn) more than anything, he moved his whole family from overseas, to a new country to a new community, all of which they are not used to, so he can perform an important job of helping and bringing our community together in ways which we were not together before. So you say he gets a big fat check for doing so, OF COURSE HE DOES!!!!!! Dont all of you get paid at the end of the week sometimes for not even doing anything at all, why shouldnt he get paid for his services?

Do us all a favor, get off his back, stop bad mouthing him for being who he is and doing his job, he is no different than you Issac and Andrew, he is standing up for what HE BELIEVES IN.

You all want to blame someone for your problems in your life, go sleep on a couch and talk to your shrink.

Lynn Norwick ~ January 21st, 2010

Dear All,

I would like to say that the next issue of Scrolls is going to be about Identity- a topic that many of our community members have been discussing on this board and seem to have strong feelings about. Actually, any of you who feel frustrated on the side of Andrew and Issac or against, I welcome you to share your thought in an article and send it to my email: lynn.norwick@gmail.com. We want to include your thought in our next issue. Please remember that we cannot accept any anonymous entries. Also email me if you have any questions and spread the word!

Thanks,

Lynne

why? ~ January 21st, 2010

But, it's like saying someone jumped off a bridge so i'm going to do it too. There must be another reason that you do it.

Regardless, now is the time to start repenting. Maybe you can start a "movement" amongst your peers and have them start repenting as well. G-d is forgiving, and hopefully, with time, your wife will be too.

Don't be scared and do what you think is right/best.

Good luck to you

love ~ January 21st, 2010

To jboy and kartaqi bisexual- Please remember that you deserve to be happy. Although you may not be ready to come out, you can always live your life the way you please. I recommend approaching kartaqis who are already out and confiding in them. Maybe talking to someone who understands your pain and has been through it will help. Dont give up and please dont let any of these harsh words bring you down. G-d made you the way you are for a reason. Please dont believe that you cannot be gay & religious. You do not have to give up Judaism because you are gay.

James Kamins ~ January 21st, 2010

[profanity]

Answer to Why? ~ January 21st, 2010

I assume it all comes back to a form of sex addiction. I actually, know of a kartaqi sex addict who is in therapy and medication for his problem.

It shouldnt be so hard to believe, this problem very much so can exist in our community and is in no way limited to men!

hello ~ January 21st, 2010

James,

You are making a fool of yourself. Have some dignity and self respect

James Kamins ~ January 21st, 2010

People directed me here as apparently someone is posting here under my name. Kindly stop.

Why? ~ January 21st, 2010

I am sorry to hear that, and I hope the problem will be solved.

Silence Do-Good ~ January 21st, 2010

One point I think people in this forum are missing.

A lot of notion has been made about a person's right to live their life how they choose. But doing things like "bringing a cheeseburger into synagogue" is crossing the line.

You should be made aware that Isaac and Andrew didn't try to make their lives public. They didn't walk into synagogue, they didn't invite kartaqis to their wedding, and they didn't ask our rabbi to do anything for the ceremony.

It was us who decided to butt in. A kartaqi found this website and told everyone about it. We infected their lives, not the other way around.

For those of you who don't understand the name I used please google it, I find myself to be pretty clever ;)

James Kamins ~ January 21st, 2010

I have no interest at all in getting involved in discussions on the forum, but I'm being told there were posts using my name. They are not me, please remove them

disgusted ~ January 21st, 2010

You people don't realize what damage you are doing. You are all selfish and truly disgusting. Just because you have confessions to make (for example: you work on jewelry district and cheat on your wife) it doesn't give you the right to post it here in front of hundreds of women who have husbands who work on jewelry district and are now panicked and depressed and calling their husbands and potentially getting into a fight that shouldn't even be happening. If you are so called religious or even care about other people, then why dont you think about a concept called "*shalom bayit*" (peace in the household) because you sure as hell are ruining that for a lot of people. I have tons of friends who told me that after reading this website, they called their husbands crying and praying that their husbands are not cheating on them. These women dont deserve this, and just because you are sick in your head and you cheat on your wife, or you think its OK to write these comments saying how unhappy you are, you are basically ruining the lives and marriages of other people. (Believe it or not, it could be the relationships of your parents, sister, brother, cousin, best friend, etc.) If you are such a smart and noble man Isaac, then make the right decision and take this discussion board down. I don't think you wanted your marriage to cause such trauma in this community. If you did, then you honestly should be ashamed of yourself.

Stop being so selfish people.

Email

From: Carl

To: Isaac

Date: 1/21/2010 12:02:32 P.M.

Subject: A BIG problem has been created...

Hi, I'm Carl, I have no idea who you are, I just need to address something to you. I absolutely respect your opinions and how you live your life, and wish you lots of luck. The thing is your message boards have been a vehicle for some good, but unfortunately lots of bad. Marriages are being ruined as I write this email to you. The Rabbi of our community, who wished you and your husband well-being, is going through a hard time and having his reputation ruined. I understand free speech is great, but when it is coming at the expense of marriages, something needs to be done. I think you know what is right. Please be assured that I am not connected in any way to any of the community rabbi, boards, committees, etc, and I wasn't sent here by anybody, I am only seeing things with my own eyes:

"You people don't realize what damage you are doing. You are all selfish and truly disgusting. Just because you have confessions to make (for example: you work on jewelry district and cheat on your wife) it doesn't give you the right to post it here in front of hundreds of women who have husbands who work on jewelry district and are now panicked and depressed and calling their husbands and potentially getting into a fight that shouldn't even be happening. If you are so called religious or even care about other people, then why dont you think about a concept called *shalom bayit* (peace within home) because you sure as hell are ruining that for a lot of people. I have tons of friends who told me that after reading this website, they called their husbands crying and praying that their husbands are not cheating on them. These women don't deserve this, and just because you are sick in your head and you cheat on your wife, or you think its OK to write these comments saying how unhappy you are, you are basically ruining the lives and marriages of other people. (Believe it or not, it could be the relationships of your parents, sister, brother, cousin, best friend, etc.)"

I'm sure you did not intend for this, but it only gets worse, this message board is also creating animosity between Kartaqis and another community of Jews.

I am 24 years old and 2 of my non-Kartaqi friends just told me that they have been putting up fake stories on this message board for the past 48 hours just to stir up some drama. This discussion board is completely ridiculous and I have a feeling 75% of the entries are based on *lashon hara* or just made up completely. Please know that what you have been reading is not necessarily real. I would out these 2 non-Kartaqi boys but they would come right back and destroy my name. What more can I do?

I know you are a good man and will know what the right thing to do is! The fact that due to false statements marriages are being ruined greatly bothers me, and I know it bothers you too. So I beg that you remove the message board asap. Please do not share my name with anybody as I don't want to get involved in all the ruckus that was unintentionally created with your message board.

Your friend,

Carl

Email

From: Isaac

To: Carl

Date: 1/21/2010 2:34:20 P.M.

Subject: Re: A BIG problem has been created...

Indeed a tool of honest and free democratic discussion has been morphed into something I never intended. Surely, I never wanted any harm to come to the Central Board or the Rabbi. I am looking into ways to tone things down, or transfer the blog elsewhere away from my auspices. Please advise.

Email

From: Doug

To:　　　Isaac, Sarah

Date:　　1/21/2010 2:57:03 P.M.

Subject:　Connecting

Hey Isaac!,

Sarah and I have been monitoring your site constantly and are in complete awe to whats happening.

Years ago, I had put up a blog venting my frustrations with the central board and the communities direction. My posts created a rather large burst of comments similar to whats happening on your site. The only difference was that I posted anonymously and my feedback wasn't as rampant as yours.

I'm also part of a web committee the community has formed that is trying to update the various community websites and bring them up to speed. I'm working closely with a rather moderate CB member in doing this. Last night, he called me suggesting we figure a way to carry the discussion over from your site to kartaqi.org. I think we all agree that this is a very bad idea. It will only create another media outlet endorsed by the Central Board.

My suggestion is to create a new blog.

This blog will firstly be independent from any authority with an agenda to push. It will also have a series of editors and administrators, preferably with varying viewpoints. These editors will balance each other out so nobody can claim the blog is an extension of the CB or right/left thinkers. The hard part would be curating the editors willing to take on this task. We can recruit writers from your site, or the Scrolls.

These editors cannot post anonymously. As helpful and therapeutic as your site has been for many people, posting anonymously is not credible. It is leading to issues on your site now which is hurting integrity. The editors will post whatever they please and/or think is currently a hot topic. They can post polls on community issues such as CB approval ratings, Gay rights, weather converting to judaism for marriage is acceptable, etc..

Posts from editors can be commented on by the entire community (anonymously if they wish). And obviously filtered to remove rubbish.

The admins can be a mix of anyone. As long as they remain journalistic and professional. CB members, left/right thinkers, rabbi?... anyone

I was thinking of calling it "The Unofficial Kartaqi Weblog" - or "TUKW" - Free speech.

The idea is to have system with checks & balances. By doing so, we can lay conspiracy theories by either party to rest.

PS - Sarah, I agree that we should not mix the content. This site will be new.

What do you guys think? any suggestions to add?

Email

From: Sarah

To: Doug; Isaac

Date: 1/21/2010 3:00:16 P.M.

Subject: Re: Connecting

Love the idea. Doug, I think once you have it up then Isaac can put a message on his board saying his board is closed for biz and direct everyone to the below. That way the content stays separate and the integrity isn't hurt either way. But we need to do it fast. How fast can you set up this sit and are there friends you can work on this with who are not intimidated by CB and open minded?

Email

From: Isaac

To: Sarah; Doug

Date: 1/21/2010 3:07:37 P.M.

Subject: Re: Connecting

I like the idea of new blog with neutral and varied moderators. Just that my site is bursting, and we should act fast. Tell me where the site is, and I will redirect all people there.

Email

From: Sarah

To: Isaac, Doug

Date: 1/21/2010 3:10:40 P.M

Subject: Re: Connecting

Doug – why don't you set it up with the name you mentioned and for now Isaac directs people there.

Isaac – I would leave up your site but stop new postings and just direct them to the blog that doug is creating

For now doug – you can let it flow and discuss with others what to do. I wouldn't worry about editing. You can write that it is an independent body and an extension of what started on Isaacs blog but Isaac is no longer moderating or connected.

Isaac – you must leave the content up as I feel that people still need a chance to get the full picture of what happened

Lets see how this goes – if it gets out of control then we can source more help but with some laws in the masthead of the new blog I think we will minimize that

Email

From: Doug

To: Isaac, Sarah

Date: 1/21/2010 3:47:24 P.M.

Subject: Re: Connecting

before you post anything. (I will be open to getting emails at a different address). I just got off the phone with my contact from the CB. Freddy Horton. He's one of the younger more moderate thinkers on the board. Trust me in that, he is very neutral in his position. He also agrees that a blog like this should be created. He went further to say that he doesn't think a CB member should even be allowed to edit the site.

Regardless. He wants me to arrange a conference call between us. He asked me to ask your permission.

If we can all agree to a conference call, we can come to some sort of closure today!

I'm going to have the site up shortly. I'll add you as an admin so you can check it out

The Discussion Board had blossomed into something beyond I or anyone else could have imagined. I wasn't sure if the amount of support was enough to outweigh the additional animosity that could come out of it. Additionally, monitoring and managing the discussion was beyond my capacity, both logistically and stylistically. It was time I found a satisfactory end to the whole thing. Transferring the custody to neutral persons seemed like the perfect answer.

Discussion Board

Answer to disgusted ~ January 21st, 2010

Disgusted, you make a good point. However, I guess these people have had these feelings inside of them for a long time, and don't know who to go to or how to get it out. They are using this forum as an outlet, and that is a start in improving themselves.

You are right, it can cause problems. However, as a concerned kartaqi, you/we should think of other ways in which people could express themselves. They are crying out for help, and u should take that into consideration.

Answer to disgusted ~ January 21st, 2010

Its a sad situation, i feel very bad for those women who are upset. However, chances are that if a simple forum with anonymous subscribers is upsetting these women, maybe they have a reason to be upset.

They should have nothing to worry about if they are secure about their marriage and husband. If they are calling their husbands in a panic, maybe they have found a reason to accuse them!?

UNDER ~ January 21st, 2010

Disgusted, Thank You for your post. You are so correct. Please stop ruining people's lives and our Heritage.

Sorry Disgusted ~ January 21st, 2010

Disgusted - I feel for you and your friends' situation. Everyone's panicking but think about all those people who have a guilty conscience and have nowhere else to let it all out but this discussion board. Our community is so controlling and threatening that sadly, this is the only opportunity people have to spread their feelings

guilty and honest ~ January 21st, 2010

OK guys, I need to come clean...I got caught. I didnt mean for my post to get so blown out of proportion. I personally am not one of those men who has had affairs on jewelry district but I hear about it all the time. I just feel bad for Isaac and what he's going through and wanted to make a point that there are worse things going on in this community, we just dont know about because its behind closed doors.

Reality ~ January 21st, 2010

Disgusted: I think we need to understand that the man who confessed to cheating has nobody to speak to. The Kartaqi Community has no counselors and he is probably ashamed to go to the Rabbi because as he said he is a religious man. So he has to do it anonymously. And the point he made was that we are punishing Isaac when there is a bigger problem in the community which is adultery. You must accept this and cannot expect people not to express how they feel. Accept the reality. And move on. If you are blessed with a good husband then chances are he is not cheating. But leave the man who had the courage to confess alone please. And the hundreds of people that are in awe of Isaac for finally giving everyone a voice. Thank you Isaac and please do not take this board down. People need to express themselves.

Very Important ~ January 21st, 2010

I am 24 years old and 2 of my Zameeni friends just told me that they have been putting up fake stories on this message board for the past 48 hours just to stir up some drama.

This discussion board is completely ridiculous and I have a feeling 75% of the entries are based on *lashon hara* or just made up completely.

Please know that what you have been reading is not necessarily real.

I would out these 2 Zameeni boys but they would come right back and destroy my name. What more can I do?

Money Talks ~ January 21st, 2010

I've read all the posts, and I just want to say that I no longer will be donating to this synagogue. I'm voting with my wallet. I can no longer relate to the ideology of our synagogue.

Guilty and Honest ~ January 21st, 2010

To guilty and honest nr 2 who took over my name just now. I think it is wrong for you to use my name and lie to the world and write on my behalf telling them you are coming clean. You just posted as me and that is not right. Whatever I said in my previous posts came from the bottom of my heart and a confession I made that I cheat and that Isaac should not be the one punished. It took a lot of courage for me to write about it. And the reason I do not think anyone is doing anything about the adultery is because some of the men are from the rich families in the community so the leaders are afraid to say anything because they are scared not to get donations. This is the way our Community works. We do not say bad things about men that cheat ever. We hide it. So it happens and the ones that do it like me don't get punished for it. But Isaac gets punished for being gay?

So for everyone on this board. I am telling the truth and not coming clean as guilty and honest nr 2 just said. My posts are the truth and may G-D understand my need to confess and forgive me.

This will be my last post as all I wanted to do is say there are worse problems in the Community than gays. We must bring in counselors to help the men that cheat behind the wives back. It is a big problem.

S.H. ~ January 21st, 2010

I convinced my parents of the same thing this week. No more money. If the radicals and large donors want to fund it, let them.

Anonymous ~ January 21st, 2010

If you stop donating, then there will just be a yearly fee to have a seat, like every other synagogue in the world...

Kartaqi Youth Speaking ~ January 21st, 2010

Very Important: I am very Kartaqi and my friends and I have been posting on this board over the past 2 days and we know even who many of the others are who have posted good stuff. We share our fake names so we know it is real. My mom has posted and my 3 uncles and my cousins. So do not try and scare away the people from this board by saying its the Zameenis. Don't blame everything bad that happens to Kartaqis on others. We have to be real. We have a crisis and no matter what tricks you use to bring down this board. It will not happen. Isaac, please listen to the voice of the youth and don't bring down this board.

guilty and honest ~ January 21st, 2010

This blog has become a mockery. I am the original "guilty and honest" I wrote that post just to show a point. I have personally never cheated...and if I did I would never admit it on this discussion board. I was just trying to make a point that you cannot get mad at Isaac for being gay when none of us knew about it when all of us are probably doing worse things ourselves.

to any body else who wants to pretend to be "Guilty and Honest" PLEAST STOP!!!

check values ~ January 21st, 2010

To Very Important

Why are you friends with those guys? Why would you be friends with someone who would destroy your name?

Doesn't that say so much about our community? I advise that you stop considering these people who post fake stories here as friends. They are not worth anything...even a chewing gum stuck to the sole of your shoe is worth more than these two (if indeed they exist).

BRUTAL ~ January 21st, 2010

Honestly, I think this is the most disgusting discussion board i have ever read in my life. The problem here is not gay people, or people who cheat, its YOU! Kartaqis are so up each other's asses 24/7 that instead of working on themselves & working on their own relationships they sit there in there stupid cliques and talk about who is dating who, & why is this person gay, & why did this girl marry that guy he has no money, & this boy was adopted so he shouldn't get married in this community, or why did so and so's mom wear that dress when shes 500 pounds, & why did that man come to synagogue after his daughter just got brutally beaten up. MIND YOUR OWN DAM BUSINESS. Sitting here & posting your problems is one thing, but instead your making everyone paranoid & destroying peoples marriages as we speak. Some of you idiots can sit here all day & argue whether being gay is ok or not ok. But at the end of the day..guess what? NOONE CARES. I thought very highly of this kartaqi community, i was proud to tell people where i was from. But now i am ashamed.

S.H. ~ January 21st, 2010

A yearly fee is the way to go. Then the few families who think they are kings and have hijacked the direction of the community will have less sway. We need a democracy, not clerics

Anonymous ~ January 21st, 2010

ok the whole guilty and honest sh*t is getting old. No one cares. You're the one with the effed up life. Take care of it with your wife (if it happened). If it didnt, go work. It's the middle of the day! Stop wasting your time here and being retarded

anonymous ~ January 21st, 2010

We will not be donating either. For what?

DONT BE SO GULLIBLE PEOPLE ~ January 21st, 2010

for those wives who are worrying about cheating husbands on jewelry district: there are people slandering by posing as others and immature high school kids trying to be funny posting on this site: so did it ever occur to you that the "cheating husband" post is just someone trying to make trouble or push their "the kartaqi crisis is not the gay issue, its everything else" agenda on everyone else and cause a mass hysteria. anyone here can pretend they are someone else. i doubt any kartaqi man would admit to cheating on a blog where they feel unprotected by the security of the site, so clearly these are pranks to rile people up. same goes for gays, no gay person will come out on this site, and the same poster could assume different identities each time with the same admissions to make the issue seem far more rampant than it truly is. we are dealing with one of the most slandering and "*lashon hara*" speaking communities around, dont forget that.

oy! ~ January 21st, 2010

G-d!!!!!! Whatever came of us!

MESSIAH MESSIAH MESSIAH ....oh yuy yuy yuy yuy yuy

Guilty and Honest ~ January 21st, 2010

guilty and honest nr2: i stated clearly that I will not post again but you have hijacked my name. All I asked is for people to understand many men cheat and that we need counselors and have nobody to talk to. If your wife is calling you and that is your way to calm her down so be it. My wife doesn't know I cheat and I hope she never finds out. But I have a problem and the Community is not giving me a helpline for it because they are afraid. This is why so much bad happens in our Community. So if you want to hijack my name please do it but please understand that I am telling the truth and that if you put me and the many men that I know who cheat in a court of law you would see how serious the problem is. I would advise you to stop this conversation and accept the fact that there is a major problem we have and speak to the leadership about it so it does not get worse.

Messiah ~ January 21st, 2010

Leave me alone (*in Kartaqi language*)...you guys arent worthy. Like what's gonna happen if I come? You guys wont change.

MOST PEOPLE ~ January 21st, 2010

I AGREE. I WOULD SAY THAT 95% OF THESE COMMENTS ARE MADE BY IMMATURE IMBICLES TRYING TO RILE THINGS UP AND CAUSE EVEN MORE HATRED AMONG FELLOW JEWS. *LASHON HARA* ALSO MEANS TALKING ABOUT PEOPLE WHOSE NAMES YOU DON'T MENTION/and GROUPS of people. WHEN YOU SAY: CENTRAL BOARD, RABBI, WIVES(even though youre not mentioning actual names, you are still KILLING them and DESTROYING ppl and lives with your careless comments). GROW UP AND SOLVE YOUR OWN ISSUES

happy ~ January 21st, 2010

I am a 24 year old girl. I got married at 21 and I am probably the happiest person in the world. I love my husband and he is obsessed with me.

Instead of people writing horror stories I am sharing inspiring stories!

My husband has taught me to grow and be a better person and I hope I have done the same to him. We have one beautiful son and another child on the way. Everyday of our my life is so rewarding. I finished college and I do plan on working again when the time is right.

Although it is a hard economy and life is not as easy as it used to (we are going to be moving in with his parents soon) life is life and I still couldnt be more grateful for everything I have.

Being jewish is the best thing that happened to me and being kartaqi is also great. Think about the times when certain people in our community were sick and we all pulled together and had Psalms readings and challah bakings and speeches etc in their honor. Think about the times a parent or grandparent has passed away and all the people who showed up to pay their respects. I have never seen anything like that in my life.

Please, people, start writing your inspirational positive stories and not your confessions of guilt and personal problems.

confused ~ January 21st, 2010

I am literally laughing on the floor right now

WHAT LEADERSHIP??????? WHERE DO YOU PEOPLE LIVE? BECAUSE I LIVE IN GREEN HILLS AND I AM KARTAQI AND I DONT KNOW OF ANY LEADERSHIP.

I WAKE UP EVERY MORNING BRUSH MY TEETH, AND PEE AND I NEVER SAW A LEADER STANDING IN MY BATHROOM TELLING ME TO DO SO.

Still on the floor laughing

WhatsWrongWithYou? ~ January 21st, 2010

Are you telling us that there are ACTUALLY people out there who think Kartaqi Men dont cheat on their wives?

Are you people for real? Not all men cheat, obviously...but to say their confessions are a lie?...and high school kids are messing around pretending to be these "cheaters"?

Get Real...kartaqi men brag about it...some of them are damn proud of it!

Just a mom ~ January 21st, 2010

Dear All: I am new to this board and a mother of 5 children. I love my community and my friends and I respect people, all people. I think we are learning that we need to have a place to speak out. Let's have leaders decide to have an official Kartaqi discussion board for everyone. We know there is a crisis going on. We need a solution. Please post if you have good ideas for a solution so that we can move forward to a better community.

Vegas ~ January 21st, 2010

What happens in Vegas stays in Vegas

concerned ~ January 21st, 2010

I know for a fact that there are many gay people in our community who love the community and need a place to feel safe.

Suggestion: how about working with gay kartaqis instead of kicking them out of the community? maybe we could start a support group? if the central board, rabbi, and other leaders of our community are so confident, why not be open minded to such ideas? what do you have to lose? if you are all so certain about your theories, try to convince us.

vegas2 ~ January 21st, 2010

what happens in your ass stays in your ass

Really confused ~ January 21st, 2010

I dont see why all of you gay people arent coming out then...want to be independent and hate this community? You wont care about coming out. You think it's not a sin and you shouldnt be looked down upon...you shouldnt have a reason to stay in the closet

happy too but honest too ~ January 21st, 2010

happy: thank you for sharing your wonderful story and I agree there are also some positive stories in the community but we are bombarded with those everywhere, in the Scrolls, the websites, Shalom magazine, facebook, the weeklies. Everybody shows their lives are perfect. This is the first time we as Kartaqis have had a chance to share our true stories. It is healthy for us. So let the truth rule and find comfort that there are enough outlets for us Kartaqis to share joy and happiness and show perfection.

agreement ~ January 21st, 2010

I agree. There are plenty of positive things about the community as well and it would be a shame not to acknowledge them, foremost our commitment to our families and our love for traditions.

We must find a way to unify but in order to do so, we must open our hearts and accept those who do not seek to hurt others.

Isaac is a real inspiration. He is educated; a renowned doctor who is seriously committed to helping so many people; and a family man who stood by his father's side and helped his every step until he decided to move to Israel. He happens to be gay, but in my book, he is more of a quality Kartaqi than many others.

Shabbat Shalom ~ January 21st, 2010

My family is donating to Haiti and to Israel. Nothing for our Synagogue this year.

Comment on agreement ~ January 21st, 2010

Agreement, we need more kind-hearted and open-minded people like you. Good for you.

concerned ~ January 21st, 2010

we are not coming out because we are scared to be kicked out of the community. we love our community dearly despite its flaws. we believe that this community is beautifully united and has great values. however, the central board and rabbi have made it pretty clear that we will not be welcome if we do come out. this is just one of the many reasons gay kartaqis hesitate to come out

HeadonStraight ~ January 21st, 2010

Your heads are going to explode (*in Kartaqi language*)!

Up to the gills ~ January 21st, 2010

Nice...punish the synagogue, by not donating because someone chose to be gay or someone chose to cheat on his wife.

Pick your battles what does one have to with the other?

happy ~ January 21st, 2010

In response to happy and honest: Why depress people more with sad stories. You never heard of the book "chicken soup for the soul" its great inspirational stories that put a smile on your face and appreciate life.

Why depress everyone further with your problems when you can talk about your happiness.

Godric Gryffindor ~ January 21st, 2010

Damn you Salazaar, your evil ways will never win over hogwarts

yeah right! ~ January 21st, 2010

Submit your secrets to PostSecret.com

happy and honest ~ January 21st, 2010

Happy: That's the problem with our Community. We are never encouraged to show our true self or tell our problems. It builds up in us. We always have to show we are happy. Have you ever seen someone not smiling even if they are suffering inside? That is the Kartaqi way. Talking about what bothers us is healthy and not depressing.

wow ~ January 21st, 2010

You know I am posting comments and they are not coming up or being taken off completely.

no profanity, just different views from some people on this forum, funny how its being filtered right???

Talk about ONE-SIDED!

anonymous ~ January 21st, 2010

Being gay is a sin.

Up to the gills! - I 100% agree with you

Kebab House ~ January 21st, 2010

wow: Don't talk nonsense. The minute you press "submit" the post shows up. Nobody is filtering unless you do profanity.

If ~ January 21st, 2010

I hope you are all proud of yourselves, the very few of us who were actually pouring out our hearts, will no longer be believed.

happy ~ January 21st, 2010

In response to happy and honest: "Talking about what bothers us is healthy and not depressing."-happy and honest

I think you should talk about what bothers you to your psychologist or therapist or someone who is a professional that can help you. Or confide in a friend you trust. And YES it is VERY depressing to hear other people's problems. I understand you shouldn't keep stuff bottled up but why vent on a public forum when no one here can help you

Tracker ~ January 21st, 2010

Guess what everyone...I know quite a lot about computers and everyone who posted can be tracked using their IP address. By getting their IP address, I found out their actual address through their service provider and because most of you are in the Kartaqi phonebook, I know who you are. Don't be foolish. You're never really "anonymous" nowadays.

Have a good day.

"THE SITUATION" ~ January 21st, 2010

DISCUSSION BOARD IS THE NEW FACEBOOK, I CHECK IT MORE OFTEN!!!

Kebab House ~ January 21st, 2010

Tracker: Go to About Discussion Board section of the site, nobody can track anyone. Not even Isaac. I am sure Isaac would not even if he could. He is a gentleman. Stop the scare tactics

kjkj ~ January 21st, 2010

I CANT STOP CRACKING UP FROM THIS WEBSITE. HYSTERICAL

"The Situation" ~ January 21st, 2010

I wish there was a "like" button [referring to a feature on Facebook]

Hey ~ January 21st, 2010

Tony!

OMG ~ January 21st, 2010

I cant wait to go to synagogue this week and for it to be exactly the same (ie. fake hellos and convos) because no one has a backbone. AHHH SO excited!

Kevin ~ January 21st, 2010

ALL THE GAYS STEP UP TO THE PLATE AND COME OUT OF THE CLOSET IN SYNAGOGUE THIS SHABBAT.

Dr to Kartaqis ~ January 21st, 2010

I am not Kartaqi. I am an American physician who lives in Green Hills and am a Dr to many Kartaqis. One of my patients told me about this board. I have been reading it and have some advice for you. I hope you will not be offended. Many Jewish Communities have help phone lines and counselors for their members. It is so helpful for young people and adults and even the elderly to have someone they can talk to. As a medical professional I think you need to bring in a team to help people. Nobody lives a life without problems but many suffer in silence. Do not let your members suffer in silence. Try and help by bringing in mental health professionals and setting up a confidential system for them to seek the help.

Miss you ~ January 21st, 2010

To the girl who recently got engaged..I still have feelings for you! Reach out to me. I miss you - You left too soon

At his point Thursday afternoon I was in the middle of seeing patients in the office. I had a run of patients, and was not able to check the Discussion Board for about an hour. Once I got back to my computer, there were more than 70 new messages in just one hour. I had to skim through all those entries quickly just to make sure there was no profanity. I had the sense that things were getting out of control, everything was developing so fast. I thought it was a good idea to take a short break.

Discussion Board

ISAAC NAMDAR ~ January 21st, 2010

WOW! There are so many voices here, and people have so much to say.

I am still saddened that many here have used this medium for slander, or have created unnecessary friction among the community.

I am proposing a cool down period of a couple of hours, probably till 5PM. You can read old posting, but new postings will not go through until after 5PM.

I am also again apologizing sincerely to our Rabbi and all members of the Board if many comments in this forum have made negative remarks about them. That for sure was never my intention.

I am also proposing that we come up with an alternate location for this discussion board, one that is not under my domain name. I am asking everyone to put your heads together and come up with acceptable solutions. Silencing the people is not the solution, but we need a more constructive forum for discussion.

Thanks for your understanding.

Email

From: Jerome

To: Isaac

Date: 1/21/2010 3:52:46 P.M.

Subject: Hi

I am so glad you suggested a two-hour break from the site. I think it's a good idea for people to simmer a little.

Email

From: Isaac

To: Jerome

Date: 1/21/2010 4:45:05 P.M

Subject: Re: Hi

Thanks, I agree we need to cool off a bit. I actually set up a conference to see how I can transfer it over to someone else. I guess it became a bit of a monster.

Facebook Message

From: Ron

To: Isaac

Date: January 21 at 5:23pm

You must be going crazy with the site, i can imagine how much work it could be. Dont give up ...you are helping a lot of people

At 6 PM I had a conference call with Doug and Freddy Horton, a Central Board member. Freddy and I went to the same college, and had known each other since then. Occasionally, when seeing each other in synagogue or at a wedding or other community event, we would exchange hellos. He is now a member of the Central Board, and perhaps represents some of the younger voices in our community.

After a few pleasantries, we got to business. We all easily agreed that the Discussion Board on my website was never intended to air out everyone's laundry, and it was set up only for my own communication with others. I apologized to Freddy, and asked him to carry the message of apology to others on the CB and Rabbi Levy. I never meant to create a medium to be used for slander and ridicule. I made it clear to him that revenge was never the intention.

We also agreed that with Doug's knowledge of internet technology, we can quickly set up an alternate discussion board, and direct all traffic there. Doug indicated he will look for more moderators who can post topics for debate, and perhaps some of the editorial staff from Scrolls are best suited for this role.

Once all the logistics were ironed out, the conversation turned to a lighter note and Freddy asked me about the honeymoon pictures he saw on my original website before I took down the pictures. He was really impressed by the location. I told him the name of the island and the resort, how to get there, prices, etc.

Although I maintained my calm through this last piece of conversation, I was completely taken back by what I just heard. Freddy, a member of the Central Board, the same panel that decided gays should be strictly banished from our community, and numerous other judgments pertaining to what is proper code of behavior, just admitted to me he went behind my back and got into my business without being invited to do so. He was no different than all the other nosey people who made it their business to dissect my life into pieces while I had done my best to shield them from information they might not find agreeable. As a member of a panel deciding proper behavior, he should have known better and not go through my site page by page and then have the audacity to discuss it with me openly as though he were my best friend. Just mind-boggling!

Email

From: Andrew

To: Laura, Sharon, Isaac

Date: 1/21/2010 6:36:53 P.M

Subject: Hi

I had not gotten involved as I don't understand all the cultural pieces but I sat down yesterday and read lots of it and all I can say is unbelievable. This thing has quickly taken on a life of its own. I am truly mixed as I am happy isaac is living freely and open but sad that he is no longer welcome at his traditional synagogue. We will join another synagogue together that is more welcoming to keep close to the faith as I don't want this to diminish isaacs traditions and faith.

All will work out and I am sorry if there has been any backlash to any of you as we clearly didn't intend for this to happen please express this to your mom and Nathan.

Right now we are trying to figure out where to move this forum blog to as it is too hard to host and I don't want isaac to be more disliked in his community than now...although the way he was treated was awful and I hurt when hatred and discrimination is projected on the most amazing man in the world!

Lots of love. Andrew

Email

From: Sarah

To: Isaac

Date: 1/21/2010 7:09:11 P.M.

Subject: Re:

Isaac a few people have emailed me if you could at least finish posting what has come in during the few hours of hiatus. They wrote stuff and want it on the board badly. Could you do that and then a final statement when the new board link is up? otherwise they wont let me alone!

The following is only a portion of a series of emails that circulated among a group of us as we tried to figure out the terms of the new weblog. Although the reader might find it a long and laborious process to read through them one by one, I am including (most of) them here to showcase the amount of incoming correspondences I had to sort through in addition to an unstoppable debate on the Discussion Board. Oh, and I had to attend a three hour dinner in the middle of all this, so I was out of commission for a few hours and had to do some serious catch up after I got back home.

Email

From: Doug

To: Isaac, Sarah, Janice, Veronica, Joshua

Date: 1/21/2010 7:46:34 P.M.

Subject: Re:

To Janice and Veronica.

Hello Isaac. Meet our first few editors who are going to free you from the monster you've created!

It's been decided amongst several parties to migrate the discussion (and all future topics) to a neutral blog.

http://kartaqiweblog.blogspot.com/

Please keep that url to yourself for now.

I understand Scrolls wanted to work with Isaac and because of Scroll's ties with the CB, they cannot. You can interview him here. This site has no CB oversight. It has no political tilt either. As a matter of fact, I'm trying to balance out it's ideology with editors of varying backgrounds. As an editor, you have free rein to post whatever you wish is appropriate. No one will stop you. But we would also like to have a mix of editors with ideas that differ from yours too. If you know of someone, please get them involved.

Keep in mind that even though this is a 'kartaqi' site. and it is approved by the CB (well at least one member unofficially). It is not publicly endorsed by the central board. And it should remain that way.

PS - I've cc'd Joshua here as well. He has created a forum (bit different than a blog) as a substitute to Isaac's site. We will use the forum (by linking to it) for long and trailing topics that are not suitable for a blog.

http://boards2go.com/boards/board.cgi/Kartaqi

PPS - I've also added Sarah to the message. She's been integral in the entire process from the beginning. Though she may not step in as an editor, i'm hoping she can linger around and suggest topics and maybe even do some guest posts on occasion (the same goes for the doc).

With your permissions, I would like to add you as editors to the newly formed blog. Once underway, Isaac can put a stop to the postings on his page.

Email

From: Isaac

To: Doug; Sarah, Veronica, Janice, Joshua

Date: 1/21/2010 7:49:59 P.M.

Subject: Re:

Great work. I see that my child will be in good hands, LOL.

Please tell me ASAP when you are ready for people to start posting there so I can make the announcement. Do you think it will be tonight?

Email

From: Sarah

To: Isaac; Doug; Veronica; Janice; Joshua

Date: 1/21/2010 7:51:57 P.M.

Subject: Re:

Congrats to you all and for Isaac to opening this forum. I am not suggesting you make this blog about the gay hysteria we have had but I encourage you to address that entry. It is alarming and it covers the core issue of acceptance in a civil way even if not in a religious manner.

Other topics are scattered throughout Isaacs blog: from parenting, to gossip, to adultery, to molestation. You have serious stuff and light stuff so go for it. Great journalists (which I always wanted to be) would eat up this material as journalists in my mind (the top ones) are the biggest agents of change ie my hero Anderson Cooper :-)

Let me know if you ever need help

Email

From: Carl

To: Isaac

Date: 1/21/2010 8:13:29 P.M.

Subject: Re: A BIG problem has been created...

What I would do is shut down the blog and inform people of several existing message boards they can speak on.

Email

From: Janice

To: Doug; Sarah; Isaac; Joshua; Veronica

Date: 1/21/2010 8:15:09 P.M.

Subject: Re:

I am leaving my house right now...but I think Isaac should certainly do the honors. Should we request some guidelines and some idea of what this is all about? And inform them beforehand that any ridiculous/offensive comments will be removed, so they shouldn't bother. Whoever is writing the first post, email out a copy so the rest of us can see it and approve before we make our big splash. I'm excited to see where this goes.

Email

From: Sarah

To: Doug, Veronica, Janice, Joshua; Isaac

Date: 1/21/2010 8:19:52 P.M.

Subject: Re:

You guys go for it! Only you have the ability to create a movement that prevents great minds like Isaac to be excommunicated. I don't consider myself a great mind but had this movement happened in my day and age maybe I would still be living in Green Hills and not left the community. In many ways I was driven out for lack of respect woman got for education and career so you may want to address that too as I get emails from many young woman crying for help for me to speak to their parents.

Good Luck to You!

Email

From: Isaac

To: Doug; Sarah; Janice, Veronica; Joshua

Date: 1/21/2010 8:27:10 P.M.

Subject: Re:

I will be glad to write the first post, giving it a sort of passing of the baton. What's our "go live" time estimate?

Email

From: Sarah

To: Isaac; Doug: Janice; Veronica; Joshua

Date: 1/21/2010 8:30:07 P.M.

Subject: Re:

Isaac, a passing on of the baton from you would be amazing plus you are an excellent writer with a moderate approach in your style. Perfect

Email

From: Veronica

To: Isaac; Sarah; Doug; Joshua; Veronica

Date: 1/21/2010 8:38:33 P.M.

Subject: Re:

Hi Everyone! I am just getting up to speed with all these e-mails. Issac- I commend you- what has happened this week has changed the lives of so many Kartaqis- especially the youth! I have been writing articles to help stir change (in a positive manner) and never in my life thought I would see this kind of reaction and out of all things to bring it on- your marriage! If there is anything I can do for the new blog, please call on me. I intend to start writing my articles again- Veronica I was going to send you a draft for Scrolls. Also, will be posting on new blog- so please just let me know what you need me to do so change can start now!!!

Email

From: Doug

To: Isaac; Sarah; Veronica; Joshua; Janice

Date: 1/21/2010 8:41:49 P.M.

Subject: Re:

Isaac,

I just sent you an invite to be an editor on the blog. It seems the girls are a bit hesitant to fire things off (I would be also). And i sense you are very anxious to lay your site to rest and get on with your new life! And you have quite the following on your site that really trust you. The blogger user interface is fairly straight forward. When you post, please try to re-iterate that the site was created to be balanced.

It became obvious that the new blog will need some work before it is ready for traffic. The transfer was not going to be as imminent as I had imagined. I reopened the discussion board to keep the momentum going. There was a need for some overlap time to allow for a smoother transition.

Discussion Board

"Miss you" ~ January 21st, 2010

Isaac...please put my comment up! I need her to see it

prince ~ January 21st, 2010

There are so many closeted men in the kartaqi community - both single and married. They are probably reading this now, in private of course. Its not easy living a double life, nor is it healthy. But when other people become involved (for example naive kartaqi girls dying to get married) that is when lines are crossed and unhealthy becomes unethical. No one is asking you to come out of the closet, just don't lure anyone else inside the closet with you - because one day, you will run out of air and both of you will suffer. If you want to live a lie the rest of your life, that is your prerogative, don't make others suffer because you're too much of a pussy to live openly.

SO KARTAQI MOTHERS, OPEN YOUR EYES - CHECK UP ON YOUR HUSBANDS MORE OFTEN, INSTALL GPS ON THEIR CAR, LOVE YOUR CHILDREN NO MATTER WHO THEY WANT TO HAVE SEX WITH - THEY

ARE A PART OF YOU WHETHER YOU LIKE IT OR NOT.

AND FOR THE RECORD, ALL YOU UNEDUCATED CLOSED MINDED RETARDS SHOULD KNOW THAT YOU ARE BORN GAY - SO IT CAN'T BE A SIN.

"GOD BLESS"

an interested kartaqi ~ January 21st, 2010

hi isaac, i have a question which may be too personal to answer but i will ask any way for the sake of discussion. how observant of a jew are you and what fears do u have of the repercussions that comes with choosing a gay lifestyle, in regards to g-d, religion, and the afterlife? An orthodox community does what it must to preserve its orthodox heritage and unalterable laws, and that is understandable, but do you, or have you ever, find yourself in a self struggle with being gay and jewish/observant? if so, how do you overcome that?

ISAAC NAMDAR ~ January 21st, 2010

I am working rigorously with a few community members to set up an independent weblog. However, due to the activity seen here, we will need moderators to monitor activity there. We need people from all ends of the spectrum to make the process transparent and effective.

If you are interested in volunteering for this, please write me an email to Namdar@aol.com, and I will forward your name to the set up people.

McCain for tolerance ~ January 21st, 2010

Cindy McCain and Meghan McCain, John McCain's wife and daughter just came out with an ad today supporting gay marriage. This is the wife and daughter of our Republican presidential candidate. If they can be so open-minded, when their own husband and father was running on the platform against gay marriage, then why can't the rest of you

McCain for tolerance ~ January 21st, 2010

http://www.politicsdaily.com/2010/01/21/cindy-mccain-poses-for-ad-supporting-gay-marriage/?icid=main|htmlws-main-n|dl5|link3|http://

Skeptic ~ January 21st, 2010

You know why a new board won't work out? Because G-d knows who's going to be behind that and we won't know if we'll truly be anonymous

How Come No Speech About Adultery? ~ January 21st, 2010

I wonder, will Rabbi Levy give a speech about adultery soon? Because adultery is a much more prevalent problem in our community than homosexuality. Why was there a speech about gays but not about straight husbands who cheat on their wives? According to the Torah, adultery is a sin too. But I don't see Rabbi Levy giving speeches about that. We wouldn't want to offend the majority of the congregation, now would we? Rabbi Levy, we are waiting for your speech on adultery.

sad man. lets be happy ~ January 21st, 2010

PLEASE STOP THE MADNESS.

we should be grateful to have community. we are all so fortunate...

BUT: we also have flaws. and that OK.

we get it: people cheat, some women flirt, some men go to bangkok and have fun, some teenagers dont have single value, some people only care about money, some people gay, some people hate their spouse, some people get abused, some people are sexually abused (by dads) ,some people only care about looks... that doesn't mean we are all like this, and we should all cry about it. Maybe its time to change.

Mothers, TEACH your children the importance of finding the right spouse, not just someone that would make your family look pretty and nice.

Fathers, teach your children manners, respecting others, greeting others politely and proper conduct.

When I came from Kartaq, my generation had true jewish values. what happened to this generation?

my niece (teenager) ask me what something meant- she learned in class- i was so sad to hear.

lets STOP problem now!!!

it not late!!!!!!!

synagogue ~ January 21st, 2010

what should we wear to the big event

do i have time for a nose job

this is huge

nonsense ~ January 21st, 2010

this blog is ridiculous.

any moron, including doctors, who believe even half the garbage posted here should think again. my 16 year old cousin made believe he was an 18 year old girl yesterday and had 50 responses to his story.

and for the 25-50% of posts that have some truth to them, shame on you all. this is not the way to express yourselves.

now respond to me calling me names so my elation can continue.

No Name ~ January 21st, 2010

Dear readers of this discussion board. This is a serious post, and not some phony, faux attempt to get attention or stir conversation. I would please please ask you to honor and understand my decision to remain anonymous. I don't want you to respond to my post, I just want my voice to be heard.

I have nothing but respect for the Kartaqi community, for the way we celebrate our traditions and maintain our commitment to Judaism and to the values of family. It's really true, I sometimes think of us as one big family.

I have always known that I was gay. Ever since I was a young kid, I knew I felt no attraction to the opposite sex.

At times, I didn't understand why I was the way I was, and how I could be different, and I had no one to turn to. No one in my family, nor anyone in the community, least of all our so-called community leaders.

I was often distraught and wished I weren't gay. I became scared of social environments, scared of even opening my mouth because other kids would accuse me of being like a girl and mocking me.

At other times, I became angry with the community, at my family -- having negative feelings about people that are not healthy and that I do not wish upon anyone.

Thankfully, at college, I was able to meet many like-minded people and learned to accept myself for who I am.

But I am still not totally comfortable. After all these years, every time I go to a wedding or come to synagogue, and hear things like "Why aren't you married yet? Your parents are getting older and you should give them a reason to be proud of you before they die," In fact, I want to die. I go home and I think of the worst things. It makes me not want to come anymore, it makes me want to close door to my room and never see people anymore. But how can I not come to synagogue and sit next to my father, pray for Israel, pray for my family's well-being and have him bless me?

How can I not come to synagogue and express my respects to the deceased and their families?

Will I not be able to say the *Kaddish* (mourner's prayer) when one day, G-d forbid, my loved ones pass?

I know the answer in my heart and I think many of you on this site know the answer too. If this means I have to find another synagogue, then so be it. Nothing can change the love and respect I have for my father, my mother, my siblings and their children. Nothing can change the relationship I have with G-d. And nothing can change me, just as much as I can't change a heterosexual, much as some members in our community like to believe that we are out to convert the world. For the record, we are not.

I know what the Torah says, and I do not expect to ever marry at our synagogue. Nor do I want to. Nor would I necessarily ever want to marry should I find the right partner, but as a human, I should be allowed to have that right. Others should not be making that decision for me.

And just on an ending note, please think twice on this site before you use profanity or words of hatred. We Kartaqis are respectful people, this is a big challenge but I know we can overcome it and come out on the side of love and acceptance, and I expect nothing less. My sincere hope is that tomorrow's Kartaqis won't have to go through the pain and anguish I did growing up, and can be free to pursue their happiness.

Cosmo ~ January 21st, 2010

Issac & Andrew a belated congratulations!

I love the discussion board. Never thought we had so much diversity in our community. I hope this will move us forward.

Question to Isaac ~ January 21st, 2010

I have a personal question to Isaac. You can choose not to answer if it is too personal. But what are your beliefs? Do you believe that homosexuality is a disease people are born with, and should they fight against that disease they have or should they be able to open up and accept it?

Also, do you believe that being homosexual is wrong, and have tried unsuccessfully to beat it? Or do you believe there is nothing wrong with it, and that you don't believe in the rules of Judaism that are against it? I'm just curious how you've made these decisions that have impacted you so greatly. You can choose not to answer if it is too personal.

Thanks.

Another gay Kartaqi ~ January 21st, 2010

I met Isaac Yesterday for coffee, this was the first time I've ever met him.

Since I only heard about his website after he already took off all this wedding photos he was kind enough to show me some of the wedding photos on his iPhone. Seeing Andrew and Isaac together in the photos it was very obvious how much happy and in love they are.

I think it's a safe assumption that this couple is so much happier together then most straight kartaqi couples are.

Isaac comes across as an extremely genuine, smart, sweet person. It was a real pleasure meeting him!

Perhaps Rabbi Levy should've also met with Isaac before judging him!

Isaac Namdar ~ January 21st, 2010

I am finalizing the details for setting up and moderating a much better organized community discussion board. I expect that the new site will be ready soon, maybe even tonight. Ideally, this new blog will have several concurrent discussion topics, so you can partake in the topic of interest to you. All previous entries on this domain will still be available for review.

I will post the new address as soon as it is possible.

Aside, Andrew has had a huge eye opener about our community this week. You should see the speed at which he has been reading all the entries.

Kartaqi Teen and her Clique ~ January 21st, 2010

My friends and I love and need this board. Don't take it down please. We read and re-read everything all the time. We are inspired there are Kartaqis looking out for us.

gay kartaqi mom ~ January 21st, 2010

I am a Gay women , I got married to a man because i wanted to seem normal but i was born this way now we have kids together , He hates me i know he goes with other s, and i am lusting after my female friends . This is not life

p.s there are others in my family who were born this way and suffering us.

2 Kartaqis Sisters ~ January 21st, 2010

No Name: I want you to know that my sister and I are reading your post and have tears in our eyes. We admire your honesty and feel your pain. Thank you for sharing this with us and never feel ashamed of who you are. Thank you Isaac for allowing this individual an outlet so he could speak. You are an amazing person. Never forget that regardless what the Community does to you one day when you can be who you are. With much love, 2 sisters who were raised by very tolerant Kartaqi parents and so happy for it.

kartaqis in support of no name ~ January 21st, 2010

No Name, who are you and even if you hide, we want you to know you are amazing for what you wrote and the understanding you have given us about your challenges. May we all be blessed with friends like you. May your post open everyone's eyes and move us forward. May you never have to fear the Community again for ostracizing you.

Kartaqi mother of four ~ January 21st, 2010

No Name, have you shared your story with anyone in your family or any Kartaqi friends? How have they responded? I want to be your friend and guide you. I am a mother of four children and wish you had the opportunity to come and speak to me. I promise you nobody would judge you. We would all support you in my family. You have broken my heart with your story and I will do what I can to help you whether today or in the future. You are loved by many, never forget that.

OMG ~ January 21st, 2010

Wow!! Seriously, this is insanity. Men that cheat- can you please please please grow up! If you can't solve your own problems then there is no help for you at all. If you have an addiction- go seek therapy- another thing Kartaqis are afraid to do- get help! If you are waiting for the Central Board to solve your marital problems then you will be waiting a long time. Also, is this cheating thing the same things as Kartaqis all being followers not leaders? So if every Kartaqi decided to jump of a bridge tomorrow, I am sure you would do the same

open-minded ~ January 21st, 2010

It's truly wonderful to see people here that are "open-minded", understanding, and have the ability to empathize. No-Name's story was touching, and that's just one of many stories out there that also reach out for help.

It's comforting to see that there are even parents on this board that are "open-minded" and kartaqi mother of four. The ability to empathize and feel other people's anguishes, rather than judging is not just an emotional gift. It is also something that can be delivered or expressed mentally.

Some people, especially elders feel that being "open-minded" is equivalent to believing the things you are aware of. To me, open-minded is equivalent to an awareness of the world around you and the things that occur in it. Beyond the awareness however, is the acceptance.

So yes, things that are considered "taboo" in our community might come as a shocker to us. But nevertheless, they do exist, and we must learn and understand how to deal with and treat our fellow friends and family when they do have problems. We should not judge, but open our minds and hearts to their problems and their feelings. Our community is built on a foundation of support, and we should not break it.

No-Name, you already see that you have many people willing to support you emotionally and mentally. I hope that we can expand our sentiments of support throughout the community and help others that are in emotional or mental anguish.

There isn't always one-side to a story. While one person is yelling and screaming about a gay person in the community, our fellow jew is sitting at home crying contemplating on whether living life is worth it because of closed-hearted and closed-minded people. You have to look at things from different perspectives and different angles before you can really judge a person. Really, sit down and think before you react in a way that you were taught by your parents to react.

Understand: There are different kinds of people in this world. Not everyone will fulfill the "kartaqi-Jewish" ideals. We can only bring them closer to our community and instill our values.

I hope I was able to shed a new perspective.

What's wrong is WRONG ~ January 21st, 2010

Another "gay Kartaqi":

You seem to take so much joy and pride in seeing how happy Isaac & Andrew are together. Well gee golly, how wonderful that must be!!

But tell me something else...

Osama Bin Laden took/takes pleasure in seeing the murder of innocent Americans. Were you flipping in joy for him on 9/11?

Or several years back, when Alternio Sanchez, "The Bike Path Rapist," raped over 15 women, did you put your thumbs up and say good for you every time that demented being indulged himself with a new victim?

Being happy with what you do does not make it right.

Do you know what was Sanchez's punishment for what he did? 75 years in prison with no parole.

The repercussions of Isaacs actions should be to be completely severed from our community. There is no room for tolerance on this topic.

The only person I feel bad for in this whole ordeal is David Namdar, Isaac's dad. That poor old man had to escape to Israel to not have to deal with the shame of having a creature of a son who takes pride in such disgusting choices. I pray that his soul may one day find peace. And I pray that your family will never be shamed the way his has been. I knew David well; he was a kind and compassionate man. It is really unfortunate what he must be going thru.

Kartaqi Dad ~ January 21st, 2010

To "What's Wrong is Wrong": You are a truly sick, demented individual. What kind of parents did you have to raise you like such an animal. You should be ashamed of your hateful and Nazi-like words. G-d will judge you for speaking so unkindly about another Jew, who happens to be a very good person. Shame on your family for making you this way. They did a very bad job

Survivor ~ January 21st, 2010

I don't mean to be disrespectful to people who form their life around their sexual orientation, but this is to all of our children who are confused and looking for purpose in life. The one and only purpose of every living thing in this life is reproduction and forming a family. Sex is only a small part of living, it is not everything. Holding your child in your arms and having a family to come home to is what life is all about. If you're looking for happiness, that's where it is. A happy sex life with another man, does not bring happiness in life

Excuse ME ~ January 21st, 2010

What's wrong is WRONG:

It's exactly people like you that don't have a mind and equate being gay to murder and rape.

You are either brazenly provocative, or astonishingly uneducated. You remind me of ahmadinejad.

1. You equate being gay to murder and rape? Someone who is gay doesn't seek to hurt or terrorize anyone. They just are who they are. As long as they are not doing anything to hurt you then it is none of your business.

2. You speak of being gay as if the person CHOOSES to be gay. You think a Jewish Kartaqi person would CHOOSE to go through the hell that people like you in the community cause them? YOU should be ashamed for judging and causing others embarrassment. The only entity in this world that has the right to judge is Hashem. And embarrassing others is a big NO-NO in the Torah. So maybe you should evaluate your thought process and your character.

Grow up, and most importantly, Grow a brain.

you speak of tolerance as if "the gay" are going to creep up on you in the middle of the night and rape you or bomb ur house. Seriously, RELAX. There is nothing to even "tolerate." The only thing the community needs to tolerate is nasty people like you that bring upon major negativity, and seemingly from your charter major *lashon hara*.

Learn how to give love and support

abc ~ January 21st, 2010

You are an abomination. Please change your last name to Mitchell. You are a disgusting creature.

another gay kartaqi ~ January 21st, 2010

"whats wrong is wrong" did you really just compare Isaac to Osama???? Thats very ignorant of you!

All my family knows im gay and very supportive

Don't be ignorant ~ January 21st, 2010

To Survivor:

If the only purpose to getting married is to have kids and raise a family, then should a straight man and woman who can't have kids not get married?

pissed off couldn't hold it anymore ~ January 21st, 2010

Dear Isaac and Andrew, I would like to start off by thanking you for the opportunity you took to let freedom of speech express itself. I will try to be very quick and to the point, but it will be hard.

- It's a shame that such a community as the Kartaqi one does not have its own unregulated discussion board. It's due to the fact that people are somewhat afraid of the system. Yet, your website has 3000 hits as of today, a sign that people are willing to air their voice no matter what the subject is. As the movie Gladiator puts it, "power of the mob".

- The single, most tragic fact in this whole situation has nothing to do with homosexuality. In my humble opinion, people failed to analyze that we are here blogging on your site today because community members don't mind their own business. So for each one of you, starting from the single person who wrote the original E-mail spreading the website out, to all the others who forwarded along and created this chain reaction, you have committed a greater sin of *Lashon Hara*. Therefore, before mocking other people for their behavior you should think of your own. There is no way to track e-mails yet, but I am sure G-d up there knows who you are.

- In regards to the issue of 'Shalom magazine" and other magazines published by community members (not necessarily by the community), containing anti-homosexual propaganda, I would like to ask the writers a question: Did homosexual behavior offended you, personally, in any way? Did gays campaign outside your house and offended your family? Did they demand you acceptance, did they excessively bother you or take away much of your time? The answer to all these questions is probably NO. So I ask you, why the hell would you write such articles? How about writing about the many problems our community has in order to fix them, as homosexuals never demanded anything from the community? (on a side note, that whole issue of 'Shalom' magazine was a piece of art. I wanted to keep it for my future children to show them what NOT to read, by I was compelled to use it in other ways I cannot describe on this blog)

- Our community suffers from a disease called "Not my family" or "immune status". You may have heard about it, it's when something that is thought to be out of the ordinary (anything from being homosexual to consuming drugs, drinking and driving, raping cases, divorce, or even kids hooking up in high school, dorming in college, eating non kosher, not living in Green Hills, buying a second apartment that is not in Miami, etc. etc.) happens to a Kartaqi family. Kartaqis are immune, they found the antidote to all the evil in the world, love each other and live in a wonderful bubble. It's the same reason why if Kartaqi kids are out with other Kartaqi kids they can come home at 5 am ("Oh you are with so and so, I know his parents, you would never drink and drive or smoke pot") but if they go out with anyone else they have a an early curfew ("Who are you going there with? Don't go into places I wouldn't go! Come home early, call me...."). This way of thinking is degrading to the people that, for whatever reason, fall in the categories above mentioned.

- I really don't know if homosexuality is something people are born with or that grows in you. Doctors did not figure this out yet, so I don't know why would we. What I know that if Isaac and Andrew decided to spend the rest of their life together, they have the right to do so and be happy. Again, this probably falls under the category "did Isaac or Andrew do anything to personally harm you? No? So what gives you the right to flood their website, look at every single picture and comment, send their link out to your friends?" MIND YOUR OWN BUSINESS and you will notice the world will be a better place. (Isaac and Andrew, this is the part where I should apologize on behalf of other people for their behavior, but I won't. They have to. If they don't, as you mentioned in your point # 3 in the 'previous message' section, they will deal with it eventually).

- If you read any newspaper last week, you know that Haiti was hit by a terrible natural disaster that killed 100,000 people. If you read your local news, Green Hills had to deal with many burglaries. The world is changing, bad things happen every day, and instead of focusing on current events (or raising money for Haiti) I have to hear the Rabbi speaking about the issue of being homosexual in the community. Now, I know that the Rabbi did not choose to speak about this argument himself (he is way too smart and, as he repeated many times, he knows that it's a delicate matter also for potential lawsuits) but it demonstrates the very poor judgment of the people in the Central Board who pushed so hard for this issue to come out. Now you will deal with the consequences because it backfired, and because you deal with issues in very inappropriate manners. Do I expect any orthodox Rabbi to support homosexuality? No. Do I expect our Rabbi to bring this issue out on a Shabbat because community members started to spread rumors and talk s—t about other people? Not in a million years.

Thank you.

Mom of two ~ January 21st, 2010

To "Excuse Me", you make an EXCELLENT POINT! The only person who should be ashamed of themselves is "What's Wrong Is Wrong." What a horrific person.

Survivor ~ January 21st, 2010

Again, don't mean to be disrespectful to people who have let their sexual desires rule their life, but a good therapist at the right age when teenagers who shouldn't even be having sex, think they are genetically attracted to the same sex, may help them overcome their serious issues and get to the route of their problems.

Shortbread ~ January 21st, 2010

To 'pissed off couldn't hold it in anymore, you are a genius. I love you post and everyone HAS to read it. To 'What's wrong is wrong', I dread the fact that we may be related since most Kartaqis are. You need help, you belong in a mental institute for your remarks or go get a degree in history so you understand the true meaning of what you posted. If you had any smarts you would know that you compare Osama only with Osama and Hitler only with Hitler. These are murderers and sick people. How could you

Mom of two ~ January 21st, 2010

To "Pissed Off Couldn't Hold It Anymore", fantastic post! Bravo. Thank goodness for intelligent people.

great point ~ January 21st, 2010

pissed off couldn't hold it in anymore...Who are you? i think i fell in love!

Survivor ~ January 21st, 2010

To Don't Be Ignorant

How many couples do you know that get married at a later age who at least one of them doesn't have a child from a prior marriage?

Grandmother to Be ~ January 21st, 2010

To "Pissed Off Couldn't Hold it in anymore", wow what a post. I am going to cut and paste it and send it to my three children, my son-in-law, and translate it in kartaqi for my parents.

To whats wrong is wrong, who raised you? I know we have terrible parenting in the Kartaqis in many cases, but this???

Young Zameeni Jew ~ January 21st, 2010

I'm writing as an outsider looking in; looking in and already knowing what's going on here. I am not Kartaqi. I am not a part of the community I have watched afar and admired for its cohesion, emphasis on family and togetherness, and most importantly its persistence through severe persecution in Kartaq, which I have studied at length. I have always thought highly of Kartaqis because I love Judaism, and in turn I love people who love Judaism (like the Kartaqi people do.) Having had many Kartaqi friends, I have gotten a rare glimpse into the culture and tradition that sets Kartaqis apart from us other Jews, and I think it comes down to cohesiveness, which breeds success (and has done so for Jews in foreign lands throughout history). If you young guys lose cohesiveness by ousting certain people, you are violating the best thing about Judaism - that you're never alone. You can't leave this guy alone. I'm Jewish, I'm gay and that's not a problem for me. I can't even imagine being "excommunicated" by my family - that was never even a possibility with my parents. Everyone knows, and everyone loves me the same - it CAN work. It's up to all the young people who are going to move up and take over presently to make a choice not to be exclusive about members when it comes to Jews. The practice of homosexuality (like heterosexuality) does not have to be

342

public, and there are ways of interpreting even the Torah to say that marriage is not always between one man and one woman. If exclusion starts happening, there's no end to it. Jews should stick together no matter what.

Kartaqi Teacher ~ January 21st, 2010

I am a teacher and obviously take education very seriously. How about for those of you who are so antagonistic to Isaac in your posts about gay marriage being against religion, you look at it from a civil rights point of view. If it's against the religion then at least accept that in the United States we have something called civil rights where we are taught (and that is what I teach at school) to accept people regardless of race, religion, color, sexual orientation etc. We are Jews but we live in this great country so we also must respect the laws of this country. We cannot make our own laws when it comes to civil rights.

Survivor ~ January 21st, 2010

What's wrong with all this support. I don't understand. Isaac, I admire all your achievements and I think you are a genius. But I wish you weren't gay. I wished you had a average normal semi happy/unhappy life like us. Attended social events sometimes, had a boring life like most of us.

Let's all face it, we all hope to g-d to have children that accomplish what you have professionally, but none of us wish your sexual orientation on our children.

Nevertheless, I do wish you lots of happiness and I'm sure if I knew you I would have loved you and would have liked to be your friend.

Sarah ~ January 21st, 2010

To What's Wrong Is Wrong:

I would like to direct you to an organization called Facing History and

Ourselves at facinghistory.org.

My husband and I are extremely involved with this cause and I serve on the board of this amazing organization whose mission it is to engage students of diverse backgrounds in an examination of racism, prejudice, and anti-Semitism in order to promote the development of a more humane and informed citizenry. (Anyone interested to get involved or have your schools teach the curriculum please let me know)

I along with several other Kartaqi families grew up in post-war Europe and know first-hand what it is like to be discriminated against. It is not a pretty sight and I am sure many on this board have been as shocked by your comments as I have. Which is why I was propelled to post.

Vladamir Ramanovic ~ January 21st, 2010

Hello I am Vladamir hear me roar

kartaqi gay mom ~ January 21st, 2010

i was born gay but got married to look normal , my husband hates me and goes with others , i lust after my female friends !!!!! what kind of a life is this???? I wish i came out long time ago like issac . Btw there are others in my family who are gay and also miserable

a great idea ~ January 21st, 2010

Rabbi Levy wrote on his daily E mail: There is NO sin in the Torah that has many prohibitions related to as LASHON HARA...So i have great idea : Why dont we have a hot line that when ever u hear some one does *lashon hara* we call that # ...if the panel decides its true , we put their names up on the board . I promise you all these gossip will stop in a few days FOR ever. Bec this is where all are problems are coming from

great idea ~ January 21st, 2010

Let me clarify....if the panel finds out that the person did actually do *lashon hara* , then we make a board of shame and put their names up

Bad Idea ~ January 21st, 2010

Putting people to shame is against the Jewish religion. It's not right to embarrass others

kurtaqwi~ January 21st, 2010

I mast say my reding an riting was impruved becas of al this.

tank you to all.

Hailey Hoffman ~ January 21st, 2010

Dear NO NAME,

I'm sorry for your pain and wish you much strength and peace through the rest of your journey. May it have a happy ending :)

great idea ~ January 21st, 2010

But *lashon hara* is killing us all , much bigger sin according to torah than being gay...so why are we picking on Gays???

support no name ~ January 21st, 2010

Dear no name...no one should go through what you are going through, i hope that this site has given you hope and courage to face your true identity . We will be proud of you one day soon

I got home late from my dinner meeting. I had to monitor all the new entries on the taxi ride home from the small screen of my smartphone. Luckily, there were no new profanities that needed to be modified. There were a few inspiring entries, and one very disturbing one. I also received an email invite from Doug to log onto the new blog and post the official kick-off entry. I sat down and wrote my kick-off post for the new blog that night, then copied it onto my own website to serve as a bridge. Below is the text of that entry.

Discussion Board

Isaac Namdar ~ January 22nd, 2010

I have been overwhelmed by the amount of interest in my discussion board at here at mitchell-Namdar.com this past week. Although I had originally intended the discussion board to be a tool of communication for people trying to reach me after my outing, it seems that many in the community were glad to utilize a new tool of free speech afforded to them. I was delighted to see people make their case, and often offer eloquent arguments on both sides of various issues. Many in the community have thanked me both personally and through the postings for having the opportunity to have their voice heard without the fear of repercussion.

However, the discussion board had grown into a much larger entity than yours truly can handle. Additionally, I was not elected, nor did I volunteer to be the moderator of the community's free speech. The time has come for me to pass the baton of this great tool I created (by chance) to a more appropriate forum.

Thanks to the special efforts of Sarah and Doug, we were able to establish a new weblog to accommodate the volume of postings coming in. We are hoping that there will be a smooth transition of ideas and discussion to the new site. Also, the weblog will be set up with several administrators who will have the ability to moderate fairly, while the community at large can make their input at any time. An extra feature is that we are hoping to organize the discussion into specific topics, and you can choose to follow as many topics as you wish rather than have to go through every post to find those interesting to you. Please be advised that this weblog is not under the auspices of any elected or non-elected entity of our community, and is a totally independent site.

With the hopes of building a new tool of free speech, and improving on what I accidentally created, I am hereby endorsing the first version of the community weblog. I hope you will all find your new site as comfortable as you were on my website. I am sure that it will take a few days for the weblog to take shape and have enough postings to make it relevant and interesting.

I would also like to assure you that all the previously posted entries here on mitchell-Namdar.com will be available for viewing, and will not be erased. The Discussion Board here will remain open only for issues directly affecting me, and I will reserve the right to publish those entries I consider relevant, and respond as needed. It is in no way intended to compete with the new weblog here.

I may choose to follow some of the threads there in the future, or make my own remarks from time to time. In the meantime, I bid you all farewell and happy blogging. It has been an honor to serve as your temporary moderator (even if by default).

The new weblog's address is http://kartaqiweblog.blogspot.com

Isaac Namdar, MD

Isaac Namdar ~ January 22nd, 2010

I am also planning on offering my analysis of the events of the past week and the way it affected me and the community. You can expect a posting tomorrow afternoon, before Shabbat entry.

Email

From: Isaac

To: Doug; Sarah; Veronica; Joshua; Janice

Date: 1/21/2010 11:56:18 P.M.

Subject: Re:

I made my initial kickoff posting. Please review. I will now post on my site to redirect all traffic.

In the meantime, I was concerned about what would happen this coming Shabbat morning. Everyone has been talking about the discussion board all week, and it became such a more important issue than the shock of discovering my sexuality ever was. A lot of new discoveries have been made. If the Rabbi felt compelled to talk about homosexuality last week, it is only natural he would offer his two cents about this new phenomenon. Again, he would have the captive audience of all the congregants, and I did not want to become the subject of further condemnation.

I thought it was best to have a pre-emptive response. By offering my 'sermon' in the form of an open letter, I could argue my side and plant some seeds before people hear the other again side Saturday morning. I needed to post it on the discussion board some time on Friday. Yet, as things were developing in such a fast pace, I didn't want to post it too early in the day and let subsequent events change people's attitudes. I decided to formulate a letter, post it online Friday afternoon shortly before Shabbat entry, and then shut down new entries for Shabbat.

Finding the right words is always a hard task. While I wanted to maintain my composure, I also wanted to talk from the heart and address all the issues that went into play. I was up until 3:30 in the morning working on the first draft.

At 1:30 in the morning I got a surprising email.

Email

From: Anonymous.****@gmail.com

To: Isaac

Date: 1/22/2010 1:36:44 A.M. (note the early AM time!)

Subject: Message posted

Dear Isaac,

I am writing this letter to you in shame. There was a post I had made on your site a couple hours ago which I really regret posting. I am so embarrassed by what I said, that I don't even have enough decency to reveal my true identity. But i wanted to write to you know to express how sorry I am, and to request that the post I had made be removed from the Mitchell-Namdar site.

Even with keeping my identity in discretion, I am embarrassed to admit to you that I am "What's Wrong is Wrong."

(Firstly, just for verification, b/c I am requesting the post be deleted, i guess it is necessary to prove it was indeed me - If you'd like to do so, I'm pretty sure the name I used to create that user name was "truth." And while I don't remember what email address I made up for the post, i do recall going for an @aol.com username. Anyhow, I just wanted to get that out of the way so you know that this is indeed me emailing you)...

I learned about your website and the discussion forum on it during my train ride home tonight. As I began to read the posts, I was increasingly filled with shock, anger, sadness, and overall disappointment. I only read for 20 minutes before exploding and deciding to comment. I wrote those horrific comments in pure hatred and anger. It was evil and malicious of me. It was meant to cause harm. But that is not me, and I fear that I have crossed a line and may have deeply hurt you with my remarks. It is past 1:00AM but i cannot fall asleep now knowing that I may have caused you harm. Now if possible, I am hoping you can delete the post I had posted and replace it with a comment stating what I'd like to tell you now on the record. I have cooled down now, and would like my genuine and (somewhat) more rational thoughts to be presented. (This way ppl will also know that i had requested to remove those comments, and they won't complain to you for "censoring.")

Isaac,

My comments earlier were written in pure anger, and were completely irrational. For one thing, comparing you to Osama Bin Laden is preposterous, and was plain stupid of me. I know you well, and I'm sure you know me well too. And I'd like to publicly vouch for the fact that you are one of the nicest people I know. I've envied your level of education ever since your college days. But in the past week, I have lost complete respect for you. Is that your problem? No. It is simply something I have to deal with. And this has nothing to do with religion either; i do not know, nor do I care much about the religious issues at play here. I just personally feel that your decision, even if it be due to a genetic impulse, is

morally reprehensible. Now are you still one of the nicest people I know?
100%. One thing that is for certain is that the way to go about discussing
this is not to do so in hatred and anger. I don't know how to deal with
this. I was hoping I won't ever have to. But I am sorry for my original
hurtful statements. That's what was really WRONG...

Email

From: Isaac

To: Anonymous.****@gmail.com

Date: 1/22/2010 1:47:08 A.M.

Subject: Re: message posted

I am actually still up, trying to formulate my analysis posting that I will publish
tomorrow afternoon. It is taking me quite some time to choose the right words.

I really appreciate your courage to contact me and apologize for your words. It
takes a true man to admit to his mistakes. I, on my end, am sorry if my actions
this week or in the past, caused you to feel offended personally or generally.
Perhaps once all the dust settles, we can reconnect and I will be glad to discuss
with you any topics that caused your anger. People usually are most scared of the
unknown. If you let me explain myself to you, perhaps I can soften the edges a
bit.

I am no blogger or journalist, but have learned a thing or two this week. The only
way to maintain my integrity about the discussion board is to keep it transparent.
Therefore I cannot simple go back and delete a comment as though it never
existed, especially since numerous references were made to your post. What I
recommend is that you generate a retraction letter or a clarification, and I will
add that as an addendum. Email me your statement, and I will attach it to the
original post.

Friday, January 22, 2010

Email

From: Anonymous.****@gmail.com

To: Isaac

Date: 1/22/2010 8:32:18 A.M.

Subject: Re: message posted

Isaac,

Thank you for your quick response. Your response shows me that you are being strong about this all, and I hope you continue to be so. And I understand your desire to keep the discussion forum transparent, but I am hoping you can at least delete (or let me alter) the second half of my original comments. I love your father so so much, and bringing him into the debate was awful of me. He does not deserve that. In his respect, I really hope you can delete that part of my comment or (let me) alter it somehow. It seems like most comments on my post referenced my first irrational point. So if you keep that up, please add an addendum quoting the second half of the apology I sent you last night.

Again, I am sorry for the pain I may have caused, and hope one day you can forgive me. When I am ready, maybe we can even sit down one day and have coffee together to discuss this.

Be well,

Email

From: Isaac

To: Anonymous.****@gmail.com

Date: 1/22/2010 8:56:20 A.M.

Dude, I will lose 100% credibility if I alter entries, even at the request of the responder. I will gladly add any addendum, so that the train of thought and course is completely transparent.

Give me the exact text of your addendum and I will incorporate it for you. Send me an email this AM.

And let me know when u are ready for that cup of coffee.

Email

From: Anonymous.****@gmail.com

To: Isaac

Date: 1/22/2010 10:40:00 A.M

Subject: Re: message posted

Sorry for the late response,

But if you can add an addendum, please put the following apology after my original comments on your blog.

Isaac,

My comments earlier were written in pure anger, and were completely irrational. For one thing, comparing you to Osama Bin Laden is preposterous, and was plain stupid of me. I know you well, and I'm sure you know me well too. And I'd like to publicly vouch for the fact that you are one of the nicest people I know. I've envied your level of education ever since your college days. But in the past week, I have lost complete respect for you. Is that your problem? No. It is simply something I have to deal with. And this has nothing to do with religion either; i do not know, nor do I care much about the religious issues at play here. I just personally feel that your decision, even if it be due to a genetic impulse, is morally reprehensible. Now are you still one of the nicest people I know? 100%. One thing that is for certain is that the way to go about discussing this is not to do so in hatred and anger. I don't know how to deal with this. I was hoping I won't ever have to. I dread the fact that my nephews and nieces are being raised in such a liberal society. But C'es la Vis. We must learn to deal with it appropriately. But I am sorry for my original hurtful statements. That's what was really WRONG...

I then attached the above paragraph to his original Discussion Board entry as an addendum.

Email

From:　　Isaac

To:　　Sarah; Doug; Joshua; Veronica; Janice

Date:　　1/22/2010 10:54:59 A.M.

Subject:　　Re:

Until we figure things out, I kept the site open to keep the momentum going. I will probably run it till Shabbat entry, and then deactivate again to allow people to reflect during Shabbat. Hopefully this weekend we can hash things out and have a product to offer to everyone.

I never knew what power can do to you, I can just willingly turn on and off such a powerful tool as I please. Power corrupts, LOL

In the meantime, Joshua, an independent activist of sorts, opened a second weblog to address the community's needs. That site was under his sole supervision, and he did not reveal his identity as the moderator. He used his pen name Silence Do-Good, which I later found was also Benjamin Franklin's pen name for a while.

Discussion Board

Sharon ~ January 22nd, 2010

Hi Everyone, My name is Sharon, and I'm Isaac's niece. I've been reading your posts these past few days, and I had to respond on behalf of my family. First, to "what's wrong is wrong" - You should be ashamed of yourself. Who do you think you are to even bring up my grandfather's name??

Since I was a child, my uncle Isaac was a hero to us, the pride of the family. with everything he had to go through, he built an amazing life for himself, one we should all look up to. from a young age, he has been supporting my family, in ways you can't even imagine. He would do EVERYTHING for us. Do any of you think that has changed because he's gay??? I feel sorry for the small minded ppl who are a part of this community, one which my uncle has done so much for. This community that pushes ppl like me away and away due to actions like this. We have a new and wonderful addition to our family, Andrew. I can only wish all of us to find an inspiring love and commitment like Isaac and Andrew have. Uncles - we love you.

shabbat shalom ~ January 22nd, 2010

after a chaotic week..

i would just like t say shabbat shalom to my dear community.

may you all have a restful and peaceful shabbat...

lashon hara free

hiiii ~ January 22nd, 2010

this site is amazzzing

proud kartaqi jew ~ January 22nd, 2010

I really think u r all crazy!!!! Whats the matter with you? We live in a community and like every other jewish community in this world we need to have rules and laws in order to live in perfect harmony with each other.

Of course like every other groups we have a lot of problems but believe me the pros are more than the cons.

I respect the decision of Mr Namdar to get marry with another man. But I think we have to set boundaries for our children thats why there was a turmoil in the community for the pictures. It was a scandal and everyone including me got shocked.

The state of NY doesnt legalize yet the gay marriage and a lot of americans still cannot accept the idea that their daughter/son is gay.

So I dont understand why so many people considers our community as a bigot and someone also compared us like the taliban mullah.

We have to respect each other without making mockery of others if they are different from us.

Given the fact that we live in a heterosexual society some people get alarmed about differences in others. But dont act so liberal in anonymous when in real life u r chickens.

Stop complaining!!! Instead act!

Nobody forces an 18 years old girl to get marry if she doesnt want.

And if a woman has a problem with her husband she cannot blame the community.

The major problem that we have is the peer pressure and competition with each other, like having big mansions when we cannot afford even a quarter of it.

In this time of recession that 95% of the people have a sort of financial problem its simply ridiculous to throw a lavishing party for just an engagement.

I say bravo to the people that r real, that do whatever they can do, not what is the standard in the community like throwing parties that r really unnecessary and getting loan from a bank just because everyone in their "clique" did.

Mr Namdar accept our apology if u got offended in the beginning

But u have to understand that our jewish heritage and torah dont allow homosexuality, and I agree with someone saying that rabbi Levy speech was a little bit harsh but u have to understand his point of view. We still live in a society that doesnt accept fully homosexuality. I have a lot of american friends and they would be shocked to hear that their kids are gay.

So dont condemn the community pretending U r so liberal. U r not!!!

Reading different comments i was impressed by one stating that LASHON HARA is the worst sin. Agree 100%

Dazed & Confused ~ January 22nd, 2010

I understand very well, that we are being encouraged to post our comments on the new blog site, but since people are still frequenting this website, I thought I'd drop by with a message.

Sharon, you have incredible uncle(s) and what "whats wrong is wrong" said is just an old man blabbing, because he's probably senile.

My main shout out is to "No Name", I know Im behind on the readings, but your post has really hit me hard. I have realized that in my recent past I have developed the same symptoms you have. I, too feel like doing the unmentionable when I realize how my family would handle hearing that I am gay.

To "Kartaqi Mother of Four", I wish my mother was like you. You seem to care a lot about "No Name"s situation.

Isaac Namdar ~ January 22nd, 2010

It seems that the new weblog still needs some structure and setting up before we can officially migrate. There have been several postings here, and numerous people have approached the weblog group to keep this site running for the time being.

I am keeping this blog open for discussion, probably until Shabbat entry. At that time I will post my own commentary as a final posting.

What's wrong is WRONG ~ January 22nd, 2010

The following is a copy of a message I sent directly to Dr. Namdar late last night. I first learned about this website and discussion board on the train ride home last night. I commented after 20 minutes of reading thru the posts, when I was still in an angry and irrational mode. I later felt obliged to apologize for my misconduct, and I am posting a copy of my letter to Isaac here now, for all those in addition to Isaac and his family who were offended by my words, to know that I am sorry.

Isaac,

My comments earlier were written in pure anger, and were completely irrational. For one thing, comparing you to Osama Bin Laden is preposterous, and was plain stupid of me. I know you well, and I'm sure you know me well too. And I'd like to publicly vouch for the fact that you are one of the nicest people I know. I've envied your level of education ever since your college days. But in the past week, I have lost complete respect for you. Is that your problem? No. It is simply something I have to deal with. And this has nothing to do with religion either; i do not know, nor do I care much about the religious issues at play here. I just personally feel that your decision, even if it be due to a genetic impulse, is morally reprehensible. Now are you still one of the nicest people I know? 100%. One thing that is for certain is that the way to go about discussing this is not to do so in hatred and anger. I don't know how to deal with this. I was hoping I won't ever have to. I dread the fact that my nephews and nieces are being raised in such a liberal society. But C'est la Vis. We must learn to deal with it appropriately. But I am sorry for my original hurtful statements. That's what was really WRONG...

Kartaqi Mom of 3 and Wife and Sister ~ January 22nd, 2010

What's wrong is wrong: you deserve credit for your apology. It is genuine and helps us understand where you were coming from. Hopefully as this board grows we will help more people that don't accept gay marriage (and yes it isnt legal in our state but many of us are not campaigning for gay marriage but for respect) to respect Isaac and not demonize him.

Sharon - your words are beautiful and we all should have an uncle like Isaac. I don't know Isaac but he should be judged by the content of his character, not by his sexual orientation. And he has proven to many of us in the Community that he cares for us deeply and respects us and is an outstanding human being.

No Name: I still can't stop thinking about you. How can we do you right?

To everyone, Shabbat Shalom. This has been an amazing movement. Keep it going for us moms, our children, our grandchildren and our elderlies.

ChallahBaker ~ January 22nd, 2010

Finally...everybody got quiet. I feel like we should set up a night for challah baking. This has been cancerous to our community. Repent Repent Repent. Your tongues will buuuuuuurn

Shortbread ~ January 22nd, 2010

ChallahBaker: We are having a serious discussion here and you suggest Challah baking? How about a helpline for Kartaqis, some counselors, psychologists. I will come to your Challah baking which I truly respect as a religious mother but not before the Community comes to us with some real solutions to the issues we are witnessing here.

You think we can help 'no name' by baking challah. Will that make that boy straight? Come on now. We need to help our Community not pretend nothing is wrong.

Allah ~ January 22nd, 2010

The creator of the universe specifically mentions to stone people like you two. Have fun in this life (before you get stoned), but be prepared for the afterlife. The idea of this life is to resist sin, no matter which sin you choose. Everyone has temptations to violate certain sins, but they hold back. The creator's rules are genius if we understand them or not. Narrow-minded people like you should understand that if people follow your pathetic logic on an aggregate level, the world will end. The rules were made to perfection; apparently, you weren't

Veronica ~ January 22nd, 2010

"Kartaqi American" -check it out at
http://kartaqiweblog.blogspot.com/

Most of you know me because of my articles in Scrolls magazine- my column called "Into the Light"- I started the column as a means of raising awareness of serious issues plaguing our community and spark educated conversation, and hopefully inspire people to lead happier lifestyles. For the most part I received positive feedback about my articles, from young mothers, to single guys, to my mother's friends, and even my own grandparents, (though some of my grandmother's friends had told her- stop your granddaughter she is ruining her reputation!). My first post on this blog is not going to be about a specific topic such as "The Social Effects of the Cliques"- this first post is simply about me and my relationship with the Kartaqi Community.

I was raised in this community from birth, coming from two of the largest Kartaqi families. The first time I remembered having to make a choice about my relationship with the community came at the age of 10. My mother with all the best intentions tried to put me into a "group" to expand my social network in the Kartaqi community. Let's just say it did not end on a happy note. I may not have had the backbone at the time; I just could not keep up with this group of girls! I felt very isolated when hanging out with them, never fitting into conversations or understanding why a few of them tried to exclude me or choose to play pranks on people- this kind of behavior I was not ok with. I made a decision, I told my mother, I want out of the group. It was then my decision was made- I wanted nothing to do with the community! A bold decision for a ten-year old- but it was made. Throughout my teen years I mainly socialized with Americans and I was ok with that. I formed some of my closest friendships at the point in my life. I had a few Kartaqi friends here and there, and even made a fresh attempt at starting a new group with more like-minded

Kartaqi girls, but it turned out to be a failure.

As a college student I made my way back into the community and became much more active. I joined the KYC and for the first time in a long time I felt connected again and found my purpose, to help the community by writing articles. Writing those articles worked as therapy for me as it reminded me of the good this community has and how foolish I had been all those years being a rebellious teen!

Now as a 27-year-old woman I am finally satisfied with the person I am. I am confident, happy, and know myself. At 27 I consider myself to be above anything a JEW and then an American-Kartaqi. I know that without my unique and interesting heritage I would not be who I am. I am proud of myself because I transformed all of my self-doubt into positive energy. I took the good of my Kartaqi lineage such as respecting family, to fear g-d, to accept and to forgive and took the best of my American homeland such as getting a great education, being an independent, free thinking woman, having a career I am confident about and an outlet to call my own. I took the positives of both and melded then into a woman I am very proud- it took me a very long time to be proud of her and I would not change me for anything!

My mini biography does have a purpose. Though I still do not feel 100% at home in my community- I still keep one foot in and one foot out. I have realized that turning my back on my community is not something I can do. There are many things I don't agree with that go on but I am still a Kartaqi through and through. On that note, I would like to present you all with this idea, the only way change will come to this community, without tarnishing our faith or forgetting about our very special lineage is by using my analogy from above, to take the good from both of our cultures! We have to face the fact that our backyard is America. We are Kartaqi-Americans! We cannot hide in a bubble and pretend like we live in our own little Kartaqi cocoon. We are exposed to American culture, be it on TV, magazines, and members of our own congregation. Adapting to American culture does not mean the end of the community- it is called being progressive. We must accept tolerance, accept that our children may marry Jews outside the community, and yes, woman can have careers and can be AMAZING mothers too!! This is all possible, but we have to remember that we have to extract the good from both cultures, if we learn to do that there is no doubt in my mind that we will be the BEST community, an example for all other Jewish communities. Let's make that dream a reality, instead of just preaching that we are!

Thank you.

ChallahBaker ~ January 22nd, 2010

Sugarlips, we should be baking up until Yom Kippur. Not for 'no name' but for your sorry a$$ and for whoever else is spewing *lashon hara* left and right.

Mommy ~ January 22nd, 2010

Challah Baker two of my friends having the cancer sickness. Please not compare nothing to cancer. Is terrible thing cancer. This board is good for all the Kartaqi. Challah baking is good too. We go always when synagogue ask but I scared when you say this board is cancer.

Cute ~ January 22nd, 2010

Allah, what the hell are *YOU* doing here ???

proud kartaqi jew ~ January 22nd, 2010

This is to "shortbread", its true we r having a serious discussion here but what do u expect the community to do? Straighten up a homosexual when this is the problem of the whole society.

I really feel bad for "no name " but the only thing we should do is respect for others.

If a person is gay shouldnt marry with a straight person because they gonna be miserable together for the rest of their life. Even though I dont agree with gay marriage we need to have tolerance for them and Mr Namdar found his happiness this way so we have to respect it but im not gonna flaunt his example to my children, and PLEASE dont ridicule your community for the sake of saying something.

Our beautiful heritage, tradition and community is old more than 200 years and the beauty of it is that in times of sorrow and problems we r all united.

SHABBATH SHALOM TO ALL

Lynn Norwick ~ January 22nd, 2010

check out my first post on http://kartaqiweblog.blogspot.com/ here is a copy below:

Welcome!!

Hi everyone,

I am Lynn Norwick and I am so excited to be part of this amazing outreach effort on behalf of the community at large. Many of you anonymously or maybe even joking posted to the Mitchell-Namdar discussion board and the over-arching theme to the posts is that some of us feel like we have lost ourselves within the community here in Green Hills. My objective in joining this cast of characters is to: 1. perhaps share my opinions on different issues so that you can identify with me positively or negatively and comment below or 2. give you all an opportunity to voice your own opinions without any fear of consequence. The names of the administrators are the only ones that must not be anonymous, everyone else can be. I encourage everyone to join the discussion, but please be respectful. And if you are one of the people who were making a mockery of the Mitchell-Namdar board by lying to be funny or by being disrespectful to other humans, do not do that here. That's the end of my intro--

Last year the KYC started a new program called the Monthly Lecture Series. Every month, new Jewish month, people host Rabbi Levy and send an open invitation to community members at their home where they can eat, socialize, and listen to a lesson about a chosen topic. Last night we were at James Kamins home (great hosts!) and Rabbi Levy accompanied by Rabbi Cohen (a new Rabbi in town) spoke about the Evil Eye/ Ayin Hara. I won't go on about the details of the discussion, but in the end Rabbi Levy offered a type of cure for the Evil Eye.

He said that the Evil Eye exists if there are people giving it to others, so why don't we work on ourselves and become better people so that we are not the ones wishing for bad things to happen to others. He said we should all practice being better people, being happy for the successes of our friends. How beautiful. Another thing he said is that unfortunately we live in a society that breeds envy. Where people live grand lifestyles, where the media structure is based on consumption and all we want is to get more stuff. And you getting more stuff and boasting about it in public causes most of the public to become jealous. So, he said, live a more humble lifestyle. Enjoy the fruits of your honest labor, by all means, but some people live to make other jealous. They do things specifically to show- off about it to other people and make them envious. His suggestion was to become more modest people.

I could not agree more. Actually I think this topic is very relevant to many of the posts on Mitchell-Namdar. Many people have been cast out of a group of friends or have been picked on because they just didn't have the right stuff. Beyond that, people have been bullied and gossiped about because of the envy of others. How many times have us women sat together and discussed someone going out with the other and perhaps "he is too good for her"? How many times has someone around you earned a higher mark in school and yet, "how could she get an A, I am much smarter than her?" We have all been there. Whether we have said it out loud or not, we have. Rabbi Levy's message of treating your neighbors the way you want to be treated (I think that's the commandment?) is an important one. If you want privacy in your life, do not prod into the lives of others. If you want people to respect you for all of your accomplishments, respect others and congratulate them on theirs. So this is the remedy guys, and I hope some of you try and see if it works. But I think it's true, if you smile at the world, the world smiles back.

Silence DoGood ~ January 22nd, 2010

Hey everyone. There is a new forum starting here...

yy.vc.Kartaqi

Its confidential just like this one.

Freddy Horton ~ January 22nd, 2010

The Central Board DOES NOT try to shut down web sites or discussion boards. It is easy to post an anonymous message making and accusation, but that doesnt make it a fact. (with that out of the way, I can now say what I want)

I have read every single post here (up to around last night) and I have to say that I am amazed by the level of intellect in all of you and the genuine emotion I see towards the Kartaqi community. Even the posts about negative qualities of the community show that you care.

Community living has its pros and cons. Being a Kartaqi means the pros are exaggerated and so are the cons. I am first to admit that this community, its Central Board, the KYC, our synagogue boards, or any community member for that matter, is not perfect. We are all humans and we try to do what we think is best for our community.

If you think there is something wrong that should be changed help change it. If you think you can help the community grow intellectually then help do it. Don't blame your parents, or family and friends for anything. Your decisions, and who gets to influence them, are yours to choose.

I would like to encourage, or even challenge you, to get more involved. Join, or even better, start a project in the community. Start a new Mitzvah project, or a culture club, or an enrichment program. If you have ANY ideas for the KYC or the Central Board approach them. Vote at each and every community and government election. But most important of all become a candidate in the next election and help run the community in the direction that you would like.

RESPONSE FROM ISAAC:

I am honored to have a member of our elected leadership post on this site. I agree with Mr. Horton's comments, and encourage all concerned community members to get involved on a daily basis. The way to make your voices heard is through action, not just words.

Carolina Liar ~ January 22nd, 2010

"Show Me What I'm Looking For"

this song reminds me of the gays on this board.

Please show me what I'm looking for. Save me, I'm lost. Oh Lord I've been waiting for you. I'll pay any cost. Save me from being confuuuuuused.

the grinch who stole chanuka ~ January 22nd, 2010

THIS POST WAS FROM "SHAMED KARTAQI/PROUD JEW" 2 DAYS AGO AND IS STILL THE MOST HONEST, CONSTRUCTIVE, INTELLINGENT POSTS I HAVE READ ON THIS SITE AND IS THE ONLY ONE THAT OFFERS A VALID SOLUTION, SO IT IS WORTH RE-READING AND FOR THOSE OF YOU WHO MISSED IT:

> I am going to express what it think the route problem is, as well as being open minded by criticizing both sides of the argument, but bear with me since this is going to be kind of long.

> The biggest problem of our community is that we lost our identity, being Kartaqi is not what it used to mean, especially going back centuries to see that we were built on the opposite values/standards of life we have today. For the women who post that they are unhappy in their "forced" marriages and preach "be happy at all costs, even if being gay makes you happy, so power to you"! Every community has

gays, and Rabbi Levy was right to say society desensitizes people, but the problem is that all the leadership the CB appoints (cough*controls*cough) is basically going to be politically correct and approach this the way the CB decides, which is to blame society, which is only a small part of the big picture. But nobody has the balls to blame the real issue, and that issue is the parenting. In a few years when more Kartaqi homes get foreclosed and people close down their businesses because these same parents spoiled their kids to the point where their kids are not equipped to survive in the real world on their own, and they cannot maintain this competitive material lifestyle, something worse will happen: we will have more criminals, mischief's, gays, drug addicts, atheists, assimilations, etc than ever.

Another extreme is the overexposure that every Kartaqi feels like they are followed by a paparazzi when they want to just go buy food, yet most of them love it and live for the attention and drama, so they are hypocrites (yes I'm talking to you too, self-righteous yentah reader!). We are overexposed to each other, hence the low marriage rate. Facebook, making 500 lavish engagement parties and after-parties, and clubbing together just makes it worse. People know too much about the materialistic outer shell of their Kartaqi "friend" and label them as such, yet barely know this "friend" deeply by treating them with true care. I say "friend" in parentheses because hanging out, competing, slandering, and jealousy within EVERY "clique" doesn't constitute friendship. If you want to see real friendship, then go talk to soldiers in the Israeli army who risk their lives for their fellow soldiers and people.

My personal belief is that Homosexuality should not be shoved down people's throats, but neither should heterosexuality. That is why our sages command us to keep laws of *Nida* (separation), not just at home, but even outside we should not take part in public displays of affection with our significant other. This is a private thing, and all that can come out of that is jealousy from people who don't have that. I respect the liberal position to speak their minds; however I am upset that these same liberal people are bringing up how people speak "Lashon Hara", and claim everyone is a hypocrite for breaking the torah in other ways i.e. driving on Shabbat, keeping kosher etc. (which are all valid points, by the way). But Judaism isn't an all or nothing religion and we cant start nitpicking who keeps what and who doesn't, because we should all start changing from within before trying to change others. That being said, if a homosexual is using the torah to support his argument then color me confused.

Now to my last and MOST IMPORTANT point: the biggest problem facing our community is the rampant "Lashon Hara" being spread. This very thing, along with "Sin'at Chinam/Hatred of Fellow Jews", destroyed our temple (Beit Hamikdash) and put us in exile. And now history is repeating itself.

"Lashon Hara" is responsible for the lack of values and downward spiral the community has taken, but what upsets me is that the closet gays and liberals are the same people who love the juicy gossip, love spreading "Lashon Hara" and ruining people's (even their own "friends") reputations and lives. A lot of these people that are complaining have many reasons to be upset that they cannot be open, however its not because of fear of tarnishing their reputation, in fact most inner circles already suspect or know who's gay, but its these same gays and/or liberals who hide behind a computer screen and bash the community for its negative traits while they are too cowardly to speak out in person, are the same ones who should be held responsible for bringing down the once positive spiritual energy of our community. Their real fear is that they will lose their social status and cliques a.k.a. avenues for gossip and slander. There is no other fear besides that, because having a traditional family with kids is not the priority for them anyways: Which brings me to these women who complain about their forced marriages by parents.

No matter how much pressure your parents put on you, you still made the decision to marry young for riches and status and it's in your hands to decide to leave, and if you have kids you are responsible to do what's best for the family. Give your husbands an ultimatum to change or you will leave them, but you must also change, especially with your demand for money and material and also if you flirt/sleep with other men. Its easy to blame parents for everything , and in this case its warranted, but you ultimately made the decision to get married and finally a few years later you realized you are living a life devoid of meaning and happiness (maybe your husband wasn't as rich and popular as intended by your premeditation), you choose to blame others. Yes they were wrong and have a backwards way of thinking, but people you must "make the bed you sleep in".

At least this Namdar guy moved away and had the balls to make his own decisions. I do not condone those decisions, but they are not mine to make, and if the community has bylaws that's normal and should be respected (but you still have free speech), a line should be drawn somewhere because eventually this will lead to other things such as marrying Christians and forcing us to accept them as community members. The institution of marriage is of holy matrimony intended for having children, whether or not you believe in G-d, I cant remember the last time a baby came out of a guy, clearly getting married is unnecessary, its just a way to rub it in. but again, its his right because the country allows it and nobody should slam him. He may have put up this site but it's his property and he did not intend to get ratted on by some gossiper who did not think before he acted so "zealously" (but he is a Jew and we must forgive him and not slander him as well).

For the record I think the community has more pros than cons, but we've lost our way. And to prove this isn't a one sided opinion, I mostly blame the parents and older generation that paved the superficial way for us. Even the right wingers are to blame. You send your kids to public schools, mock spirituality, teach competitiveness, spoil your kids, name them 'Tristan' or 'Mason', and then one day that child wants to marry a guy you freak out thinking "what will my clique say?!" and try to convince this child that marrying Jewish is important. Umm, at what point did you make Judaism important to this child? Judaism has nothing to do with going to Synagogue to socialize. Most people are breaking not some but ALL 10 commandments. Speaking any form of *lashon hara* is the biggest form of jealousy and the worst sin since our sages teach us that "Derech Eretz Kadma Le'Torah/Proper Behavior Must Come Before Torah" and the fact that jealousy is one of the 10 commandments (along with KEEPING SHABBAT), that suggests the level of importance it has (more so than keeping Kosher, going to Synagogue and putting on Tefillin, since they are not on that list of 10). These ritualistic and symbolic things we do, known as mitzvoth are mainly done as reminders that a form of action must follow beliefs and values. So in my opinion learn-it-up should be every night and the only thing learned should be "Shmirat HaLashon/Guarding Your Tongue" by the Chafetz Chaim, until it's ingrained in the ENTIRE communities heads! I know none of you have the balls to ask for forgiveness to those you have slandered, because in many cases it has spread to far and deep. But you will answer to the Judge of this world one day, so at least start by making this change and sticking to it, while teaching your children the same, and having the courage to stop others from gossiping when you see it, since it is an equal sin to hear it.

To finish my point: Everyone gives their sons "Brit Milah", the mitzvah symbolizing the importance of keeping the sexual organ pure from sin. Yet the words in literal Hebrew mean "covenant of words/speech" and it is the 1st thing we implement on a newborn, implying that all sin of impurity starts and ends with self control of desires, and the main 2 parts of our bodies we sin with are the mouth and sexual organ. This is a kabalistic concept that will take hours to delve into, but Google it if you want. The point is that EVERYONE needs to look themselves in the mirror and not wait for the CB to clean up the mess of our predecessors, but the changes must come from each person. Kartaqi is just a temporary title, when you all figure out that we are Jews first and identify yourselves as such, maybe then you can start criticizing others. But for now, the only thing to do is dropping everything and committing ourselves to AVOIDING "LASHON HARA" AT ALL COSTS!!

Veronica ~ January 22nd, 2010

Wow. This is this is the most constructive part of this whole blog! We are starting to get somewhere now...great post Mr. Freddy Horton. Thank you for recognizing the positive voices on these pages...constructive change will come, I am sure of it now!

Shabbat Shalom.

Wow ~ January 22nd, 2010

Shamed Kartaqi/Proud Jew - very inspiring and touching words. It's so refreshing to hear a view of someone with their head on straight. Thank you! Even though, unfortunately, people won't live their life by what you said, just know that you've made a difference in mine

talkin smack ~ January 22nd, 2010

shamed kartaqi/proud jew....that was unbelievable...words of wisdom about the REAL UNDERLYING PROBLEM as we can see by all the slandering that came after your original post, you stand CORRECT!

Truthful ~ January 22nd, 2010

Dear shamed kartaqi/proud jew. you truly get it. why can't you and people like you be our leaders. The central board and presidium (or whatever they call the top members) have failed us. We need people like you.

Isaac Namdar ~ January 22nd, 2010

I was just talking with one of my cousins. We joked around and said maybe after all that happened, I should run for the Central Board next time. That was so funny!

Don't worry, it is only a joke, no such intentions here. Just trying to be funny.

hypocrisy ~ January 22nd, 2010

Isaac, I just want to know one thing: you claim you tried to disassociate with the community by "not inviting any kartaqis to your wedding" and "not telling anyone about your pictures/website", yet you create this board to not only legitimize your situation, but also interact with your community now more than ever!! So tell us, what exactly are you trying to do?

Martin ~ January 22nd, 2010

Yea..don't push it.

pushing it ~ January 22nd, 2010

hypocrisy: Isaac never invited us to his board. he generously let us post on it. And we love it.

No Name ~ January 22nd, 2010

This posting is intended for Kartaqi Mother of Four, Support No Name, Kartaqis in Support of No Name, 2 Kartaqi Sisters, Hailey Hoffman, and everyone else who has thought about my earlier words.

I am completely humbled by your responses. It just underscored how wonderful so many people in our community are, and that, ultimately, we have so many reasons to be proud of being Kartaqi. One day, when your grandchildren grow up and tell their children about their heritage, I can assure you they won't be talking about the edicts and the excommunications of our leadership. They will talk about you and your open and understanding heart.

I just wanted to clarify that despite all the challenges I have faced growing up, despite of all the doubts I still carry around with myself, I now consider myself to be in a very good place. Don't get me wrong. It's not easy. I still often think about leaving to get as far away from Green Hills and the Kartaqi community. I have considered moving to Israel, where, ironically, I feel so much more comfortable as a gay man than I ever did among Kartaqis. But how could I just pack my bags and leave my parents, who are increasingly reliant on the support of their children as they age?

While I have not come out to my family yet, I have had much support from my friends, and as I get older, I realize that running away is no solution. I would just take all that baggage with me.

In time, I hope to find solutions, and like I said, if that means I cannot come to our synagogue anymore, then so be it. I'd be sad, but I have learned through this blog — and that's really what I wanted to tell everyone — that there will always be a seat kept for me at some shabbat dinner and a *seder* (Passover dinner) at a wonderful home. I will always have a family.

This board has been really inspiring to me. Thank you, and Shabbat Shalom.

Jim Farthing ~ January 22nd, 2010

My Dear Friends Isaac and Andrew: Hate and discrimination are the property of those who espouse that agenda. Here in any House of God it's an unacceptable gift, and one you do not have to receive. Please do not let ignorance, small-mindedness, religious rhetoric and intolerance cloud that every man in this country is created equally, DESERVING equal rights. You are both Brave, Strong, Talented, and Giving Men, and you deserve every happiness. Pray for those who fear and lack knowledge of their own humanity and imperfection. I applaud your tolerance and willingness to indulge their thoughts and expressions here! I can only suggest that loved-ones and family who fail to support you both in your life together are in fact neither. Jim

Isaac Namdar ~ January 22nd, 2010

Almost done proofreading my commentary letter. Will post here soon. 3.5 pages of single-spaced

Email

From: Joshua

To: Isaac; Doug; Veronica; Janice; Sarah

Date: 1/22/2010 11:18:34 A.M.

Subject: Re:

Take it easy there Fidel...

I think the issue here is not what tool can best accomplish the task at hand (I think we are all aware of which tool is best used for which task), rather I believe the issue is what task we are interested in accomplishing.

We have two choices. We either wish to continue this discussion in all of it's hate-filled, venom spewing, core shaking, brutally honest glory, or we can choose to find a new and more civilized model for the community to discuss issues.

I have made it clear that I wish for the former. I think that without the ugliness and the shock factor, that this movement will die. It will die quickly and quietly.

Doug's blog is a great idea. I think an independent blog with articles not controlled by the CB will certainly be a good thing. However if our intention here is to continue Fidel's.....er.....Isaac's revolution, we must do it in a forum before it is too late.

VIVA LA REVOLUCION!!!!!

Email

From: Sarah

To: Janice; Veronica; Doug; Joshua; Isaac

Date: 1/22/2010 11:35:45 A.M.

Subject: Re:

Ok guys – I want to alert you to why keeping Isaacs board open is so critical and effective for change. Read the message from psychopath whats wrong is wrong that just came up. Because of some solid response to his hate mongering he took time to think about his irrational behavior and posted an apology. This is what changes people's minds. That's why Isaacs board must keep on going and you young people need to create another vehicle that works side by side with the goal.

The hatemongers that read the apology may or may not start to become more understanding but at least you are making them think.

Check out the post

Email

From: Anonymous.****@gmail.com

To: Isaac

Date: 1/22/2010 11:47:53 A.M.

Subject: Re: message posted

Thanks.

I look forward to making amends with you in due time. I will try to learn and grow from this whole situation. And I look forward to reading your closing statement.

All the best,

Discussion Board

orli ~ January 22rd, 2010

Isaac and Andrew

I salute you for voicing your feelings and questioning the community's behavior only through dialog a change can be made.

I know Isaac for many years, he is one my most cherished friends.

I have seen him struggle with himself and finally few years ago he met Andrew and learned to accept himself for who he is; and doing so with such respect to his family's feelings and its traditions.

I am guttered by the way he and Andrew were treated, I hope for you that it would never be one of your family members who would be treated that way.

Instead of excluding Isaac and Andrew you should have been embracing them.

Orli

Judaism 101 ~ January 22rd, 2010

In my opinion, what is going on in this website is utterly disgusting. Also, I believe Mr. Namdar is enjoying every second of our debates over homosexuality. There should be no debates going on, Judaism does not condone marriage of the same sex. For Mr. Namdar to come and quote excerpts from the torah stating that we should not be judging him is repulsive. Religion is based off of tradition, it is not something that can be changed based off of the reforms of the society. The Torah has been consistent throughout its existence, through difficult or luxurious times. Just because we have entered a new age of liberal ideas does not mean that we can channel those ideas into altering the messages of the torah. Furthermore, for the people who do agree with Mr. Namdar, you can keep your opinions to yourself rather than indoctrinating the youth of our community. I also believe that we should put our energy in something more vital rather than debate over a topic that does not require a debate at all.

To try to even prove that homosexuality is accepted by our religion is a mockery of the Torah.

Here are some quotes from the Torah:

Leviticus 18:22 states, "Do not lie with a male as one lies with a woman, it is an abhorrence."

Leviticus 20:13 states, "A man who lies with a man as one lies with a woman, they have both done an abomination; they shall be put to death, their blood is upon themselves."

In Genesis 19:5, the people of Sodom stated, "Where are the men who came to you tonight? Bring them out to us that we may have relations with them." As a result, G-d destroyed Sodom and Gomorrah because of their sins. Through these biblical sources, one can strongly conclude that the Torah condemns those that have sexual relations with other men and that sexual relations between men are forbidden, similar to that of adultery and incest, and even punishable by death.

In conclusion, the Torah is very strict about any type of sexual relationship between men even if it is the loving, committed, and exclusive homosexuality of contemporary society. Therefore, Jewish ethics prohibits all types and forms of homosexuality. You must either be willing to accept what the Torah states or leave our community. There are plenty of other reformed communities that would accept you with open arms.

P.S. It has been debated that homosexuality is a genetic disorder due to imbalanced hormones. Our religion accepts that homosexuality exists, but it does not accept acting upon it. With that being said you have no right to try to manipulate the torah in a way that your actions upon your homosexuality is acceptable.

A wise man once said: "You are responsible for your own actions." Due to your personal decisions in life, you have sacrificed your membership in our community.

cable car ~ January 22rd, 2010

Judaism 101, you are DISGUSTING. I hope I am not related to you but I probably am because all Kartaqis are related. They all intermarry and that is not normal either

crazy1 ~ January 22rd, 2010

I think judaism 101 wrote the most honest and truthful comment. He is absolutely right.

boycottsynagogue ~ January 22th, 2010

crazy1 -- you picked a perfect alias. People like Judaism101 will be the reason the community will fall apart.

Judaism 101 ~ January 22th, 2010

Religion-a specific fundamental set of beliefs and practices generally agreed upon by a number of persons or sects

Fundamental-serving as an original or generating source

Now that you have received the absolute definition of Religion and the further definition of fundamental you know that these posts should not be going on at all. No one should be supporting this outburst of liberal ideas and directing them towards religion. As you can see, religion is based off of fundamental ideas and fundamental means original or generating source. These ideas of homosexuality are absolutely not original at all, they have been adopted by society due to the surfacing of new ideas. Religion, specifically Judaism, is based upon tradition, not on the reforms of society. Therefore, for all of you supporting Mr. Namdar forming this website to boast about his homosexuality, you should all be ashamed of yourselves.

As for Mr. Namdar, you had no right to create such a despicable problem between the community members. Please cease these abominable activities and turn to a reformed Jewish community. The

Kartaqi community is based off of tradition, which obviously you are not.

RESPONE FROM ISAAC:

I am honored to have provided you with this medium of free speech so that you can express your honest opinion. I find it ironic that although you are representing the moral and traditional religious view, you choose to hide your identity, yet it was OK for the entire community to dissect every element of my private life publicly.

ForJudaism101 ~ January 22th, 2010

In Judaism, suicide is of the gravest of sins. It is taken so seriously, that the individual cannot be buried in a Jewish cemetery nor is anyone allowed to mourn for him.

Mr. Namdar's website has prevented suicide amongst 1-3 Kartaqi men and possibly women because they are not able to come out to their family and community. They have put kept their own happiness in the dark and the pressure has brought horrible thoughts to them. Thoughts of suicide.

After being able to use this website to anonymously spill out their hearts, they have realized that they are not alone and even though they may never know the identity of their fellow Kartaqi who's in the same shoes as them, still Mr. Namdar's discussion board has given them a reason to live (at least a little bit longer).

So, Judaism 101, what do you think? Should the discussion board have gone down and the community would have had to experience one of the worst events possible? The suicide of a lost soul(s)?

cosmo ~ January 22nd, 2010

Isaac this blog cannot be replaced. The other one made me vomit. It's business as usual

Kebab House ~ January 22nd, 2010

cosmo: i FULLY agree with you. Isaac please don't let us down.

Hailey Hoffman ~ January 22nd, 2010

Shabbat Shalom to all

All through Friday, in between seeing patients and monitoring the Discussion Board, I kept revising my analysis letter. Finally, almost before sundown, I had the final version ready. I posted the comments below, and then deactivated new comments for the time being.

Discussion Board

Isaac Namdar ~ January 22nd, 2010

Shabbat Shalom to all!

It's been a very interesting couple of weeks for Andrew and I. We went from virtual unknowns to ironically become the most talked-about couple of our community. I think we got more press than any other wedding in our community, and more people looked at our pictures than anyone could imagine. People are now on a first name basis with Andrew, even though none of you ever met him. Even WE think it is odd.

What started as a behind-the-back outing, slowly morphed into many reiterations and evolved faster than anyone could keep pace. The novelty of the first same-sex marriage wore off within days when the Discussion Board became a major component. And therein lays the most surprising factor: how 600 postings, left on the wedding website of the most recent outcast of the community, changed the dynamics of our community so much in such a short amount of time.

Allow me to recap how we ended up with a Discussion Board, and the ramification of how things turned out. As you all know by now, Andrew and I got married last year after 6 years together, and had a small party for our close circle of friends and family to celebrate. We used our domain Mitchell-Namdar.com to post information and pictures for our friends. Andrew and I are fully transparent to those around us about our lives together and our relationship, and we do not live in a bubble. That's why we did not feel that we should take extraordinary efforts to password protect the site, any more than any of you tried to be secretive about YOUR weddings. Being fully respectful for the norms of our community, however, we decided not to parade our relationship in front the congregation, although many of you knew about the situation to various degrees. Although neither one of us believes in secrecy, we were willing to voluntarily adhere to our community's don't-ask-don't-tell policy in order to maintain calm, respect and peace.

Recently, a member of the community who shares the same last name, was apparently doing some online tinkering when he came up on our wedding website. Not recognizing either one of us personally, through a process that is still not known to us, he shared the information with others in the community. Within hours, 1000 website visits were registered onto the host, and people who did not even know us personally allowed themselves to browse through every detail of our lives.

Once this was told to us, we took down the original site to allow us some privacy. Instead, we quickly put up a one-page response to the events. Soon, many friends and family contacted us to express their support and love no matter what the circumstances. That's also when we realized that there must be a lot of hurt and questions, and in order to keep the channels of communication open, especially if someone may want to contact us anonymously, we started the Discussion Board. AND THAT IS THE FIRST AND ONLY PURPOSE OF OUR DISCUSSION BOARD: TO HELP BUILD BRIDGES.

During the next few days, we got approximately 100 visits to the site daily. Most were curious to see our response, a few left messages. And then came last Shabbat! A speech was given, the content of which is still not fully known to us. But judging by the sudden rush to our website, we think that many were surprised, dismayed, or otherwise not in agreement. I did not invite anyone to keep visiting my site. But people came to my site *because* of that speech, and *despite* that speech. The pace of visits escalated, and many more comments were left. Some were sympathetic, some were not.

And then the Discussion Board went from being a medium of communication with us exclusively, to take its own form. People felt comfortable to share, and opened up about many things they previously did not want to talk about in public. We are still humbled that you all came to OUR site to do some opening up. There were 3400 visits, and 600 postings (I had to keep updating these numbers as I kept proofreading my letter). As many of you know, I have not been a terribly active and engaged member of the community, and have lived my life with some privacy in the city. Ironically, since the community was strongly cautioned not to associate with me in any capacity, I have had more contact and involvement with the community than the rest of the 41 years of my life combined! I even got quite a few patient referrals from the whole ordeal.

Yes, there was some profanity on the Discussion Board, and many went off topic. Many unfortunately used the forum to create additional controversy. Most unfortunately, some used the forum to insult the leadership of our community and its Rabbi, who give of themselves selflessly to maintain the values of our community.

Therefore, I am taking this platform to publicly apologize to our Rabbi, our Central Board, and all public servants and leaders, if the contents posted on my website by others were derogatory to them and minimized from the outstanding job they have done for us all for years. I highly value you as individuals and collectively as the leaders of our community.

Once I realized that the Discussion Board has left its original mission and morphed into a much-needed forum for free speech, I tried to find a more suitable host for the entity. Therefore, the location of our community's discussion board is in the process of being moved from this website to another neutral location.

My analysis of what happened is as such: although my name was never mentioned once in last Shabbat's speech, it was very clear to all present who was the topic of discussion. I do sincerely believe that the speech was trying to be true to the *Halacha*, the same tradition that has guided us for many generations. What I think was missing was the human factor. I am after all a human being. I am someone's son and someone's brother. As a community, I am YOUR son and YOUR brother. It is easy to make a one-sided argument against me in my absence, especially when it comes from a Rabbi I did not have a close relationship with. I am sure if he had known me personally, his tone would have been different.

I grew up in a loving Persian Jewish family with deep traditions. Not only did they teach me Biblical Judaism, but they also taught me *chesed* (grace), charity, *rachamim* (mercy), social justice, and compassion. They taught me to open my heart and love all those around me. They taught me to not only respect my elders, but my juniors as well. They taught me that no matter who transgresses me, always try to be the better person, and never shame your counterpart. They taught me the value of education, a huge Jewish value. They taught me to be happy with my destiny. But most importantly, they taught me to be true to myself.

I am going to pre-apologize if the contents of the paragraph that follows this one many seem confrontational with the most esteemed and learned member our leadership. At first reading your will surely be appalled how a sinner has the audacity to question the contents of the weekly sermon of our community's spiritual leader. How dare he even think he can have any dialogue after everything he has done? I encourage you to read the paragraph once. Then read it again, or a third time. This time read it not as yourself, but put yourself in my shoes. Read it as a mother with unconditional love for her child. Read it with humanity, not rage. Also, as you will see, although I am not naming which Rabbi I am talking about, everyone knows whom the argument is directed at, much the same way that everyone knew all the references of last week's speech were directed at me even though we never said which homosexual we are talking about.

Our dear Rabbi, although I did not hear your speech directly, I got enough information from others to get some overall impression. As a spiritual man, how come Chesed and compassion were not the main points when treating such a delicate topic? Why did the congregants get the feeling that I was dehumanized? How come we couldn't separate the sin from the sinner? As the embodiment of social justice, which is the main feature of our religion, how come you couldn't calm everyone's anxiety by offering insight rather than exclusion? How come you didn't treat me as though I was YOUR son or YOUR brother? By making me an entity rather than a person, are you not trivializing the extreme pain and anguish I have suffered all my life trying to reconcile my Orthodox upbringing with my inner self? Why did you not try to make your speech more well balanced by devoting at least a portion of the time to the million instances of *lashon hara*, invasion of my privacy, gossip, and all the faggot jokes that ensued after my outing? Are those not sins? Were all those sins not committed right there in the sanctuary in front of the holy ark all last week? Were the collective actions and treatment of the matter not worthy of any review? Was I the only sinner that week? Although I didn't expect any conciliatory or forgiving language from an Orthodox speech on homosexuality, I did expect to be treated like a human being, like your son. Again, I apologize for my line of questioning. I am not doubting you, or your best intentions for the preservations of our community. But discussion, respect, and understanding are the cornerstones of any civilized society.

Andrew grew up in a very loving and accepting family. He is the purest and most humane soul you can imagine. If he finds a spider in our house, he will take the spider and release it back into the woods behind our house. He and his family donate hundreds of thousands of dollars every year to various charities (sorry guys, don't expect any donations from him anytime soon), and host charity events in their stores that raise tens of millions of dollars every year (don't expect anything there either). The events of this week were his first introduction into the intricate workings of our community, although he has already changed his name to Mitchell-Namdar (yes, he is the only natural blond Namdar in the world). As he was feverishly reading all the posts this past week, I saw the kind of rage and pain in his eyes I have never seen before. It was completely beyond his apprehension how could an entire community be told to behave in manner that did not respect the dignity of a fellow human being. Honestly, I did not have an answer for him.

Allow me to preface my next point by reminding all that I am far from being a mastermind. I am not a politician, a public figure, or well-versed in public relations. I am also not a computer genius. I am a simple and generally nice person. I am most definitely not one of those doctors with a G-d complex. Most who know me personally can attest that I never demand attention or presence when in the company of others. In fact, I generally shy away from attention as much as I can.

During last week's speech, my life and lifestyle were put under a magnifying glass. Again, even though my name was never mentioned, it was clear to all who was the target. There was an unequivocal denunciation of the summary of all who I am, and the community was encouraged to focus only on my sins that day. My family and friends were encouraged to shun me my solely based on my sexual orientation. Congregants were encouraged to redirect me to another synagogue even if one day I wanted to come back (not to mention we frivolously belittled our fellow Jews in the Reform synagogue by dragging them into the conversation through no fault of their own). A one-sided argument was given, and the results were unanimous.

And here we get to the punch line of my entire discussion here. Through no planning or special skill, the Discussion Board I had created for personal communication suddenly became the main attraction of the community. The most amazing thing that happened is that the Discussion Board, again through no wisdom on my end, became a virtual mirror that threw the judgments and condemnations previously thrown at me right back to those pointing a finger. It allowed the community to look at itself in the 'mirror' and realize that to some extent we all have flaws, and we all have broken the rules from time to time. We all have daily inner struggles we have to overcome. We all have previously broken a commandment or two, and will unfortunately probably do it again in the future. Basically, we are all human. We are all Jewish and proud of our heritage. And no matter what and how much any one of us has done, we all belong together. That we all have learned to live with each other's imperfections, and sometimes we even get a kick out of it. We are all a holy community, and nothing or nobody can take that away from us. The phrase holy community has obviously two components: holy, and community. The holy is perfectly known to us. But it is the community that keeps us together. And without community, the holy would not exist in a vacuum. And as such, none of us has the right to be more equal or worthy of belonging to the community than the next person. And nobody has the right to alienate you from your community, because we all learned this week that none of us is perfect. And none of us can claim ownership of the community more than anybody else.

I hope I am wrong, but I have a premonition that tomorrow in the synagogue, there will be some reference by the conservative voices that the community was warned against associating with me in any form, and since you all came to my website to visit the Discussion Board, and got yourselves tainted with a sin, especially since there was a big picture of two guys kissing on the front page, the ensuing chaos resulted. And that I am a troublemaker, and instead of disappearing quietly and in shame, I somehow dragged everybody else down with me. And that now the floodgates are open and other gay and lesbians may come out of the closet, and then we added infidelity and forced arranged marriages into the mix just to make it more crazy. And so much more *Lashon Hara*. A true Sodom! All because of this one troublemaker! And that if you all listened and didn't associate with me and visit my website, all would be fine. Well, as we learned from the mirror analogy above, all these problems have existed amongst all of us for years, and shoving them under the carpet only made them worse. Instead of thinking of me as the odd one out, think of me as the one who decided that above all, you need to be true to yourself. Only then you can take the task of being true to others. Lead by example, not by judgment. Although I never thought of myself as a pioneer, many have applauded me this past week for being more in peace with myself than most of you have been with yourselves. As much as our community cherishes itself for its cohesiveness, we need to attend to every individual's mental health before we can all band together and label ourselves a community.

Before I finish, I am extending my hand to every one of you in peace. Although I was mocked and ridiculed at times, was the target of bashing, came under the scrutiny of our elders and leaders, had my privacy invaded, was singled out among an entire village of less than perfect congregants (sorry again), and was the direct target of a very passionate speech, I realize that I too am not perfect. And I will take this opportunity to learn and grow. And I thank you all for bringing those imperfections to my attention so I can be a better person every day. I pray that every single one of you do the same and take a personal inventory of yourselves. Let's all emerge from this experience better people. And let my parting gift to you be the freedom of speech we all experienced this week. I am hopeful that the new weblog will continue the work that was started on my website. I have written the kick-off first posting, and it is now yours to populate.

Andrew and I will continue to live our lives among those who are accepting of us, in our homes in the city and in the country. Should our paths cross in the future, I hope our interactions will be mutually respectful.

Shabbat Shalom,

Isaac Namdar, MD

Isaac Namdar ~ January 22nd, 2010

The posting above is my analysis of what happened here this week. Please take a moment to read it.

Also, in observance of Shabbat, I am disabling new comments from getting published. Not because I am personally *Shomer Shabbat*, but because I do believe Shabbat is time for reflection. You can still read through old postings, and again, reflect.

Isaac Namdar ~ January 22th, 2010

The following letter was mailed to our Rabbi and the Central Board:

Dear Rabbi and Sirs:

I am writing this open letter of apology to ask for you forgiveness on many levels. I am fully respectful of the mandate trusted in you to defend the values of our community, and I am even more mindful of the daily challenges and obstacles that you all have to overcome in order to accomplish those goals. Although at times it may seem like you are doing a thankless job, the entire community is indebted to you forever for all that you do for them.

Firstly, although you and I don't agree on issues pertaining to my lifestyle, I am fully respectful of the societal, religious, and historical reasons for your positions. Being fully aware of the ramification, I was content to live my life in peace and privacy in both geographical and cultural isolation relative to the rest of the community. Unfortunately, the clash happened when a third party went behind my back and flaunted my lifestyle in front of everybody's eyes. I fully regret if I caused unnecessary commotion in the community, or if I gave you an additional challenge to deal with in your long list of objectives.

The Discussion Board on my website, the same domain where many in the community first learned about my lifestyle, turned out to be a phenomenon nobody anticipated. As stated elsewhere, the first and only purpose of the discussion board was for people to be able to reach me directly, with support or disdain, in a transparent and anonymous way. However, many found the forum to be a vehicle of free speech. Unfortunately, some people abused this free speech to express hurtful opinions about you. Although I cannot control the free speech of others, I ask for your forgiveness if it seemed that my site at times may have turned into a medium of attack on you. As you may have seen from my own entries, I repeatedly tried to remind people to be civilized in their discussions, and to observe the respect that our community leaders so obviously deserve.

Lastly, I need to express my deepest apologies to our Rabbi. I regret that since I was living my life pretty much away from the community, I never got to know you personally and form any kind of personal relations with you; the loss is purely mine. From afar, I have always admired the sense of community you have been instilling in our lives. I recently published a statement on my website, and in it there was some questions directed to you. I tried my best to clarify that I was by no means trying to question your judgment or undermine your authority. I was simply trying to have a dialogue with you, since a face to face discussion at this time seemed impossible. Again, I beg your forgiveness if you got the notion that the tone or the content was inappropriate. That was never my intention.

I am hoping that you will all accept my heartfelt apologies.

Sincerely,

Isaac Namdar, MD

So Then What Happened?

It was the Saturday after the storm. Going to the synagogue and confronting everyone was out of question. However, I would have liked to be a fly on the wall just to see what happened there. I wanted to know if people were still going to talk about me or the Discussion Board. Will the Rabbi address the magnitude of the consequences, or will he find a different topic to divert everyone's attention? I sat home, with a major case of butterflies all morning, waiting for people to get home from morning services.

At 2 PM, I sent a few emails to Thomas, Ron, and Ellen. I knew they were attending services, and would fill me in. Apparently the Rabbi talked about Alcoholism, another taboo subject in our community. My guess is someone got caught with drinking while driving, and there might have been another mini-crisis of sorts. The only remarkable theme that emerged from the feedback is that indeed there were very few young people in the synagogue that day; they boycotted services that day. The synagogue was half empty. I was actually very uncomfortable that due to circumstances surrounding me, people refrained from participating in prayer services. That was never my wish, and I regret that it happened.

As sunset approached, I was debating if I should keep the Discussion Board closed, or if I should re-open it. I got a few messages such as: "Isaac, please open the blog, we have so many problems!" I also monitored the two other blogs recently set up, and there were a few messages there such as: "when does Mitchell-Namdar re-open?"

At 9 PM, I re-opened the board. Right away people started posting, more in line with previous comments, from both ends of the spectrum. A few commented that since they boycotted services that morning, would anyone who attended care to elaborate what happened.

Over the next couple of days, Sarah, Doug, Joshua and myself tried to redirect as many people from my site to the other blogs. Several key postings were copied from my site into the new ones to stimulate conversation. Several new eloquent new entries were also posted by editorial staff to diversify the content. Slowly, some of the more moderate voices migrated away, and traffic slowed down.

A couple of days later, most of the visitors to the site were ultra-religious people who compared homosexuality to bestiality and incest, with only a few sane commentators and myself offering counter-arguments. Just to get a feeling for how crazy these last few people were, I posted a multiple choice question as follows:

Discussion Board

Isaac Namdar ~ January 26th, 2010

As your moderator, allow me to pose a general question for discussion. I personally never CHOSE to be gay, same way that most of you don't perceive your heterosexuality as a choice. I grew up having those feelings, and decided to act on them in my own way.

Now put yourselves in my shoes. Supposing that YOU grew up in our community and felt that you are more attracted to the same sex than to the opposite sex. What would you do with your life? Let me give you a few permutations, but feel free to offer your own solution:

1. Take your secret to your grave. Homosexuality is not accepted in our community or religion. Marry a woman, have kids. Perhaps make an excuse later why you no longer want to have sexual relations with your wife; three kids is enough sex!

2. Try to make the best of it. In order to remain part of community and religion, get married to a woman. Maybe find some secret outlets for your urges when she does not suspect.

3. Can't imagine yourself getting married to a woman. You can't ruin her life as well as yours. Every time family sees you they bug you how come you are not married and that time is running out. Eventually they give up on you and stop asking.

4. Try to be true to yourself. Follow your own path and find a same-sex partner, marriage or not. And since the community's traditions cannot openly accept you, create some distance so you can have your privacy.

5. Life is too short. You are who you are. Find a partner, settle down.

Be 100% honest and open about it. Your cousins invite you for dinners and weddings, you go as a couple. Still maintain respect and don't bring him to synagogue, but YOU go regularly.

So please let's hear what each one of you would do if you were gay. Or what do you think your child should do if he were gay?

There were a few responses, mostly in line with the response below:

Discussion Board

poll answer ~ January 26th, 2010

I would go, and I would like my kids to go with option number one. You can find a less feminine girl to make it easier.

That's when I realized that I was dealing with some zealot fanatics with no common sense. Arguing with them was futile. I decided that I needed to bring the Discussion Board to a final resolution in order to preserve my own sanity. I had said my piece, I made my point, and now it was time for put an end to it and move on. I needed to put this whole thing behind me, and restore some sense of normalcy to my life.

I first offered that since there are now two alternate blogs where people can post anonymously, I was changing the format on my site so that only postings with full disclosure of names will get published. There were absolutely no new postings for the next 24 hours. My final posting was as such:

> Due to lack of interest on behalf of visitors to the site to participate in a transparent discussion, where all parties express their opinions with full disclosure of their identities, this Discussion Board is retiring.
>
> You can visit one of the other Boards at http://kartaqiweblog.blogspot.com and yy.vc.kartaqi. A greater selection of topics is available on those sites for your consideration.
>
> I am not going to exchange half-hearted pleasantries and say it has been a pleasure to serve as the moderator here. The Discussion

Board left its original mission, and the task of moderating fairly was beyond my capability. However, it has been an honor to interact with so many of you, and learn your viewpoints.

To the other Namdar, who sent out the email revealing my original website with the pictures to the rest of the community, I will be forever indebted to you. Since I was originally willing to adhere to our community's don't ask / don't tell policy, I had strained many of my friendships and relationship by voluntarily withdrawing myself from community and family activities. However, my newfound transparent life has allowed me to revive many of those relations again. The outpouring of support and love from the more moderate people in the community was more than I could ever imagine.

Should any of you have more outstanding issues you would like to discuss, you can always reach me by email.

My dilemma at this point was whether to keep all the entries available for review, or should I hide the discussion pages altogether. At that point I was still getting 250-300 visitors daily to the site even though no new entries were possible and most people were redirected to the new sites.

The main factor influencing my decision was that since I had minimal need in keeping in touch with the community even *before* all hell broke loose, and especially now that I have been 'banished", I needed to come up with an exit strategy from the situation. I needed, for my own sake, to reduce my ties and move on. I never aimed to be a motivator for change for those people, and there is no sense in taking that thankless job now. Although many regarded me as a pioneer, I did not need to further entangle myself with the inner struggles of a community I was no longer involved with. The politics of Green Hills and the polarizations of the religious and the secular elements there was not something I needed to deal with.

So, I disabled the Discussion Board from viewing. By then there were another 1500 website visits since my analysis letter. Altogether, there were 739 separate entries on the Discussion Board, and more than 6000 visits to the website as I am writing this paragraph. Two weeks later, I was still getting 20 visitors per day, and people still approach me almost daily through email. Some people in the periphery of the community, as well many Zameenis who missed the two week window where all this happened later contacted me to express support.

Interestingly, after the Discussion Board was closed, many of the frequent bloggers with recognized aliases individually contacted me and revealed their true identities. None of them were from the conservative end of the spectrum of the debate.

Before you read this next paragraph, take a deep breath, as I am sure your jaw will drop to the floor. On Friday, February 5th, Rabbi Levy responded by email to my apology letter addressed to him and members of the Central Board! He told me that he had been out of town for one week, and he could not respond sooner. He was relieved to hear that I was not trying to provoke or instigate the community, and that I too was a victim of hysteria as things at times got out of control on my website. We exchanged a couple of more emails. He tried to stick to a strict biblical view, and I pointed out the inconsistencies of isolating out homosexuality out of proportion to other taboos mentioned in the Bible that we now ignore and take for granted. In my last email to him, I mentioned to him that in no way is he obligated to keep the online conversation since he has a full community to lead, and that is the last time I heard from him (for a while).

Just before Passover I felt a big emotional turmoil. Will the same Zameeni cousins who usually invite me for the Seder dinner once again invite me? Or will they be afraid of exposing their adolescent children to me? Will they invite me by myself or will they make a bold move and invite Andrew as well? Where will I go for services on the morning of the holiday? I did get invited to my Zameeni cousins again. And I attended a progressive synagogue in the City where I had gone rarely for services. However, there was an unsettled feeling in me the whole time, as this was the first major holiday I was celebrating as an outcast. After the morning services, I felt very depressed and lonely. I felt detached, amputated. I found comfort in writing the letter below, and I posted it on my website. I also made a link on facebook for people to read the article should they be interested.

> I have been on an interesting spiritual journey for most of the last year. First, my sister passed away last Shavouth after battling breast cancer for 17 years. Then, my brother-in-law became suddenly ill from recurrent brain cancer and died rapidly and dramatically. While I was still grappling internally to come to terms with two big losses in my family, the news of my sexuality got out to my community. Needless to say, this did not sit well with the leadership of the community. In the midst of a great community-wide debate, as many members of community examined their own beliefs and prejudices, there were a few speeches 'encouraging' me to seek another synagogue to worship in.

It is true that nobody ever contacted me directly with any edicts or message of excommunication. I never got any official correspondence telling me to stay away. Neither did other members of the community receive any mailing similar to the 'Green Letter' previously mass mailed after a different incident. In fact, the only people who ever got in touch with me directly were those who wanted to express their empathy and support. However, the consequences of the speeches given were ever so clear to everyone.

I had fully come to terms that my private life would not seamlessly blend with our community's customs. Out of respect, I made a point of not exposing the community to my lifestyle and never made an issue of it. And out of dignity, I had also decided it would not be appropriate to deny my sexuality and marry one of your daughters and make her miserable in the process as I try to secure a respectable lifestyle in our community. Yet, like any normal human being, I too have the instinct and the need to love and be loved by another person. I was successful in managing this entirely outside of the geographic and social boundaries of our community.

But I never gave up on my background. I take great pride in my identity and heritage. I fully bask myself in all the customs I grew up with. We keep fully kosher homes, both in Manhattan and in Connecticut. We celebrate Shabbat every week. We maintain separate cookware and dishes for Passover, and go through great effort to make our homes ready for Passover the way I learned from my mother. When appropriate, I make a point of educating my American friends about Israel and Jewish values.

I also did not give up on my community. I tried to walk a fine line of maintaining a life I felt comfortable with, yet try to keep in touch with those dear to me in the community. I attended services in our synagogue on major holidays and some Shabbats. I satisfied my spiritual needs in a place that felt like home to me. I remember attending services among these same people, with the same cousins and relatives, ever since I was a baby in Iran. Once we all moved from Iran to the United States, the familiar faces and practices provided a comfort level to all of us as we prayed and celebrated our religion together. To me, Judaism meant celebrating the holidays and all of life's important moments together as one people, as one big extended family.

However, the speeches given this past January changed all that. I was not there to hear what was exactly said. Yet the message was so predictable, I could have written the speech myself. The podium was used to showcase the differences, not the similarities. It was used to divide, not to unite. The podium was used to make me and others like me an outcast. It was used to send a strong message about zero tolerance policy.

Ironically, that message is so contrary to some of the main features of Judaism. Central to the principles of Judaism is social justice. We are thought to be kind and embrace the sick, the alien, the orphan, the destitute, the slave, and anyone whose luck in life is less than yours. Not surprisingly, compared to Christians and Muslims, Jews in the United and in Israel have the highest percentage of support for gay rights. Which is amazing when you think those numbers include a large percentage of very Orthodox and Hassidic Jews that would skew the average to the other side.

Nonetheless, I am a pacifist and a non-confrontational person. I heard the message loud and clear. Since then, I have been looking to get my spiritual needs met in alternate settings. Fortunately, there is a wide array of synagogues in New York City that would receive me with open arms. I had visited several of them even before the speeches, and knew there will always be a place for me to worship. I have even taken the effort of acquainting myself with some of the rabbis in these minyans. They were shocked to hear how I was encouraged to leave my ancestral place of worship because of my sexuality, yet were glad to see that I had enough Jewish zeal in me not to give up on my faith.

On the first day of Passover I attended one of the more well known egalitarian Conservative synagogues on the Upper West Side. It is a magnificent sanctuary that magically captures the spirit of Eastern European aesthetics, where most of the congregants can trace their heritage to, while providing a modern and functional space to worship in. The intricate mosaics around the Holy Ark, cascading with the same motif around several columns throughout the open space truly evokes the kind of artisanship that is not seen commonly in the New World. There are elaborate stained glass windows and panes in all four directions, capturing many stories of Jewish faith and history. The congregants sit together as a family unit, and the parents personally see that their offspring is following the rituals and getting the most out of the experience. Little kids often follow along the same prayer book as their parents and seek guidance in following the prayers correctly. Nobody talks during the services, except to chant in unison to the text of the prayers. You hear some of the most beautiful melodies in their prayers. It is the same melodies that inspired composers who wrote pretty much everything on Broadway and much of American popular music in the twentieth century. And when the melodies get a bit more upbeat, you see congregants break out in spontaneous dance in the aisles, neighbor with neighbor, mother with son. It is so easy to lose yourself in the spirit of the moment and pray with *kavanah* (intent) like you have never done before.

It was exactly at this moment of sheer religious ecstasy, while we were all breathing in the spirit of freedom as told in the story of Passover, welcoming Spring and a new awakening of the seasons, surrounded by hundreds of the most gentle and kind Jews ever so ready to receive me with open arms, that I realized I don't belong here. This is not the Judaism I know. This is not what I grew up with. These words in this prayer book are not the version that I can otherwise almost recite by heart. Those people across the aisle are not my cousins or relatives. The customs here are almost as foreign to me as if they are a different religion altogether.

The situation is especially worse since my Sephardic upbringing is much different than the overwhelming Ashkenazi domination of progressive Jewry. As I approach middle age, I was not necessarily looking for a new congregation or religious identity. But now that I am faced with that challenge, I find it hard to accept that my beloved Sephardic identity is mutually exclusive with progressive Jewry. It is absurd that I need to transition from being a closeted gay person in a Sephardic community to become a closeted Sephardic Jew in a progressive community.

I also find it hard to accept that for many, my sexuality is the sole attribute by which I am judged. I am a compassionate doctor with excellent bedside manners that all my patients and referring doctors rave about. I am a Zionist with a special bond with the country I spent my youth in. I am a philanthropist with varied causes I feel compassionate about. I am a very adoring son, a loving brother, and an uncle who loves to spoil his nieces and nephews every chance I get. I love keeping fit, and some of my favorite activities are to rollerblade and bike in the Central Park. I am a gracious host, and I love to make my invited guests feel like they are royalty. I have independently and willingly maintained a significant degree of religious observance that is on par with my upbringing and the norms of most people in the community, although many others in my situation have felt betrayed by organized religion and have abandoned their faith altogether. Are these all not attributes worth considering when judging me as a person? If my sexuality is such a strong factor that it can single-handedly disqualify me as a member of our community, is the converse true that any heterosexual person is automatically deemed an outstanding member worth of full membership with accolades regardless of their other attributes? Do we not judge a person as a sum of ALL he is? We all have many personal attributes, and none of them automatically influences our other attributes. My choice of profession does not dictate my political affiliation. My choice of home state does not automatically determine what car I drive. And my sexuality does not determine my religious views and observance. It is this special combination of all the characteristics in each one of us that makes us unique.

For those who still argue otherwise, can someone please show me the edict or passage in Torah that specifically argues homosexuality is an automatic disqualifier, compared to all the do's and don'ts? Does being homosexual automatically disqualify you from having a spirituality and observance of G-d? How does my sexuality strip me away from my natural born Sephardic identity? Truth be told, is the magnitude of the response truly proportional to the sin from a religious perspective, or is it more of a social stigma that is blown out of proportion compared to other taboos? Are our religious leaders then advocating social stigma instead of fighting them?

I know that some may argue that one of the main doctrines of Judaism is the commandments to be fruitful of multiply. I will argue with you solidly that I can fully adhere to this commandment as well even with my own situation, and the two are not mutually exclusive at all.

The people whom this essay is aimed at are all first generation immigrants who escaped their ancestral homes simply because they were Jews. They did not commit any crime or transgression. They were not out to convert the local Muslim majority. They did not want to change or otherwise influence the laws of the country their ancestors had lived in since the first Temple's destruction. All they wanted to was to have the freedom to live life as true Jews without fear of persecution. But as they saw their mere existence threatened, they escaped to the United States. This land of freedom welcomed us with open arms, and let us practice our religion and customs with pride and with complete transparency. This story of passage to freedom is especially poignant in these days of Passover as we celebrate our other passage to freedom three and half millennia ago. As we sit together with our large families and read the Haggadah cover to cover, telling the story of freedom to our children, are we forgetting the lesson that nobody is allowed to take away any kind of freedom from anybody else? Are we ignoring the very foundation of our religion, which argues for letting everybody live in harmony despite our differences? It was right there, in the Torah portion for the first day of Passover, that we read we shall treat every human being with the same degree of respect. It said the same civil rights shall apply to all people regardless of their standing in society. I find it ironic that some people are using this same most cherished and beloved religion of mine to ostracize me and prevent me from practicing my religion in a place where I feel most at home. Since when did we allow others to determine for us how religious and spiritual we can be? How can any of us allow others to tell us where and when can we practice our religion? Isn't this the same oppression we escaped from in Egypt and then again in Iran?

In a congregation where the only determinant of membership is your bloodline, contrary to other dues-based congregations in the United States, who had decided there was a mechanism to strip you away from your bloodline? Where was it clearly stated that certain actions will lead to one's automatic disqualification from that bloodline? How can one even revoke a bloodline??? And even if you could, where was the due process and fair hearing that made it possible?

As a doctor, I am all too familiar with human suffering. I have had to tell countless people that they have cancer; some of them family members who had trusted their care to me. I have had to console countless parents about their child's birth defects. I had to reconstruct people's faces after facial trauma from foul play, gun shots, or other disasters. I had to devise treatment plans for patients with life-threatening infections or organ failures. Additionally, we all have witnessed what tsunamis, earthquakes, floods, tornados, and other natural disasters can do to humanity. In light of all that, who are we as human beings to give ourselves license to add any kind of misery to someone else's life? How dare we use the name of our holy G-d to invoke hate, violence, threats, banishments, or any other mode of making another fellow human feel unloved, unwanted, or an outcast? Who are we to designate any of us as agents of G-d, carrying his judgments on Earth before any of us is due for a judgment in the Heavens? What authority does any human being have to tell me I cannot pray with my bloodline brethren in the same synagogue I grew up in?

As a doctor, I also know never to abandon my patients. Even if a patient becomes problematic, abusive, belligerent, or engages me in a lawsuit, I cannot give up on his medical care unless I find another accepting doctor to attend to his concerns. I can never simply tell him not to come to my office, and that he is on his own. Yet that is exactly what happened to me by the spiritual and lay leadership of my community. In their own terminology, it was made clear that all sides are better off if I never return to my synagogue. Nobody bothered to make sure I have another acceptable alternative to meet my spiritual needs. Does society really expect less from our clergy, men of religion, men of G-d, than we do of our doctors?

This coming Shavouth is my sister's one year anniversary. Normally, I would be planning a *didan* (prayer service) in our synagogue in her honor. I would conclude my Kaddish for her in the presence of cousins and other family, as they answer amen to my Kaddish verses in respect to her memory. Perhaps a few words could have been said by one of the rabbis of the community in trying to explain how a woman who suffered so much in her life from other issues finally died at such a young age. Now that I have been 'disinvited' from my own synagogue, where am I supposed to go to mourn for my loss? Are there going to be enough strangers in a strange synagogue to answer amen to my Kaddish? How is a rabbi who did not know my family supposed to shed some light on my loss? Which relative is going to make some of the customary foods we serve at these ceremonies, and who is going to even appreciate those ethnic foods? How am I supposed to fulfill my duty and do my best to pay honor to my dead sister in a manner that befits her memory? Is this unforgiving brand of Judaism really what I miss so much, or is it some totalitarian perversion of the customs and religion that I love so much? How cruel can you be to look me in the eyes and advise me against having a didan at my community's synagogue for my sister?

During this joyous holiday of liberty, I implore you all to look inside yourselves and see if any of you have done things to take away liberties from others around you. Have you stripped anyone of their dignity? Have you made life more miserable for someone despite what fate G-d has already allocated to them? Have you acted in a way that was less than respectful to others? Did that behavior make that person feel less than comfortable in their own skin? Have you singled out anyone recently and made them the subject of ridicule in the eyes of others? Did this ridicule later get back to the person under discussion in a way that made life even more miserable for them? Have you recently taken away anyone's right to have respect in the eyes of the public? Have you taken away anybody's right to be a member of your group or society? Do you know anybody who has? I personally know of a few people who are guilty of quite a few of the above transgressions. They all still enjoy a cherished and revered place in the eyes of our community. They all have 'permission' to come and pray in our community's synagogue; I don't.

There were many emotional responses to the letter. Quite a few friends told me they cried as they finished reading it. Some cousins spent more than an hour translating the letter for their parents. My business partner's wife, also a Zameeni, offered to host the *didan* in her house and fulfill all the customs we do in such memorial services.

During the Passover holiday, Mr. and Mrs. Jacobson (the President of the Kartaqi community in Israel), who are close friends of my family and a second cousin, visited my sister's home in Tel Aviv. At some point the discussion turned to the recent events surrounding my outing. Mr. Jacobson reiterated that he was dumbfounded when he got the email from the leadership of the Kartaqis in the United States to officially appraise him of the situation. He said that he did not know what should be his reaction to this matter, especially since he knows me personally and also since I don't live in Israel, and therefore I am technically not under his jurisdiction as a community member. At the same time he also expressed discontent with me that I had a lavish wedding only a few days after my brother-in-law's death! At that point my sister figured out that it was the impression of many that my wedding had occurred right when the news broke out. The people who did not bother to clarify the facts were under the impression that I had a gay wedding, advertised it to everyone on purpose, and that I was so heartless that I threw the wedding party only days after my brother-in-law's death. Apparently this amount of misinformation is what fueled so much of the negative response.

Mr. Jacobson was astounded to hear from my sister the correct version of the facts. At that point he called me while still at my sister's house to congratulate me and to invite Andrew and I to go visit them in Israel together. He also indicated to me that he planned to call Rabbi Levy to better understand his firm and unforgiving public statements on such a delicate and private matter. In fact, the following day Mr. Jacobson and Rabbi Levy had a long distance phone conversation for more than an hour, largely dealing with my issue. At the end of the conversation, Mr. Jacobson had the impression that the decision was made at the level of the Central Board, and that Rabbi Levy was told by the leadership of the Kartaqis to demonstrate zero tolerance policy. When confronted by the question of what should I do in a few weeks when I was supposed to carry out the one-year anniversary ceremonies for the death of sister, Rabbi Levy said it is for the best interest of all parties if I found my religious home in a different synagogue, and that I should forever forget my ancestral Kartaqi heritage altogether.

By April I had realized that I had not received a single piece of mail from the synagogue since January. I had not received the monthly calendars, or the new edition of Scrolls. I checked with Sarah and Jerome, and they had both received the most recent edition of Scrolls, without a single mention of the outing incident. I then emailed Janice, and she confirmed that in fact my name was removed from my community's roster. With a click of a mouse, I was forever erased from my Kartaqi ancestry. The Central Board just deleted me like I never existed.

As time went on, Andrew and I made several new friends from within the community. Several family members embraced us as a family unit, and have been inviting us to family functions together. Conversely, some other family and friends were never heard of again.

To this day, there has not been an official policy statement or edict printed and distributed to the community about the leadership's views on homosexuality and how to deal with homosexuals. Nothing similar to the famous 'green letter' has been generated. I take it as a small victory that the fight I put up, and the campaign of education I waged, changed so many minds and otherwise made those with more narrow views refrain from further alienating me or others like me.

<u>Conclusion</u>

There are many lessons that can be learned from this story. It is a fascinating case in sociology, where a tight-knit community dealt with a crisis internally. What sets this story apart is that so much of it happened over the internet and within the privacy of people's homes. A kind of public debate occurred that could never occur in any other forum.

Now that you have read the entire account of what happened, you will surely realize that this is not a personal story of coming out, or being outed. Rather, this is the story of an entire community coming out.

Homosexual men and women, at least the ones in my generation and the generations before me, often struggle internally before coming out. Those individual struggles might sometimes make some of us self-focused. By the time most of us are ready to accept ourselves and finally declare our sexual orientation to those around us, we might be jaded and think that the process of coming out has ended. However, that's when the process of coming out starts for those dear to us. It is now *their* turn to deal with this newfound reality. They, too, have feelings and inner conflicts of how comfortable they are dealing with this situation. Their task of coming out starts when ours ends. As we saw, the community's coming out started once I was done with my wedding.

I was the first instance of an out and confident gay man in a community that prides itself on maintaining its traditions and otherwise encourages homogeneity among its members. Prior to the events in this book, I had worked out, one by one, my coming out issues with many in my immediate circle of friends and family. But the inadvertent (or not?) outing that happened behind my back forced a community of 5000 people, most of whom see themselves as one giant extended family, to come out and deal with its first case of openly gay man. The Discussion Board that I created by chance captured those struggles publicly and transparently. Hence, this book.

The Kartaqi community also always prides itself on being a perfect community. They often like to boast about their accomplishments. Years from now, when gay rights are universally accepted, and the entire discussion here would seem absurd to subsequent generations, I have a suspicion that the Kartaqi community will reference this story and claim it was on the forefront of civil rights. LOL.

As you saw, much of the underlying tone of the story was not only about the specific issue of homosexuality, but rather the civil and societal rights of anyone who is different than the norm. Is this 'different' person entitled to his privacy? As long as he is not directly harming anyone, can he live his life as he sees fit? Does the majority have a right to alienate him? Can a community strip him of his identity as a natural-born member of the community? Can they tell him or otherwise prevent him from entering a public location such as a place of worship? Does the society have the right to pick and choose which flaws and sins are more worthy of damnation than others?

For me, the many ironies encountered in this story were the main lessons to be learned.

1. Our initial website was designed to facilitate communication and make information accessible for our invited wedding guests. While there were only 600 visits to the site during the 9 months it was up in its original format, there were 1000 visits by non-invited people in just two days as the public outing occurred. There were another 6000 visits to the domain in its new format as a Discussion Board and center for community interaction.

2. Prior to the events described in this book I was not well-known among the Kartaqis. The great majority of this tight-knit community did not know me personally, and most had not even heard of me. This was a perfect scenario for me being able to disassociate myself and live my life in relative privacy. But simply because I married someone outside the community, and just because my choice of spouse was 'slightly' different than most, I became the most talked-about member of that community. There is now not a single Kartaqi who doesn't know every detail of my life.

3. Most of my life I had been content living my life outside of the natural boundaries of the Kartaqi community, and it was not entirely due to my homosexuality. Since the events in this book transpired, I have developed many new friendships I never expected. Simultaneously, many of my previous friendships have been truncated simply because of the new discovery.

4. As I slowly came out to those around me, I tried to respect the Kartaqi community's unspoken don't-ask-don't-tell policy on homosexuality. I didn't share my life with them, and instead withdrew myself from their midst. I fully anticipated that the don't-ask-don't-tell policy would be a two-way street, and they in turn would respect my privacy. Unfortunately, it was the community who did not hold its end of the bargain and interjected itself into our lives uninvited. While I understand that the first case of a gay marriage would seem a very controversial and a sensitive topic for any group of people, it did not seem that many in the community were particularly concerned how their collective actions could have an impact on me and my life. I respected the norms of the community, but they did not respect the norms of a civilized society.

5. As seen in multiple references in the Discussion Board, many people allow themselves to discuss the sexual practices of homosexuals in graphic detail openly and publicly in an attempt to delegitimize us. They specifically and intentionally try to evoke disgust in the minds of others in order to make their point. But the truth is that those same sexual practices are not the exclusive domain of homosexuals, and the same acts are frequently performed in heterosexual relations. Paradoxically, the notion of targeting a heterosexual couple and talking publicly about their sexual practices without their consent is considered to be in extremely poor taste.

6. I had no plans to expand my circle of friends within the Kartaqi community. However, especially because of my outing and the subsequent banishment, my communications with the community members has multiplied exponentially. Specifically because of the way I was outed, and the banishment ordered by the leaders, people defiantly approached me and expressed their support.

7. Most of the Kartaqi community lives within a few miles of each other in the suburb of Green Hills. They attend the same schools, shop in the same stores, and go to the same social outlets. A very strong Central Board sets the tone for many aspect of their lives. Many feel that their individuality and free speech is, and needs to be, sacrificed in order to maintain that cohesiveness. There were recently given a rarely found

medium of free speech courtesy of a member of the community that was excommunicated. The website of this newly banished member was the only place where many people felt comfortable expressing their true feelings and frustrations to each other. Neither of the two other blog sites subsequently set up captured the same level of openness and honesty. Those people felt comfortable telling their story to an outcast, but would never dare to share openly with someone who was still part of the community.

8. As tight-knit as the community may claim to be, the great majority did not feel comfortable expressing their inner thoughts openly and candidly. Almost all the comments were left anonymously. While I could understand that the more liberal minds were afraid of repercussions of expressing progressive attitudes in a religious community, even those arguing conservative values chose to maintain their anonymity. Not even validating and glorifying conservative ideals, in line with the leaders of the community and the Rabbi's official position, gave those right-wingers enough clout to reveal their identity. However, as I was the central figure of the entire ordeal, I was the only person whose identity and positions on all matters remained 100% transparent at all times. I was the only one who owned up to his views and argued from the heart.

9. My website was clearly designed from the beginning to celebrate my wedding. The fact that it was a gay wedding was an incidental co-factor, not the main theme; the same wedding site host provides services for a multitude of couples and does not discriminate on any basis. Nonetheless, my site presented itself clearly to have gay content. After the pictures were taken off, and the Discussion Board was enabled, it still had the picture of two men kissing on their wedding day as soon as the homepage loaded. The irony in this point is that even those who bashed homosexuality and all matters pertaining to me, still had to use the services of a gay website to do their deed. They were using the freedom of speech given to them by a homosexual to express their radical religious ideas and to bash me in the process. The leaders of the community would never condone having such rampant freedom of speech.

10. Simply put, people just didn't want to leave. I never invited the Kartaqis to view my site en mass, and I never forced all the comments to be left on

the Discussion Board. I never invited them into my life. But they couldn't get enough. Even after the Discussion Board retired, and the content was no longer published, people still came to visit by the masses. People just lingered in a place they found fascinating, even if they were not supposed to be there.

The nature of my interactions with many members of the Kartaqi community has obviously changed since the event of this book. Most of the older people, and some of the younger and more conservative people have shunned me overnight. Truth be told, it wasn't me who changed his behavior and attitudes because of what happened. I am the same loveable and compassionate person that I have always been. I had been gay for as long as I can remember, and the only new thing with me is that I am finally out in the open with everyone in my life. My door, and my heart, are open to all who want to keep an association with me. It is my counterparts, the religious leaders and community organizers, who reversed their behaviors and attitudes about me suddenly because of the news of my sexuality. The same people who had just seen me the week before for my brother-in-law's 30 day memorial and consoled me and the rest of the family for our loss, now closed their heart to me overnight. I would like to believe they found this course of action especially challenging since as one of few doctors in our community they admired me for who I am up until that point. Still, some of the same people who shunned me found me very approachable when they subsequently needed to consult with me about matters of medical guidance. I was the same accessible person to them as I always had been throughout my life.

Many people believe that the major civil rights battle of this generation is that of gay rights. Therefore, the story line here becomes ever so relevant to what is going on in the United States and many countries in the developed world. I hope that with the publication of this book, I will contribute my share to fight that battle and open up so many more minds to the fact that equality is the basis for our entire Constitution.

However, I am hopeful that the reader will not view this book as an isolated story in a particularly insulated community, dealing with a very specific issue. Ideally, the reader should be able to extrapolate the main plot line to any story of minority rights in any situation you might be more familiar with. This could apply to a community, village, town, state, or region of any size and background. You read a most diverse variety of opinions on several issues here; the same spectrum could be applied to any topic of discussion. Conversely, those same individual voices of pro and con could be any *one* person's individual lamentations contemplating any topic worthy of a debate.

Appendix

As more gay people choose to live openly and honestly in their various communities in the United States and overseas, and refuse to let their sexuality exclude them from any rights or relations with their family, friends, or other societal parameters, even the most conservative circles have been forced to tackle the phenomenon that gay people exist in every walk of life. They are your colleagues, your doctors, your politicians, your cousins, your children's teachers, and the soldiers fighting to protect all of us from our enemies. And yes, there are even a few hairstylists and interior decorators! In the United States, there is a growing trend even among Republicans to break rank with the Establishment and acknowledge gays and lesbians as citizens deserving of the full protection of the law with equal rights.

Within some progressive Orthodox circles, mostly of Ashkenazi origin, there has been a similar movement to define the correct treatment of openly gay and lesbian Orthodox Jews. While most Orthodox Jews still believe that homosexuals need to be excommunicated, much like the treatment I got from the leaders of my synagogue, others believe that it is extremely un-Jewish to practice any exclusionary behavior toward any person for any reason. They believe that is important to distinguish the sin from the sinner.

Unrelated and concurrent to the story in this book, a few Modern Orthodox Rabbis recently came up with a Statement of Principles as a guide for proper handling of openly gay people, and their children, within an Orthodox community. The original document was drafted by Rabbi Nathaniel Helfgot, who belongs to a progressive Orthodox synagogue in Riverdale, New York. The draft was then circulated, and a few revisions were made by Rabbi Aryeh Klapper and Rabbi Yitzchak Blau, among others. The final document was signed by approximately 150 Orthodox Rabbis.

The document is a guideline only, and has no binding power. It is also not the official position of any association of Orthodox Rabbis. Quite a few more members of the leadership of Orthodox background, ordained Rabbis and otherwise, have signed on since its initial inception.

I recently contacted Rabbi Helfgot to thank him for his visionary efforts in restoring harmony and Jewish values into an issue that has torn apart so many families and communities for such a long time. He sounded like a very humble person, grateful to do his share to introduce compassion into a hotly debated topic.

I then copied the Statement of Principals into my website. I am providing a copy here for the reader to appreciate. Below the document, you can find a list of original signatories; I did not know how to find how many others might have signed on after the document was released.

Statement of Principles from Orthodox Rabbis: Statement of Principles on the Place of Jews with a Homosexual Orientation in Our Community

We, the undersigned Orthodox rabbis, Yeshiva headmasters, Jewish educators and communal leaders affirm the following principles with regard to the place of Jews with a homosexual orientation in our community:

1. All human beings are created in the image of G-d and deserve to be treated with dignity and respect (*kevod haberiyot*). Every Jew is obligated to fulfill the entire range of *mitzvot* (plural for *mitzvah*, good deeds and commandments) between person and person in relation to persons who are homosexual or have feelings of same sex attraction. Embarrassing, harassing or demeaning someone with a homosexual orientation or same-sex attraction is a violation of Torah prohibitions that embody the deepest values of Judaism.

2. The question of whether sexual orientation is primarily genetic, or rather environmentally generated, is irrelevant to our obligation to treat human beings with same-sex attractions and orientations with dignity and respect.

3. *Halakhah* (Jewish law) sees heterosexual marriage as the ideal model and sole legitimate outlet for human sexual expression. The sensitivity and understanding we properly express for human beings with other sexual orientations does not diminish our commitment to that principle.

4. *Halakhic* Judaism views all male and female same-sex sexual interactions as prohibited. The question of whether sexual orientation is primarily genetic, or rather environmentally generated, is irrelevant to this prohibition. While *halakha* categorizes various homosexual acts with different degrees of severity and opprobrium, including *toeivah* (abomination), this does not in any way imply that

---

lesser acts are permitted. But it is critical to emphasize that *halakha* only prohibits homosexual acts; it does not prohibit orientation or feelings of same-sex attraction, and nothing in the Torah devalues the human beings who struggle with them. (We do not here address the issue of *hirhurei aveirah* (contemplating a sin), a *halakhic* category that goes beyond mere feelings and applies to all forms of sexuality and requires precise *halakhic* definition.)

5. Whatever the origin or cause of homosexual orientation, many individuals believe that for most people this orientation cannot be changed. Others believe that for most people it is a matter of free will. Similarly, while some mental health professionals and rabbis in the community strongly believe in the efficacy of "change therapies", most of the mental health community, many rabbis, and most people with a homosexual orientation feel that some of these therapies are either ineffective or potentially damaging psychologically for many patients. We affirm the religious right of those with a homosexual orientation to reject therapeutic approaches they reasonably see as useless or dangerous.

6. Jews with a homosexual orientation who live in the Orthodox community confront serious emotional, communal and psychological challenges that cause them and their families great pain and suffering. For example, homosexual orientation may greatly increase the risk of suicide among teenagers in our community. Rabbis and communities need to be sensitive and empathetic to that reality. Rabbis and mental health professionals must provide responsible and ethical assistance to congregants and clients dealing with those human challenges.

7. Jews struggling to live their lives in accordance with *halakhic* values need and deserve our support. Accordingly, we believe that the decision as to whether to be open about one's sexual orientation should be left to such individuals, who should consider their own needs and those of the community. We are opposed on ethical and moral grounds to both the "outing" of individuals who want to remain private and to coercing those who desire to be open about their orientation to keep it hidden.

8. Accordingly, Jews with homosexual orientations or same sex-attractions should be welcomed as full members of the synagogue and school community. As appropriate with regard to gender and lineage, they should participate and count ritually, be eligible for ritual synagogue honors, and generally be treated in the same fashion and under the same *halakhic* and *hashkafic* (perspective)

411

framework as any other member of the synagogue they join. Conversely, they must accept and fulfill all the responsibilities of such membership, including those generated by communal norms or broad Jewish principles that go beyond formal *halakhah*.

We do not here address what synagogues should do about accepting members who are openly practicing homosexuals and/or living with a same-sex partner. Each synagogue together with its rabbi must establish its own standard with regard to membership for open violators of *halakha*. Those standards should be applied fairly and objectively.

9. *Halakha* articulates very exacting criteria and standards of eligibility for particular religious offices, such as officially appointed cantor during the year or *baal tefillah* on the High Holidays. Among the most important of those criteria is that the entire congregation must be fully comfortable with having that person serve as its representative. This legitimately prevents even the most admirable individuals, who are otherwise perfectly fit *halakhically*, from serving in those roles. It is the responsibility of the lay and rabbinic leadership in each individual community to determine eligibility for those offices in line with those principles, the importance of maintaining communal harmony, and the unique context of its community culture.

10. Jews with a homosexual orientation or same sex attraction, even if they engage in same sex interactions, should be encouraged to fulfill *mitzvot* (good deeds) to the best of their ability. All Jews are challenged to fulfill *mitzvot* to the best of their ability, and the attitude of "all or nothing" was not the traditional approach adopted by the majority of *halakhic* thinkers and *poskim* (scholars) throughout the ages.

11. *Halakhic* Judaism cannot give its blessing and imprimatur to Jewish religious same-sex commitment ceremonies and weddings, and *halakhic* values proscribe individuals and communities from encouraging practices that grant religious legitimacy to gay marriage and couplehood. But communities should display sensitivity, acceptance and full embrace of the adopted or biological children of homosexually active Jews in the synagogue and school setting, and we encourage parents and family of homosexually partnered Jews to make every effort to maintain harmonious family relations and connections.

12. Jews who have an exclusively homosexual orientation should, under most circumstances, not be encouraged to marry someone of the other gender, as this can lead to great tragedy, unrequited love, shame, dishonesty and ruined lives. They should be directed to contribute to Jewish and general society in other meaningful ways. Any such person who is planning to marry someone of the opposite gender is *halakhically* and ethically required to fully inform their potential spouse of their sexual orientation.

We hope and pray that by sharing these thoughts we will help the Orthodox community to fully live out its commitment to the principles and values of Torah and *Halakha* as practiced and cherished by the children of Abraham, who our sages teach us are recognized by the qualities of being *rahamanim* (merciful), *bayshanim* (modest), and *gomelei hasadim* (engaging in acts of loving-kindness).

as of July 26, 2010:

Rabbi Yosef Adler
Rabbi Howard Alpert
Rabbi Joshua Amaru
Rabbi Elisha Anscelovits
Rabbi Hayyim Angel
Rabbi Marc Angel
Rabbi Maurice Appelbaum
Mrs. Nechama Goldman Barash
Rabbi Avi Baumol
Rabbi Benjamin Berger
Rabbi Dr. Shalom Berger
Rabbi Dr. Joshua Berman
Rabbi Scot Berman
Rabbi Todd Berman
Rabbi Yonah Berman
Rabbi Kenneth Birnbaum
Dr. David Bernstein
Rabbi David Bigman
Rabbi Yitzchak Blau
Rabbi Nasanayl Braun
Dr. Erica Brown
Rabbi Yuval Cherlow
Rabbi Dr. Michael Chernick
Rabbi Judah Dardik

Dr. Aubie Diamond
Ms. Yael Diamond
Rabbi Mark Dratch
Rabbi Ira Ebbin
Rabbi Rafi Eis
Mrs. Atara Eis
Mrs. Elana Sober Elzufon
Rabbi Yitzhak Etshalom
Rabbi Dr. Shaul (Seth) Farber
Ms. Rachel Feingold
Rabbi Yoel Finkelman
Rabbi Elli Fischer
Rabbi Mordy Friedman
Rabbi Jeffrey Fox
Rabbi Aaron Frank
Rabbi Aharon Frazier
Rabbi Avidan Freedman
Rabbi Barry Gelman
Rabbi Shmuel Goldin
Ms. Anne Gordon
Rabbi Mark Gottlieb
Rabbi Uri Goldstein
Rabbi Benjamin Greenberg
Mrs. Sharon Weiss-Greenberg
Rabbi Zvi Grumet
Rabbi Dr. Charles Grysman
Mrs. Lori Grysman
Rabbi Alan Haber
Dr. Aviad Hacohen
Rabbi Tully Harcsztark
Rabbi Benjamin Hecht
Rabbi Nathaniel Helfgot
Rabbi Jason Herman
Rabbi Shmuel Herzfeld
Rabbi Josh Hess
Rabbi Fred Hyman
Rabbi Eytan Kadden
Dr. Daniel Kahn
Rabbi Moshe Kahn
Rabbi Yosef Kanefsky
Rabbi Elliot Kaplowitz
Rabbi Jay Kellman
Rabbi Aryeh Klapper
Dr. Yosef Kleiner
Mrs. Judy Klitsner

Rabbi Shmuel Klitsner
Rabbi Jeff Kobrin
Dr. Aaron Koller
Rabbi Barry Kornblau
Dr. Meesh Hammer Kossoy
Rabbi Binny Krauss
Mrs. Esther Krauss
Rabbi Dr. Benny Lau
Rabbi Aaron Leibowitz
Rabbi Zvi Leshem
Rabbi Daniel Levitt
Rabbi Norman Linzer
Rabbi Dr. Martin Lockshin
Rabbi Dr. Haskel Lookstein
Rabbi Asher Lopatin
Ms. Adina Lubar
Rabbi Chaim Marder
Rabbi Joshua Maroof
Rabbi Dr. Adam Mintz
Rabbi Jonathan Morgenstern
Rabbi Dr. Yaacov Nagen (Genack)
Mrs. C.B. Neugroschl
Rabbi Itiel Oron
Rabbi Ephraim Osgood
Rabbi Yossi Pollak
Ms. Ellisa Prince
Dr. Caroline Pyser
Rabbi Daniel Reifman
Rabbi Shlomo Riskin
Rabbi Avi Robinson
Rabbi Chaim Sacknovitz
Rabbi Noam Shapiro
Rabbi Yehuda Seif
Rabbi Murray Schaum
Rabbi Hanan Schlesinger
Rabbi Adam Schier
Ms. Lisa Schlaff
Rabbi Yehuda Septimus
Dr. Shai Secunda
Dr. Moshe (Simon)Shoshan
Rabbi Yair Silverman
Rabbi Sidney Slivko
Rabbi Jeremy Stavitsky
Rabbi Adam Starr
Rabbi Chaim Strauchler

Rabbi Yehuda Sussman
Dr. Harvey Taub
Dr. Mark Teplitsky
Rabbi Joel Tessler
Rabbi Mordechai Torczyner
Rabbi Jacob Traub
Rabbi Zach Truboff
Mrs. Dara Unterberg
Rabbi Michael Unterberg
Rabbi Dr. Avie Walfish
Dr. Dina Weiner
Rabbi Ezra Weiner
Ms. Sara Weinerman
Rabbi Ari Weiss
Rabbi David Wolkenfeld
Rabbi Elie Weinstock
Rabbi Neil Winkler
Rabbi Shmuly Yanklowitz
Rabbi Ron Yosef
Rabbi Alan Yuter
Rabbi Josh Yuter
Dr. Yael Ziegler
Rabbi Dr. Stuart Zweiter

People in this Book

In order of appearance:

Isaac Namdar – me, the protagonist

Andrew Mitchell – my husband

Jacob Namdar – a member of the Kartaqi who shares the same last name. I am not aware of any direct relations to me.

Nathan – my 22 year old nephew, son of my sister Jenny. Nathan and the rest of his family live in Israel.

Jenny – my older sister. She recently lost her husband to recurrent brain cancer.

Alon Namdar – my first cousin, also lives in Israel

Rachel – wife of Keith, my second cousin.

Zach – Kartaqi gay man, previously unknown to me

Laura – my 30 year old niece, daughter of my sister Jenny

Thomas – second cousin, lives in Green Hills, used to be very close friend

Ron Namdar – second cousin, lives in Green Hills

Norman – second cousin, lives in Green Hills

Sharon – my 26 year old niece, daughter of my sister Jenny

Keith – second cousin, lives in Green Hills, husband of Rachel

Ellen – another second cousin, who lives in the city, and has ran into Andrew and I several times in the neighborhood

Rabbi Levy – the main Rabbi of the Kartaqi community

Sarah – Kartaqi woman, previously not known to me, very involved with social issues

Jerome – gay Kartaqi man, previously not known to me

Janice – Kartaqi young woman, editor of Scrolls magazine

Joshua Norwick – Kartaqi young man, previously not known to me

Naomi – Kartaqi woman, previously not known to me

Cindy – Kartaqi woman, previously chairperson of the Kartaqi Youth Committee

Doug – Kartaqi man, previously not know to me, web and internet savvy

Freddy Horton – member of the Kartaqi Central Board, went to the same college as me

Veronica – Kartaqi young woman, staff editor for Scrolls

Glossary

CB – short for Central Board

Central Board – the elected governing body of the Kartaqi community

Challah – bread used for Shabbath blessings; baking a challah is considered by some to have a cleansing and therapeutic value

Didan – memorial service for the deceased

G-d – acronym used to write the name of the Lord, so not to use His name in vain

Green Hills – imaginary name for the suburb where most of the Kartaqi community settled in the United States

Halacha – Jewish laws and customs

Hashem – another Hebrew name to refer to the Lord

Kaddish – mourners' prayer

Kartaq – an imaginary name for the name of the town in the Middle East where my ancestral family comes from

Kartaqi Youth Committee – the elected body for matters concerning the younger generation

Kashruth – Kosher-ness

Kosher – adjective used to describe foods prepared in accordance to all the Jewish dietary laws

KYC – short for Kartaqi Youth Committee

Lashon Hara – evil speech, gossip

Mitzvah – good deeds and commandments

Noghl – Kartaqi candy used mostly for weddings and celebrations

Scrolls – imaginary name for the quarterly magazine of the kartaqi community in the United States

Shabbath – Hebrew for Sabbath, the holy day for rest and prayer

Shiva – Seven days of mourning immediately after a first level relative passes away

Shomer Shabbath – observant of all the commandments pertaining to the Sabbath

Zameen – an imaginary name for the capital city in the same Middle Eastern country as Kartaq